NO PALM TREES ON CUTTYHUNK

No Palm Trees on Cuttyhunk

SURVIVING MY ADOLESCENCE

Jeffrey E. Denning

Library of Congress Control Number: 2021905191

ISBN-13 (hardback): 978-0-578-87478-4
ISBN-13 (paperback): 978-0-578-87477-7

Copyediting by Laurel Robinson – Laurel@laurelcopyeditor.com

Cover painting by Tamalin Baumgarten – www.tsbaumgarten.com
Tower Hill Road, Cuttyhunk Island, MAs, oil on panel, 2021

Cover design and typesetting by Euan Monaghan

This book was printed in the United States of America

Dedicated to the angels that save us

To honor my Cuttyhunk mentors, guardians, and friends

ACKNOWLEDGMENTS

Gratitude to the "island kids" who contributed and
helped me remember details from a bygone era that brought
life to this story. Without their interest, I could not have
replicated the setting or fullness of the characters.

Special appreciation to

Pam Baldwin

Beverly Snow

Daniel Thomson – son of Malcolm "Muggsy" Thomson

Cuttyhunk Historical Society – Allie Thurston & Bee Elmore
Liz Cary Blum – Dir. of Alumnae Relations, Pine Manor College
Carmen Ward – 1993 Dissertation, "Hetty Shepard Wheeler"

A special acknowledgment to Patty Mariano Denning,
who listened to my endless chronicles from Cuttyhunk
and encouraged me to take this six-year journey and
reconstruct events that took place over half a century ago.
Because of her, my story is richer and more meaningful.

TABLE OF CONTENTS

INTRODUCTION

Fourteen-year-old Geoff sets off with his friend to camp alone on a tiny Cape Cod island for three weeks during the summer of 1959. He quickly blends in with the island, its culture, and the people. No sooner does he begin to experience the freedom to think and make decisions for himself than he must come to grips with the realization that his conflict with his father may be driven by something more significant and powerful than Geoff can understand.

Geoff extends his visit through the summer, and his guileless nature wins over crusty old-timers who nurture his budding confidence and maturity. He lands a job, learns to sail, and experiences the rush of first love. He befriends a foul-tempered, knife-wielding cook who encourages him not to give up on himself or his father. He fears leaving the island, not knowing what awaits him. "Will my father recognize me when I get back home?"

Experience life in a unique time and place through the eyes of a boy eager to discover himself and the world. Get to know the colorful characters who grow into his unlikely mentors, guardians, and friends. Whether Geoff's confronted with a gunny sack of feisty lobsters, a pot filled with quahog guts, or the possibility of his first kiss, you'll be right there with him.

* * *

I have a nostalgic and contemplative view of the world, pondering my yesterdays while seeking wisdom to light my path forward. I enjoy storytelling, but I think I pushed the limits of my spouse's patience with stories about the islanders. She encouraged me to write about those special people from a long-ago time and place. In 2015 we set out on a journey that began with a pilgrimage to Cuttyhunk, to visit what I had not seen in more than half a century.

As the island ferry approached the channel, indiscernible speckles on the landscape became cottages, cars, trucks, and people. I stepped onto the dock and was met by awakening memories, but not surprisingly, none of the greeters looked familiar. The roads and crisscrossing pathways, however, remained untouched by time. We stopped in front of familiar cottages, and I drifted into "I remember this place" stories. From the depth of yesteryear floated faces and feelings that I had locked away. Sepia-tone memories came alive in vivid color. This place, this island, after all these years—so different, yet so much the same.

I walked through the Cuttyhunk cemetery, where I was greeted by names chiseled on the headstones of those revered people gone from us—caring people whose culture and values gave me a work ethic that guided me throughout my professional and personal life. I wrote this story from a boy's perspective so you can appreciate those I wish to honor and how they gave that boy the will to never give up on difficult or impossible relationships.

PRELUDE

The events, the setting, and the people in this book are real. Dialog reflects the soul of the feelings noted from my journals or remembered as actual conversations. In isolated cases where dialog could not be recalled, I included narrative that blended the spirit of the experience with factual background to give a richer understanding of the characters. As I wrote my story, it was challenging to put myself in the head of young Geoff without sounding too mature. I solved this annoying problem by changing how his name is spelled. Nonsensical as that seems, it worked. To preserve authenticity, all characters kept their actual names except one. Where possible, individuals or surviving family members gave permission to be included.

THE GOOD SAMARITAN

Sunset was far behind and dawn was a long way off when Peter and Geoff stepped off the train in Providence. The city slept while nocturnal desolation saturated the damp June night. The two fourteen-year-old boys stood outside the station while getting their bearings. Peter motioned with his head. "That way."

They picked up their gear and headed into the darkness. A bus roared by, swirling its wind wake around the boys. They watched the brake lights as it turned into a large parking lot. The bus station was up ahead—just as the train stationmaster had said.

Geoff waited with their gear while Peter stood in line at the only open ticket window. He felt eyes crawling over him. Sleazy-looking men walked past, inspecting him and his gear. Despite the bright lights, he felt uneasy.

"Well, the first bus to New Bedford is four hours from now," Peter said when he returned.

"Four hours? Now what?"

"Let's get some shut-eye."

"Where? Guys are sacked out all over the benches."

"I wasn't expecting this. Who woulda thought it would be packed at this hour?"

"Perhaps I could help you." Standing behind them was a skinny man with hunched shoulders, long black hair, and a cigarette cradled behind his ear. He jerked his head as his eyes darted around the station. "I couldn't help but overhear your conversation. Where'd you say you're going?"

"New Bedford," Peter said.

"All the sailors come through here. That's why it's always crowded. I could get you to New Bedford sooner, and there'd be plenty of places to sleep in that bus station. You interested?"

"How would you get us there?" Peter asked.

"By cab. I'm sure there are other guys waiting like you. If I could get them to buy in, it would cut your cost in half."

"How much?"

"By cab… twenty bucks."

"Twenty dollars? That's a lot. Bus fare is a dollar twenty-five apiece."

"Look, pal, it's not me with the problem. I'm a local and know my way around, see. I'm just trying to help. Are you interested or not? If you are, I'll check around."

The boys looked at each other and nodded. "OK, that would be great," Peter said.

The stranger left.

"That was sure nice of him. I'd feel better if we could get to New Bedford and wait there," said Geoff.

The stranger reappeared within minutes. "Hey, guys. I have some good news and some bad news. First, cabs don't run this early, but I have a friend who can take you there for only ten bucks. You still want to do it?"

"I thought you knew your way around," said Peter.

"I do. It's just earlier than I thought. C'mon, my friend's not gonna wait all night."

The boys followed the man out the door, but when they stepped out to the parking lot, Geoff stopped and dropped his gear.

"What's wrong?" Peter asked.

"It's dark."

The stranger looked over his shoulder to see the boys huddled in discussion. "What's up, guys? Don't put your gear down here. My friend's car is over there. You're not thinkin' about weaselin' out on me, are you?"

"Hang on," said Peter. "We're talking something over."

The stranger lit a cigarette, sucked it quickly and deeply, and impatiently checked his watch while looking around into the darkness.

"Of course it's dark. It's night. What's up?" said Peter in a low voice.

"Getting a bad feeling about this. In the dark, we won't know if they're taking us southeast to New Bedford or northwest to some dirt road in the woods."

"Do you want to pass on this guy's offer?"

"Yeah, let's pass."

"OK, if that's what you want. Hey, mister! We've changed our minds. Ten bucks is way over our budget. Besides, we already bought bus tickets. As much as we appreciate the offer, we've decided to wait."

"Whadda you mean?" The stranger leapt close and put an angry face into Peter's. "We had a deal, pal. I went out of my way to get my friend to help. He got out of bed for you. I can't let you welsh on me. C'mon. You owe me. Let's go."

Peter turned away from the stranger and leaned toward Geoff. "We sort of agreed to this. Maybe we should go with him."

The boys tentatively gathered their gear and began following the stranger toward a set of red brake lights on the other side of the dark parking lot.

"Hey!" came an authoritative voice from behind them.

Two policemen stood under the light in the station doorway with their hands resting on their nightsticks. When the boys looked back toward the parking lot, the early morning Good Samaritan and red brake lights were gone.

"You boys… you waiting for the bus?" one of the officers asked.

"Yeah," Peter said.

"Then I suggest you wait inside and *stay* inside until your bus leaves."

A voice over the loudspeaker hailed passengers for the 4:10 to New York. Bodies strewn over benches came alive and shuffled to the boarding area. The boys staked out a bench in a corner and barricaded themselves behind their gear. Peter leaned against a duffel bag and soon drifted off. Geoff stared into his imagination, where he saw his bloody body lying in the woods after going with the man in the parking lot.

The bus station door slammed open, pulling Geoff from his nightmare. A fresh batch of shifty-eyed con artists infested the station, scouting for unsuspecting wayfarers. Geoff clutched his knapsack and held them off with stern glares. He watched the slow motion second hand on the station clock and kept checking for signs that dawn was near.

The loudspeaker finally crackled, jolting the boys out of their doze. Time to board the bus to New Bedford. Geoff scanned for night stalkers.

Gone. Dawn had brought gray skies and a colorless landscape. The bus reeked of unbathed bodies and cigarette smoke, but the two exhausted adventurers melted into the plush seats for the fifty-minute ride. They were one step closer.

2

ISLAND LANDING

The man in Providence had said the New Bedford bus station would be quiet. He had lied. Sailors and other passengers dodged around the boys as they attempted to get their bearings. Remnant thoughts from their brush with danger in Providence stiffened them with apprehension. They knew they were targets.

"You fellas look lost," said a stooped, bearded custodian in a gray uniform. The boys braced themselves with suspicion. They didn't want to acknowledge him and put themselves at risk again, but they had no idea which way to go.

"We're heading for Pier Three," Peter said.

"Pier Three… Going to Cuttyhunk, eh?" the custodian drawled. He leaned on his broom and pointed. "Out that door, down the hill, and through a chain-link gate. You'll run right into it."

The boys scooped up their gear and stepped into New Bedford's chilly, gray June morning. Fog blanketed landmarks, signs, and anything beyond fifty feet. It sucked the sound out of the air, leaving an eerie silence that matched the colorless surroundings. The boys stumbled down the hill, constantly adjusting and hoisting a heap of gear that threatened to slide off their shoulders with every step.

Geoff felt himself steeped in the history of this nineteenth-century whaling port with its labyrinth of buildings crammed together and pressing against sidewalks so narrow that they had to walk single file. He could hear the ancient echoes of clopping horses on cobblestone streets. Heavy-looking wooden signs suspended precariously over the walkways marked the location of pubs, pipe shops, and old bookstores. Walking through the town reminded Geoff of Mystic Seaport, a reproduction of an old whaling village in Connecticut, but New Bedford was the real deal.

Peter was significantly taller than Geoff, yet both were youthfully lanky with faces still too young to feel the edge of a razor. They stopped in the thickening fog and listened for sounds that could guide them to the boat heading to Cuttyhunk Island. All they could hear was their breathing and the occasional squawking of a passing sea gull somewhere above the fog.

The narrow streets and buildings gave way to a cold and invisible landscape. If the custodian's instructions were correct, the tired-looking chain link fence marked the entrance to the pier.

"Man, I sure hope we're in the right place," Geoff said. "What a crappy time for fog."

"If we're in the wrong spot, we'll miss the boat and then we're finished!" Peter said. Geoff winced; it was too early for Peter's exaggerated sense of doom.

"Let's wait here and see if anyone else comes," said Geoff. "This doesn't look like a pier, but we're near water. I can smell it."

A few minutes later a pickup truck turned in and disappeared in the fog. The boys grabbed their gear and scrambled to follow it. When they caught up with it, the fog lifted momentarily and revealed a small orange tugboat. Soon there was a fury of activity with cars and trucks coming through the fog. People began congregating at the stern of the boat. A man walked toward them. His stature was slight, and his white hair stuck wildly out of a fiddler hat cocked to one side. Sideburns whisked over his ears, and thick white brows shaded his eyes. His face was friendly and crisscrossed with "happy" lines. He nodded as he walked by.

"Excuse me, sir," Geoff said. "We're looking for the tugboat *Alert*. Can you tell me where it is?"

The man smiled and pointed over Geoff's shoulder. "There she is. We're casting off soon. If you're going to Cuttyhunk, you'd better get your gear aboard."

"Where do we get tickets?"

"Captain comes around once we're underway."

"C'mon, Geoff, let's stow our gear," said Peter.

"I'll be right behind you. I want to look around." Geoff stood motionless, letting relief sink in. "We're here," he whispered gratefully.

Geoff walked toward the stern and watched people scurrying around the boat. Some took packages into a cabin behind the wheelhouse. Some stowed cargo and gear under benches protected by a canopy. Larger items sat on the stern in an open area. Crew deftly moved cargo from the dock to suitable stowage on the boat. They quickly filled in the empty spaces with provisions secured in cardboard boxes and tied tightly with twine. The boxes reflected what they had once held—cans of Crisco and Pet milk, boxes of Rice Krispies and Wheaties—but had been repurposed for a better fate than incineration.

"Hey, Geoff!" Peter called. "Over here. Come aboard!"

Geoff's elation and excitement gave way to the fatigue of being awake for twenty-four hours. He was ready for a long snooze, but there was too much to see to squander time sleeping.

"Hey, Pete, let's check out the boat before it heads out."

"You go. I don't want to leave our gear unattended. If it gets lost or stolen, we're finished."

"How's it gonna get lost and who would want to steal it?" Geoff looked to the gangplank and back at Peter. "I'll be back. Gotta find out how long this boat is."

Geoff stood on the dock looking back at the boat. *Alert*'s hull was white with an orange fender strip running from bow to stern. She looked something like a tugboat with her curved-up bow, wheelhouse, signal antenna, and low freeboard—but she was not as stocky as real tugboats and didn't have rope fenders draped over her bow. It didn't matter. It was the *Alert*, and it was going to Cuttyhunk.

Geoff walked up the pier and aligned his body to the bow. He began stepping off the distance—heel to toe—as if he were walking a tight rope.

"Hey, kid!" shouted a voice from somewhere on the boat. "Whadda ya doing? We're shovin' off soon." It was the white-haired man with the bushy eyebrows.

"Trying to see how long the boat is."

"Save yaw steps, kid. She's sixty-five feet."

WHO-O-O-OP! came a deep fog-penetrating sound from the *Alert*.

"Hey! Boy! Yeah, you. You comin'?" a voice from a silhouette inside the wheelhouse thundered.

Geoff leapt to attention, hustled toward the gangplank, and jumped aboard. Dock crew withdrew the gangplank and pulled in the stern line dropped into the water by the white-haired man.

WHO-O-O-OP! WHO-O-O-OP! WHO-O-O-OP! Water churned and swirled behind the boat. The smokestack belched black soot, and the smell of diesel filled the air. *Alert* edged forward, then backward as the dock crew released the lines. She headed down a fairway to the channel. *Alert* was underway.

Geoff found Peter sprawled across their gear. "They said the crossing is almost three hours, and I'm bushed!" Peter said. "I'm gonna sleep the entire way."

Alert emerged between New Bedford's fleet of fishing boats and into the channel. Geoff worked his way to the bow, soaking in the sense of adventure, the smell of the salt air, and the damp breeze in his face. The fog returned. The coastline faded into a light shadow, and soon it vanished as the flat sea gave way to growing ocean swells.

Geoff rested his chin on his arms as he leaned against the bow post. His eyelids grew heavy, and staying awake became difficult. The boat vibrated to the rhythmic *chica-chic-chic-chica-chic-chic* of the workhorse engine and lured Geoff into a standing doze.

"You might want ta find anotha place ta ride." Geoff turned to see the man with the bushy eyebrows. "We're comin' inta some seas, and you'll get soaked if ya stay up heah. We don't want to be fishin' ya out if ya get tossed ovahbawd."

Geoff stepped into a cabin lined with orange-and-white benches along the back and side and took a vacant spot next to the door. The rhythmic vibration of the engine made his eyes heavy and sapped what was left of his energy. He slumped over onto a man sitting beside him and fell into a deep sleep.

The cabin door from the wheelhouse crashed open, shaking Geoff awake. A monster of a figure came through his fuzzy vision. He sat up tall, his awakening body well ahead of his brain. The colossal figure approached and stopped in front of him. "Fayahs!" Geoff trembled as he looked up at the thundering giant. The man glared at Geoff. "Fayahs! Fayahs!"

Geoff's eyes grew wide, and his mouth dropped open. He had no idea what to do next. The enormous man grew impatient. "Fayahs!" he roared again at Geoff. Geoff's heart raced. He felt lightheaded. His seatmate leaned over and said softly, "That's Clarence, the captain. He's collecting fares. You should pay him."

"Oh, fares." Geoff nervously looked up at Clarence and stammered, "H-how much?" He put on a plastic smile to hide his anxiety.

"Fayahs!" Clarence blasted again as he glared down his nose at Geoff. "One dolla."

Geoff hurriedly reached into his pocket, concentrating on pulling out only a single dollar bill. Clarence looked at his watch and then at other passengers and placed his stern eyes back on Geoff. Geoff pulled out his fist, and money exploded from his pocket like pigeons escaping from a cage, scattering all around him. The bill in his hand was a five, not a single. Before he could blink, Clarence handed Geoff his change and moved on, thundering, "Fayahs! Fayahs!"

Geoff crawled around the floor picking up loose money while shifting his eyes to see if his cabinmates were watching. No one gave him more than a passing glance. He sat back on the bench and faded into a dream and again fell against his neighbor. *Chica-chic-chic-chica-chic-chic.*

Another snort and Geoff sat tall. "You OK, boy?" questioned the man whose shoulder had become Geoff's pillow.

"Hey, I'm sorry. I can't seem to stay awake. Been up all night."

"What kept you up?"

"Uh, coming here. My friend and I came on the night train. I'm sorry I keep falling on you."

The man looked over his shoulder to the canopied area. "Are your parents out there?"

"No."

"Where are they?"

"Back home in Connecticut."

"So, you're alone?"

"Yeah, with my friend Pete."

"How old are you, son?"

"I'm fourteen, but my birthday is in a few weeks."

"Do your folks know where you are?" The man looked at Geoff suspiciously.

"Yes, they know where I am."

"You're not a runaway, are you? You look a little scruffy, like you left home in a hurry."

"Hey, mister, I'm no runaway. Honest. I know I'm a little dirty and my clothes are a mess, but we've been traveling since last night. My father told me to watch out for drunks on the train, and I couldn't sleep because I don't know what a drunk on a train looks like. That's why I kept falling over on you. I might look scruffy, but I'm no runaway."

"Do you know anyone on the island?"

"No."

"You're out here on a boat with your friend going to a place you've never been to before, and you don't know anyone there. Parents don't usually let boys your age venture out like that."

Geoff pulled a piece of paper from his pocket, unfolded it, and handed it to the stranger. "We're supposed to find this person at a place called the Bosworth House."

The man looked at the paper and nodded. "Gladys Snow."

"You know her?"

"Of course. Everyone knows her. How did you get her name?"

"Our parents have friends who know her."

"And who are those friends?"

"The Fairchilds."

"I'm good friends with them."

"If it weren't for them, my parents would never have allowed me to come here."

"I'm sure glad you showed me that note, son."

"Why's that?"

"Runaway kids usually get into more trouble than they can handle. Before you showed me that piece of paper, I was thinking I should introduce you to the police chief once we get to the island. How long are you planning to be there?"

"Three weeks. Why are you asking me all this? You don't even know me."

"I think you'll learn things on the island that will answer that question for you."

The *chica-chic-chic-chica-chic-chic* sent Geoff back into a doze. A few minutes with his head buried in the man's shoulder brought him back to life. "Hey, did you see the size of the captain's hands? His baby finger is twice the size of my thumb! The money in his hand looked like Monopoly play money. His hands look strong enough to crush marbles. He's cool! So, Clarence is the captain?"

"Yep. He's the captain. He doesn't talk much. He minds his own business and expects you to mind yours. Best to let him speak and to respond only if he speaks to you. If he ever tells you to do something, jump to it quick."

"Clarence, the captain," Geoff mused in awe. "I thought he would have a beard or an eye patch or something like that, not a round, clean-shaven face."

"You've been reading too much *Moby-Dick*."

"Who drives the boat when the captain's collecting fares?"

"That would be Bert, the mate."

"The guy with the white hair and bushy eyebrows, right?"

"That's him. You know, if he likes you, he'll invite you to see the engine room."

"Really?"

"The engine room is his inner sanctum. Hear that rhythmic clicking? That's a well-oiled and maintained engine you're hearing. Bert keeps it as clean as a whistle. Not a drop of oil anywhere except where it's supposed to be. If you get lucky, Bert might invite you for a look-see one day. Being invited is an honor. So, what happened a while ago when you sprayed your money all over the deck?"

"My father taught me how to fold money and pull out only what I need. I guess I got nervous when Clarence stood in front of me. I need more practice."

"What else did he teach you?"

"He taught me how to make a budget, so we'd know how much money we needed for food and traveling. He taught me how to lay out clothing so we wouldn't bring too much or forget something important like a pocketknife or a poncho. And he taught me to pretend I was asleep when someone walked by us on the train. He told us we should practice setting the tent up at night so we could do it in the dark if we had to."

"Tell me about your friend Pete. Which one is he out there?"

Geoff looked through the window over his shoulder and pointed. "That's Pete, the one sleeping on that pile of gear."

"This adventure you boys are on… How'd it come about?"

"Pete's the idea guy. He was here a few years ago with his parents on their boat."

"What did he tell you about Cuttyhunk?"

"Well, first he showed me a nautical chart his father used when they came here. I liked it so much, his father got one just for me. I studied it a lot. Mostly Pete told me about swimming in the breakers. He says they can get five or six feet high and we can go bodysurfing on them. I live on Long Island Sound, and if we're lucky, the waves get six inches high on our beaches. Yeah, we're gonna swim in those breakers!"

"Be careful. Those breakers have a lot of power. They can sweep you away and turn you upside down. You can drown in them. What else did he tell you?"

"Pete really never told me about much except for the breakers. I've never been on an island before, so I really want to see what it looks like. You know, beaches and palm trees."

"Palms in the Cape? Hmm. I don't think so. Where'd you get that idea?"

"Don't islands have palm trees?"

"In the tropics, yes, but not here."

"No palm trees? Oh, well. When the captain asked for money, I hope he didn't think I was being disrespectful. I just didn't understand him. He sure gave me a dirty look."

"Welcome to the language of the Cape. You'll pick it up as you spend more time around here."

"So, do you live on the island?"

"My family is here. We have a house and spend part of the summer here. I come on weekends, but I'll be here now for a month."

Chica-chic-chic-chica-chic chic. Geoff began to drift off again.

"Wake up, my young friend. We're getting close, and I think I can give you some tips that will come in handy."

Geoff sat up, rubbed his face, and tried to focus on the man.

"You know about the Bosworth House. You'll want to find the Allen House. There's a phone there you can use. If you poke a hole in your foot, go see Lucille. She's a nurse; you'll find her at the Allen House. There are a lot of footpaths around the island. Once you learn them, you'll get around a lot faster."

The engine slowed. Cuttyhunk was near. There was a flurry of movement as passengers closed books, gathered belongings, and stood to stretch out the kinks from the long ride. Geoff sat tall and looked between passengers lining up along the deck railing. The swells subsided, and he could see the stark grayish outline of land.

"Well, I'd better go see how Pete's doing," Geoff said.

"My name is Steve Baldwin."

"My name is Geoff." He extended his hand.

"Wow! That's a strong handshake for such a young lad. Where'd you learn that?"

"My father. He taught me that when I was a little boy. 'Don't give me the dead fish,' he'd say."

"He taught you well. A strong handshake always shows character. I'm sure he's proud of you."

Geoff dropped his head and said quietly, "Well, I'm not so sure about that."

"Not so sure? You just gave me a long list of things he taught you. How can you say he's not proud of you?"

Geoff bit his lip. Saying bad things about one's father was a betrayal.

Steve squinted and looked more deeply into Geoff's eyes. "You sure you boys aren't running away?"

"No, we're not runaways."

"Well, you're running from something."

"No, sir. We came here to camp."

"Well, Geoff, your words say one thing and your face says another. It's none of my business, so we'll leave it at that. Best of luck to you boys. Have a great adventure."

Geoff stood and nodded at Steve's smile and understanding eyes, and both left the cabin. He headed to the bow and was immediately slapped with the chilly air. Drizzle formed droplets on Geoff's eyebrows and eyelashes. Once out of the cabin, he could smell the salt air again, and got his first full glimpse of the island. Other passengers congregated along the rails, pointing and talking.

Until now, Cuttyhunk had been only an image in Geoff's mind. There were no pictures, only stories Peter had related about having once visited on his family's boat. They had braved an all-night train ride, hiked through the darkness in a strange city, sat in bus stations with others he thought wanted to rob him, and searched for a pier in a fog so thick he could hardly see across the street. Now, in front of him, Geoff watched the reality of a dream taking shape.

As the captain steered *Alert* toward a jetty marking the entrance to the harbor, the shadow of the island took on definition with the white dots of buildings. Geoff saw a barren island devoid of trees, and a lone tower perched on the tallest part. This was far from what he'd expected, but just being there filled him with exhilaration. Peter needed to see this! Geoff worked his way aft.

"Pete! Wake up!"

Pete sat up, rubbed his face, and looked around, trying to shake off sleep confusion. "Man, it feels like I have acid in my eyes from being up all night. What's going on?"

"We're almost there! I can see Cuttyhunk!"

"Ah! Landfall!" Pete came alive, stood up, and stretched to see the island.

Geoff winced when he found his knapsack on the bottom of their pile of gear. He delicately retrieved it and turned away from Peter as he opened it, peeked in, and carefully pulled out a small brown paper bag.

Peter looked on from a short distance. "What's that?"

Geoff jerked to attention and quickly stuffed the bag back into the knapsack. "Oh, it's nothing."

"Nothing? The heck. What is it?"

"I was just checking to see if anything was broken."

Peter glanced to the skies and then back to Geoff. "What could break? What's in there that's so important?"

"The knapsack was under the rest of the gear, and you were on top of it all. I just wanted to make sure nothing got broken."

"What's in your knapsack that could break?"

Geoff hesitated. "Um… a flashlight."

"A flashlight? You can't break a flashlight by sitting on it. C'mon, let's go stand by the railing and see what's going on."

Alert's engine slowed as it rounded the jetty. Excitement on the boat swelled as they passed small sand dunes and oat grass swaying in the late morning breeze. The once indiscernible speckles became cars, trucks, and people. Straight ahead, a dock bulged with greeters.

Moments later, with the boat securely tied, the dock burst with excitement. Geoff watched passengers disembark, welcomed by islanders. They were generous with their hugs, handshakes, back patting, and broad smiles. Some even twirled loved ones around. He saw his crossing friend, Steve Baldwin, give a big "wraparound" hug to a woman and three girls.

Geoff found Peter standing vigilantly over their gear.

"Pete, let's get off."

"No, not yet."

"Why not?"

"This isn't our dock. I asked the mate with the bushy eyebrows where the general store was, and he told me to stay on the boat. It's going to another dock to unload that ice." Peter nodded toward a huge, partially covered block of ice.

"Wow! Look at the size of it! What's it for?"

"Keeping fish fresh and selling to boaters."

Geoff stepped to the stern and stood beside the oversized chunk of ice. He tried to wrap his arm around one side of the block, and compared its height with his.

As rapidly as the main dock had become a platform of intense activity, it fell quiet. Except for the boys, *Alert* was eerily empty. Bert casually saluted a lone man who released the lines, and the boat chugged ahead.

Geoff settled in for a long ride, but no sooner had he sat down than *Alert*'s engine slowed as she came alongside the other dock. It lacked greeters, but a man stood nearby to handle the lines. Several men in yellow rain slickers emerged from a few of the dozen fishing shacks lining one side of the dock.

"OK, boys, this is wheah ya get off," Bert said.

"Where are we?" Peter asked.

"This is the fish dock," Bert said while looking down at the gear. "This all yours, right?"

Peter nodded.

"What did ya bring?"

Bert tilted his cap and scratched his head while Peter gave him the tour. "This bag with the poles sticking out has our tent. That bag holds our camping gear—rope, stakes, a hatchet, our canteens, and our mess kits. Those two duffels have our clothing and sleeping bags. And we each have a knapsack with personal stuff."

Bert heaved the gear up to the dock. "That's a lot of geah. Enjoy yawselves campin'." He saluted and turned his attention to off-loading the ice.

Life on the fish dock was lazy. No one moved fast. Few spoke, and when they did, their voices were quiet.

The boys climbed onto the dock. Geoff said, "I gotta see how they get that huge chunk of ice off the boat. That's one heavy sucker! I'd say it's almost twenty-seven hundred pounds."

"That would be a wild guess," Pete said.

"No, an educated guess."

"Based on what? You didn't bring a measuring tape, did you?"

"My body is a measuring tape. That block is not quite three by three and about five feet tall. Ice weighs almost sixty pounds per cubic foot. Two thousand seven hundred pounds. Ta-da."

"You figured that out when you were at the stern? Pretty fast."

"Can't read worth a shit, but I can add stuff up quick."

A man on the dock swung the arm of a boom over the boat and positioned it above the ice. The men attached huge lifting tongs to the ice and hooked it to the boom. Moments later, after a few grunts from the haulers and creaking from the tired old boom, the ice sat on the dock. The men silently cut the ice into smaller blocks with speed and precision, using only ice picks.

"Did you see how they did that?" Geoff said. "Those tongs are amazing!"

"Forget the amazing tongs. We need to find the general store."

"Do you remember where it is?"

"I think so, but maybe we should ask one of those guys just in case."

The boys approached the ice cutters. "Excuse me," said Peter in a confident tone.

One man glanced curiously at the boys, gave them a stone-faced look from head to toe, and returned his attention to the dwindling ice block.

Peter cleared his throat. "Excuse me. Can someone tell me where we can find the general store?"

"Too hard to tell," said one of the men working on the ice.

The boys looked at each other and shrugged. "'Too hard to tell.' What the hell does that mean?" Geoff said quietly.

"It means later, kid. That's what the hell it means. Later."

The boys stepped back toward their gear. "Let's try one of those shacks," Geoff said.

Fishing rods, lines, lures, and an assortment of tools hung from the walls and ceiling in the first open shack. The odor of fresh catch gushed from a large icebox. Buoys hung precariously on a row of nails. Pictures of nude women filled in any leftover wall space.

Geoff whispered, "Should we really be in here?"

"Whadda ya boys want?" came a scrappy voice from a dark corner. "Come in heah so I can see who ya ah."

The boys froze. They were afraid to step in and afraid to run off. "Well? Ya comin'? If yaw not, then git outta my light."

The boys took a step forward. The girlie pictures pulled Geoff's eyes like a magnet. "Ha! Ain't ya evah seen a pictcha of a naked lady befaw?"

As the boys' eyes adjusted to the low light, a figure appeared through the dark corner. His weathered face was strewn with deep lines cut from the sides of his eyes down to his mouth. Wire-rim glasses made his eyes look larger than normal, and he had a thin white mustache. He wore khaki pants, a khaki shirt, and a baseball cap with a large, oversized bill. He was stocky and looked fit for the sea. His hands were weather beaten and scarred, and looked granite-crushing strong. In one hand he held a narrow knife with a curved blade, and in the other, a partially cut apple.

"Now that ya can see me, tell me, whadda ya want."

Peter spoke up. "We're here to camp for a few weeks, and…"

"Didn't ask why yaw heah! Asked ya what ya want."

The boys' eyes got large. The spit evaporated in their mouths. "Ah," said Peter, "we're looking for the general store."

"Yaw lookin' faw the stohwa? Up the hill." The old fisherman pointed his knife toward the entrance of the fish dock.

The boys backed out of the shack as though edging away from a protective mama bear. If the island had friendlies, they were certainly not congregating on the fish dock.

Geoff picked up his small knapsack, turned his back to Peter, and began fidgeting with its contents while glancing over his shoulder.

"You keep fooling around with your knapsack. What's so precious in there?"

"I was just adjusting things. That's all."

"Adjusting things? I don't believe you. You're hiding something. C'mon, let's get going. We need to get to the general store."

"Pete." Geoff leaned into Peter as if to whisper a secret. "The guy in that shed… His name is Bob or Ike Tilton."

"How do you know that?"

"Their names are over the door. I wonder if all the fishermen are as good-natured as him."

Peter made a half smile. "He wasn't so bad. Just a little gruff. Maybe we were supposed to ask permission before stepping into his shack. Maybe he was just in a bad mood. Maybe he doesn't like guys our age. Whatever it is, I think we should get off this dock."

They draped gear around their bodies and headed past the row of sheds toward solid ground. Most were open and appeared to be furnished the same way.

When they reached the roadway, Peter put his hand on Geoff's shoulder. "Congratulations, Geoff! We made it to Cuttyhunk!"

"So, is this Broadway?"

"Yep, Broadway it is. All we've got to do is get to the top of that hill. I think I remember where the general store is."

They passed a small shipyard with boats on trailers and skids and dismantled outboard engines on operating tables surrounded by small tools. The industrious sound of bottom scraping and sanding was omnipresent. The dreary afternoon obviously wasn't dampening the spirits of boatwrights preparing for the summer season.

A small white cottage, perched atop wooden pilings, sat close to the road just up from the dock. Green striped awnings shaded its large windows. Fastened in the corner of the gable was a sign that read "White Cottage Ice Cream—Hamburgers, Hot Dogs."

"Look, Pete, food! We haven't eaten for a long time, and my stomach clock says it's long overdue for a meal."

"No! We have more important things to do—like find the general store and make camp. Besides, we only have enough money for one meal out when we celebrate our birthdays."

"Well, it doesn't look open, so it doesn't matter," Geoff said as he pointed back to the sign. "Get a load of that. The sign says, 'Carhop Service.' Do you think that's a joke?"

Peter scoffed and continued up the road. Geoff's hope of sustenance vanished as the sight of the restaurant grew smaller over his shoulder. His stomach yelled, *Feed me! Feed me!* and his mouth watered, but there would be no hamburgers near his mouth that day.

The cloud-covered skies dropped to the ground. Color faded away. "Great!" said Peter. "It's beginning to drizzle, and we could run out of daylight before making camp. We'd better hustle."

The boys stopped in the middle of a crossroad, one that seemed disproportionately large for both the island and the intersecting roads. With their strength zapped from lack of sleep, homesickness began seeping into Geoff's spirit. Two tired boys slowly picked up their pace, hoping to soon find the general store and a suitable place to camp as they headed up the hill on a road called Broadway.

3

THE BROWN PAPER BAG

With the dock behind them, there were few distractions left to take Geoff and Peter's minds away from their fatigue, the drizzle, and the ever-increasing weight of the gear. The crossroad marked the end of flatness. Whichever direction they went, it would be uphill. The road straight ahead led to the general store.

"We're going up *that*?" said Geoff.

"Well, we've gotta get to the general store before it closes, and this is the only way I know. We can't lollygag, so try to keep up."

Peter marched ahead, seemingly oblivious to the weight he carried. Geoff groaned and winced with each step as the straps and buckles gnawed at his shoulders. His pace slowed; walking became a laborious shuffle.

"Hey, Pete! I haven't seen a single palm tree. Where are they? I'm dying to see a coconut. And while I'm thinking of it, I didn't see much sand. Where are the sandy beaches?"

"Cuttyhunk doesn't have palm trees, Geoff. Are there any palm trees in Connecticut? No. They need warm weather all year. So why did you think you'd see palm trees here?"

"Well, I just figured that when you found an island with sand, you'd find palm trees. You know, islands, palm trees, and sand go hand in hand." Geoff paused. "But you're right. Maybe that's what that Steve guy on the boat was snickering about."

"You *didn't* tell him you were expecting to find palm trees, did you?"

"Well... actually... I did."

Peter raised his eyebrows and tilted his head toward the clouds as he burst out laughing. "I can't believe you did that! What a lame brain!"

"And I suppose there are no breakers, either."

"Oh, there *are* breakers. I told you there were, but I never told you there'd be palm trees."

Moments later, Broadway's steepening incline began taking its toll. Geoff once again stopped and dropped his gear. He put his hands on his lower back and stretched. "Pete, I need to stop."

Peter stopped and looked back in disgust. "Jeez, I brought a wimp with me."

Geoff breathed deeply as he looked around. "Take a look at this view. Sure looks different from up here, doesn't it? I still can't see any palm trees."

"I'm on to you, you idiot! Tell you what. You rest, and I'll look for your palm trees. You know, I *could* be wrong. I was only here once, a few years ago. Maybe a palm tree or two has sprouted up since then. Who knows?"

"I'll tell you one thing, my image of white sandy beaches, palm trees, blue sky… all shattered. And now drizzle. It's been drizzling since we got here, and if it's like what we have back home, it promises to last for days."

"That's enough talk about drizzle!" said Peter. "Feel that? Raindrops! You jinxed us. The drizzle's turning to rain. Come on, let's go. I feel like I'm dragging you up the hill. No more stopping."

Geoff gasped with each step. "Hey, there's the Bosworth House! See the sign in that driveway?" He pointed, grinning broadly. "That's where we'll find Gladys Snow."

Peter continued without acknowledgment.

Geoff looked around for something to distract him from his pain. He looked across the harbor to see moored boats all pointing in different directions—a sign of dead calm. He reflected on what his older brother, Peter, had taught him while earning a weather merit badge and said softly, "Dead calm and drizzle—a bad combination and a sign of a slow-moving weather front."

Geoff watched the soundless *Alert* pull away from the fish dock. Thoughts of home drifted into his head, along with an inexplicable sinking feeling and sense of loneliness. He turned away from Peter and reached into his knapsack for the brown bag. He pulled it out and gazed upon it reverently, but Peter's distant voice shook him out of his thoughts. Geoff quickly stowed the package and picked up his gear.

By the time Geoff reached him, Peter had donned his poncho. He stood tall over Geoff, hands on hips, a look of impatience on his face.

Geoff reached into his gear and quickly retrieved his poncho. Ignoring Peter, he looked back down Broadway to get a sense of how much higher they were. The fish dock was hidden behind a curve in the road, but the road ahead had a less strenuous incline. Though exhausted, Geoff felt a sense of relief.

"Hey! A sign to the Allen House!"

"Who cares about the Allen House?" Pete said. "Allen House… Bosworth House… They're both the same. I don't care. We're looking for the general store!"

"But the Allen House is where the public telephone is. Steve from the boat said so."

"Well, right now we don't need a phone. What we need is the general store. Focus, Geoff! Jeez!"

"Why is getting to the general store today so important?"

"Why? You haven't heard of… *food*?"

"Well, it's not like we're going to be able to build a fire. All the wood will be wet. Besides, my mom sent me off with a bag of fried chicken."

Oops! Geoff stiffened in his tracks. He had just blurted out his best-kept secret. He looked over and saw Peter's shocked face.

"Fried chicken? Did you say *fried chicken*? You've been holding out on me! So that's what all the secrecy's been about. You've been dragging your feet *and* lying to me! I was wondering what you were hiding—telling me it was a flashlight. What a bunch of crap. Fried chicken! Get it out! I'm famished!"

Geoff winced. "Well, I'm not sure where it is in my gear."

"Of course you know where it is. You've been feeling around for it every time you stop. What's with you? You don't want to share it with me, do you?"

"What do you mean?"

"What do you mean 'what do you mean'? Why don't you just come out and say it?" Peter looked around for familiar landmarks. "That store is around here somewhere. Maybe it's part of this house. I'm gonna take a look. If it's not here, we'll try another road farther up Broadway. You stay with the gear and think about how we're going to split that chicken."

Geoff glared. *He'll never get any of Mom's fried chicken.*

Peter walked up the narrow road and came back a few moments later. "Nothing here. It must be farther up."

A man wearing a slicker and a hat approached them from the top of Broadway. Slung over his shoulder was a stack of ropes attached to a half dozen red-and-white-striped buoys. It was their first encounter with anyone since leaving the fish dock.

When the man reached the boys, he slowed; the buoys on his back stopped clacking. "You boys… new heah, aren't you?"

"Yes, sir, we are," said Peter. "We're looking for the general store. Can you help us?"

The fisherman pointed up the long straight road leading to the top of the island. "Up thaya to the right."

"Thanks, mister, but I was just up there. I couldn't find it. Which building is it?"

The man pointed again. "Thaya's only one. Right up thaya… the dohwa just past the pictcha window. But it won't do you boys no good."

"Why not?"

"Stohwa's been closed all day. You boys will have to wait till mawnin'." And off he went with his buoys rhythmically swaying and clattering.

The boys stood motionless. All they could hear were raindrops pelting their ponchos.

All the huffing and puffing to find the general store only to learn it was closed was a hard blow. Their last meal had consisted of two doughnuts each at the Providence bus station. There would be no grub until sometime the next day if Geoff remained unwilling to share his mom's fried chicken.

"Maybe he's wrong," Peter said. "Let's go check it out."

What the fisherman had pointed to looked more like a side door to someone's house than a general store. There was no sign, and not even a small weather overhang to mark the entrance. Clutter stacked inside against the picture window partially blocked the boys' view. Geoff hesitated to press his face against the glass for fear he might be peering into someone's parlor, but hunger pangs overrode his respect for privacy. Even with his nose mashed against the glass, the diminished light made it difficult to see inside.

He cupped his eyes for a better look, hoping to see something that would give them a flicker of optimism. "I see a counter and I think the back of a cash register. There are shelves behind the counter. This *is* the store!"

"It can't be. It doesn't even look like one."

Geoff continued his examination. "Maybe this is what stores look like on Cape Cod. Hey! I see a rack of bread over to the right and a bunch of brooms, too."

Peter opened the screen door, cupped his hands, and looked through the door window. "It's closed for sure. We're finished! We spent too much time screwing around on the dock. We shoulda come up the hill sooner. This is why I wanted to move quickly. *You* held us up. It's all your fault."

"*My* fault?"

"If you hadn't had to watch that block of ice come off the boat, we would have been here long ago. *You're* the one who had to look at everything along the way and take all those rests. You took four breaks comin' up this hill."

"Three, but it wouldn't have mattered anyway."

"What do you mean, it wouldn't have mattered? I didn't take the breaks. *You* did. Did you see me drop my gear? No! Did you hear *me* whining, 'I need another break. I need another break'? No! It's *your* fault. It's *all* your fault."

"What? The store wasn't even open today!"

Peter waved away Geoff's explanation, and what was left of Geoff's sense of adventure hissed out like air through a leaky balloon. He felt betrayed by the person who had brought him to the island. This long-awaited trip was fast becoming a nightmare. He was tired and dis-couraged, and his energy was spent. His best friend was turning into a malevolent dictator and an emissary of ridicule.

The boys stood in front of the store, staring at the door. Peter broke the long silence. "Well, at least we have your mom's fried chicken."

"You've *got* to be kidding! After that, you think I'm sharing anything with you?"

"I'm sorry for what I said."

"The hell! You can't run off at the mouth like that, saying anything you want, and then brush it away when you're not mad anymore. You know, in my house we aren't allowed to blow up like that because we might regret the things we say."

"Well, maybe I went a little too far…"

"'A little,' he says."

"C'mon, Geoff, we're run-down. Hard rain's a-comin'. I'm sorry I jumped all over you. Let's find a place to pitch the tent and then think about the fried chicken."

Geoff flung his arms down to shake off the raindrops. "Get the fried chicken out of your head. My mom made it for *me*, not you."

"Fine! It's out of my head. It's all yours." Peter pointed to the top of the island. "Let's keep going up this road. It doesn't look like there are any houses up there. We won't have to camp in someone's backyard."

Geoff looked up the long road to the top of the hill. It wasn't as steep as Broadway, but he could easily have been talked into pitching the tent by the door of the general store. The road was lined with four-foot granite walls all the way to the top. Peter slapped him on the shoulder. "Come on—we'll head up there, and as soon as we find a clearing, we'll hop over the wall and pitch the tent."

Peter picked up his gear and then reached for Geoff's. "Let's go. Let's get this done."

Geoff became intrigued with the granite walls. The intricate manner in which the stones fit together attested to the skill of the craftsmen who had built them. An opening to the left led to a three-story mansion sitting on its own hill surrounded by a moat of thick, healthy grass. Steadfast Peter, now burdened with all their gear, focused on finding the ideal campsite. Geoff, liberated from his share of the weight, was free to admire the workmanship.

"Pete, I wonder why this road was put here. It goes to the top of the hill, but I see nothing up there except that tower. I can't believe they built this kind of a wall just for a tower. Got any ideas?"

Peter remained silent and faithful to his mission.

"Look at these walls! They're as straight as an arrow, and I'll bet the distance from the left to the right side is identical all the way up."

No response.

"Pete, did you see how the walls don't roll up and down with the gullies? Someone did a lot of engineering on this."

Geoff was talking to the wind.

"This is some wall. It looks like it was built long ago, but they never pushed the dirt back against it. I wonder what that's all about."

Tire tracks zigged and zagged up the road, avoiding rocks, lumps, and places where the ditch jutted away from the wall. The farther they walked, the more intriguing the origin of the wall became to Geoff.

"Hey, Pete, this wall is twenty feet high in places. This is amazing!"

Peter suddenly stopped and made a 360-degree sweep. "This is where we'll pitch our tent."

"Here? In the road?"

"No, stupid, over there where we can jump the wall *and* easily climb back. There's a small meadow right on the other side of those shrubs, and it isn't sloping much. It'll be OK for now. It's below the direct line of the wind, and we'll blend in with our surroundings."

"You saw all that in a glance?"

"While you've been jumping all over the place and admiring the architecture, I've been scouting around for a place to camp. No, it didn't come suddenly. I told you we'll make camp at the first opportunity, and this is it."

Peter stacked the gear on top of the wall and jumped into the meadow. "Let's take the tent and check out what's beyond that bush. If this is a good spot, I'll come back for the rest."

They surveyed Peter's choice and nodded in agreement. "Geoff, you pitch the tent. I'll get the rest of the gear."

Geoff cleared the ground of stones and sticks, spread out the tent, and began assembling the poles and rope lines. The tent was small yet large enough to sleep two with room at the far end to stow their gear. He hurried, hoping to impress Peter with the speed at which he could complete his task. He proudly had one end up by the time Peter returned.

"Stop! Stop right now!" Peter said.

"What?"

"Don't you see what's wrong?"

Geoff checked his work. "I can't see anything."

"You can't tell?"

"Sorry. I can't."

"You can't see *anything* wrong? Wanna take another look?"

"Pete, how many times are you going to ask me that? If you're trying to make me feel stupid, you're doing a fine job."

"Well, for one, look at where the opening is."

Geoff pointed.

"Yes, it's up there, but it's supposed to be down here. Remember? When on a slope the opening is *always* supposed to be on the downhill side. I told you that. I've told you that many times."

"Well… it's *almost* flat."

"*Almost* counts in horseshoes and hand grenades. Sometimes you're a complete idiot."

All the good Peter had done in carrying the gear flickered like an end-of-life candle. Geoff thought, *That does it… None of Mom's fried chicken for him.* "You finished?" he asked.

"Only if you stop doing all those stupid things. We went over all this a dozen times. I know there's a lot to remember, but it's obvious that tent openings *always* face the downhill side."

"Look, I'm tired. You're tired. We're getting wet and cold. We're hungry and—"

"Thanks to you," Peter interjected.

Geoff pursed his lips, dropped his head, and turned away.

Peter continued. "Am I wrong?"

Geoff said nothing and set about to reposition the tent.

"Tell me if you think I'm wrong."

"Pete, let's just let it go and get this tent set up."

"What's wrong with asking if you think I'm wrong? Just tell me."

Geoff pulled up the stakes and rotated the tent.

"Ignoring me is only ticking me off. Answer my question, darn it!"

"Pete, if I say yes, you'll want to prove me wrong. If I say no, you'll gloat and push me around even more. So I'm just gonna keep my mouth shut."

Geoff continued setting up the tent, feeling Peter's scrutiny with every step. He had been a Boy Scout, and pitching tents for him was as routine as filling canteens. He considered himself good at it. So he'd missed a step about the orientation. Big deal! He darted from front to back, adjusting rope lines to make the tent snap to attention. With each step, he scowled at Peter with a look that said, *Go ahead, you son of a bitch, find something wrong.* "Does this meet with your approval? See anything else wrong?"

"Give me time and I probably will."

Chilling raindrops rolled down Geoff's back, causing him to shiver. Darker clouds settled across the island and brought a new kind of cold. Everything that could go wrong was going wrong. Being with Peter on this island was definitely proving to be a mistake. He teetered between anger and panic. There was no place else to go.

"You know, Pete, this tent is the only dry place for us on the island, and I don't want to be in it with you."

Peter raised his finger in an attempt to interrupt.

"Stop! I'm not finished. You know, you remind me of my father. I get this same kind of crap from him all the time. I don't need it. I won't let you do it to me."

"How do I remind you of your dad?"

"First he tells me what to do, and then he rides me and points out all the little things I did wrong. Do you have any idea how small and stupid that makes me feel? Here we are, a hundred and seventy miles from home, and you sound just like him. I wanted to get away from him, and now I have *you*."

Geoff looked away and walked in a circle while throwing his arms up in the air. "Look, you're treating me the same way *he* does. By coming here I thought I could get away from him, and now I'm trapped here with him for the next three weeks."

"Who's *him?*"

"My father! Aren't you listening? I set up the tent. OK, it was going the wrong way. You made a big deal about it. You didn't have anything good to say. You had to find fault. That's what makes you just like my father. With him, if it's not perfect, none of it is good. When he launches into one of his tirades, he says it's to teach me things, but I think it's to satisfy some urge to be a bully. Goddamn it! Goddamn it all to hell!"

Geoff looked toward the harbor. "Now the weather's turning to shit and you can't even see the main dock. Goddamn it."

"I didn't mean to strike a nerve. I'm sorry. I really am."

"We've been the best of friends for two years. But when you push me around and find fault with everything I do, you're not my friend anymore. It's not like you to be a bully. So why are you being one now?"

Peter slowly approached and put his hand on Geoff's shoulder. "You know, we're both very tired and grouchy. We haven't slept for two days, the drizzle's turned to rain, and we're both hungry." Peter tossed the gear inside the tent as the wind picked up and the weather took their daylight. "Come on, let's get out of this weather."

Inside the tent, Peter watched Geoff fidgeting with his gear. "Think you can find your mom's fried chicken in there?"

"So now you're gonna be nice because I have something you want? Is that it?"

"Geoff, settle down! Jeez! If you want to eat it by yourself, then go ahead. Just don't do it in front of me. Go outside or somewhere else."

"Maybe *you* should be the one to go."

"You get the chicken. I get the tent."

"God, you can be such an asshole."

"Look, if you don't want to share it with me, that's your choice. It's been sitting in your knapsack for over a day, and for all we know it's gone bad."

"You just want me to get it out so you can snatch it."

"Relax, Geoff. I'm just being honest. You can tell if it's bad by its smell. You should at least check to see if it's OK. If it's not, you can eat the whole thing. I promise. Just take a whiff. Please."

Geoff slowly felt around in the knapsack and pulled out the brown paper bag. Both boys propped themselves on their knees, hovering over the bag with the anxiety of not knowing if they would eat or fall asleep hungry. Geoff peeled back the aluminum foil, and the delicious aroma of fried chicken filled the tent, exacerbating the pangs in their stomachs. Their noses lunged toward the only meal they would get for the day, as if the smell of the chicken could satiate their need to eat.

"It's good!" proclaimed Peter.

Geoff abruptly closed the bag and cradled it close to his chest and turned away. "We're not eating my mom's fried chicken."

"Are you OK?

"I'm fine, Pete."

"Aah! I get it. You're homesick!"

"Yeah, maybe. Aren't you?"

"Nah. Now… about this fried chicken. If we don't eat it, then it *will* spoil. It's like two guys out in the desert with a canteen of water but they die from thirst because they're afraid of running out. Kinda dumb, isn't it? Look, I can understand that when you're sore about something, you can't just turn a switch and everything will be OK. I jumped on you earlier. Maybe a little too hard, but let's look at what happened today. I was so intent on getting to the general store, I missed seeing the Bosworth and the Allen House. They're important to us, and now, because of you, we know where they are. By talking to your friend on the boat you know where the telephone is. We—"

"I'm feeling like you're conning me with smooth talk. Seems to me I heard words like lame brain, complete idiot, and stupid since we started up the hill. What am I supposed to believe?"

"Believe me when I say I'm sorry. We're gonna be together for three weeks, and this is not a good way to start. I'm sure we'll have more disagreements. We're different as can be. Yeah, maybe it's me with the grandiose ideas, but you're the one who always makes them happen. C'mon, Geoff. We're both famished. It's probably why we're on each other. Let's get to that fried chicken."

Geoff gripped the bag. "I can't, Pete, I just can't." And he stuffed it back inside his knapsack.

"God, this is frustrating! OK, I get it. You feel close to your mom just by holding that chicken. Is that it?"

"So, what of it? When she gave it to me, she said, 'When you taste that chicken, think of me. I'll be with you.' And if I eat it, she'll be gone."

"Well, try this on. If you don't eat it, it will spoil, and you'll have to toss it. How would you like explaining *that* to your mom?"

Geoff reluctantly pulled out the fried chicken. If he was going to eat it at all, he had to share it with Peter.

He placed the packet of chicken between them. They looked at it in reverence as if it were discovered treasure. Geoff peeled back more of the aluminum foil, exposing four small pieces. "Well, it looks like we have two thighs and two drumsticks."

"There's not much there."

"Yeah, well, it's plenty for one."

It took only minutes to convert the bag of fried chicken to a bag of sucked-dry bones. The boys' gnawing hunger pangs subsided.

Peter fell back on his sleeping bag. "I'm bushed. I could fall asleep right now."

Raindrops that had begun as a tapping on the tent became a full-fledged drumroll, and the wind picked up strength.

"Hey, Pete," Geoff said over the increasing noise. "We're having a splat attack!"

Peter did not respond.

Geoff felt around the tent, searching for the bag of chicken bones. He grasped it like treasure, feeling every mile between himself and the security of home. Voices wandered in his head—haunting voices. The weather had created a hostile world outside, and it was closing in on him. Cool drafts seeped through the front flap zipper. Dampness chilled his body.

He climbed into his sleeping bag, shivering and unable to get warm. He turned his thoughts to home, hoping for distractions and mental images, but none came. He felt like he had forsaken his mother by eating her fried chicken. A choking lump developed in his throat. He fought the impulse to give in to it. At fourteen, boys on the cusp of young manhood were forbidden to cry. The noise of the rain on the tent overpowered all other sounds. He turned away from Peter and sobbed himself to sleep as the long, long day finally ended.

4

STEPPING BACK IN TIME

Geoff's eyes opened to the dawn of his first full day on Cuttyhunk. He lay quietly on his back, his hands cradling his head. The rain had stopped sometime during the night, and the tent had held up in the wind. The meager fuel from the fried chicken had curbed his hunger, and sleep had quieted his gnawing homesickness.

Geoff sat up, shaken by a strange sound right outside the tent. Thump! Thump! Thump! Then he heard grass being torn from its roots. Their tent was surrounded by thumping, chewing visitors. The tent quivered and shook whenever one of them brushed against a rope.

Geoff reached for the tent's flap zipper and eased it one tooth at a time until it was open enough to poke his head out. Looking back at him from only a foot away was a wide, dark eye with long black lashes. Both he and the creature froze, staring at each other.

Then Geoff exhaled and relaxed. No beast with an eye like that could pose a threat. The animal's ear twitched. She precipitously bolted, but not without tripping over a rope that yanked out a tent stake, causing the tent to collapse on the boys.

"Oh, Shit! yelled Geoff as the thunder of hooves scrambled toward the protective cover of the bayberry bushes.

Jolted out of sleep, Peter flailed as he tried to pull the fallen tent off his face. "What the heck is going on?"

"Deer!"

"Deer?"

"They were right by our tent chomping on grass. When I looked out, they bolted and one of them tripped over a stake. Jeez! I've never been so close to a deer and never seen such big eyes. And its ears were almost the size of its head. It was only inches from my face!"

The boys crawled out of their crumpled dwelling. Peter looked around, trying to come alive from his long sleep. "How long have you been awake?"

"A while." Geoff walked to the front of the tent, hooked the other end of the rope around the ground stake, and adjusted it. "There, good as new."

"Are you still homesick?"

"Huh? Why would you ask about that?"

"Well, you were pretty homesick last night. Being homesick is no fun."

"So, you know about it then."

"Yeah. I know about it. The only good thing about it is you don't throw up."

"Hell, I thought I outgrew it at Boy Scout camp."

"I don't think you really outgrow it. You just get over it faster. You never answered my question."

"Yeah, I'm much better."

"Then let's get to the order of the day. Here's what I propose: First, food! Second, find a better campsite."

Geoff checked his watch. "It's almost seven thirty. I doubt the general store is open."

"No big deal. Let's do a little exploring and then hang around the general store. We can wait there until it opens."

As the boys climbed over the wall, Geoff stopped to take in the vista. "Man, would you look at that view! Couldn't see any of this yesterday. There's no sun, but at least it won't be raining today."

"Look up, Geoff. See those clouds? I bet they have rain in them."

"Maybe, but those clouds are high, and it's clear underneath. The wind's down, and it's warm. No rain unless all that changes. I learned that from my brother. So, did you get up here when you came with your parents?"

"No," Peter said. "But here's a bit of history for you. Did you know that the name Cuttyhunk is a shortened version of an Indian word that means 'land's end,' because it's the last island in the Elizabeth Islands string? See that beach area between the barges that stick out into the water? Guess what's there."

"A beach?"

"Close. Guess again."

"No hint?"

"What was the one thing you wanted to see while we're here?"

"Ah! Palm trees, but I don't see any."

"No, dummy. Breakers! Those are *breakers*!"

"Those white waves on the beach are breakers? They don't look very big."

"They're big enough to give you a walloping. I almost got caught up in one when I was here with my family. Enough of the geography lesson. Let's go check out the tower."

The boys walked to the top of the hill and looked up the base of a metal tower that stood about fifty feet tall. Sitting on top was a small shed-like structure with windows and a metal walkway all around it.

"It doesn't look like anyone's in it," said Geoff.

Just then, a small door opened, and a man stepped out. He leaned over and looked down at the boys. Geoff waved. The man nodded and looked away.

Peter slapped Geoff's arm. "Yep, no one's up there all right. C'mon, let's go get some chow."

The boys bounced down the road and soon found themselves in front of the general store.

"I still say this place looks more like the back door to someone's house," Geoff said.

A man inside fidgeted with the lock and opened the door. He was average height and thin, with long smile lines on his cheeks. "Morning, boys! You're here early. You need something from the store?"

"We're here to buy breakfast provisions," Geoff said.

"You fellas off a boat?"

"No, we're here camping," Peter said. "We'd like to buy some bread, peanut butter, and cookies."

"Where are you camping?"

"Last night we camped up the hill by the tower, but we're gonna move to the beach," said Peter.

"Yeah, and we haven't eaten hardly anything since *very* early yesterday morning," Geoff said. "When we got here yesterday, you were closed."

"Yep, closed up early. Nothing from the mainland, and the season hasn't started yet. We don't open till ten, but I'm guessing you were hoping you could buy your breakfast provisions right now. Am I right?"

"Yes, sir! You got that right!" said Geoff with growing anticipation.

The man stepped aside and held the door while motioning for the boys to enter. "You want to make peanut butter and jelly sandwiches, eh? Bread's here. You'll find peanut butter and jelly on the shelf over there."

The boys wandered through the dark store. The smell of old, damp wood reminded Geoff of a village store way back in his boyhood. Canned and boxed goods crammed the wooden shelving: canned soup, canned vegetables, canned Spam, condensed milk, canned fruit. Cans, cans, cans—everywhere. A large industrial-size refrigerator with glass doors held all things perishable. Without its humming, the store would have been as quiet as a country bar on Sunday morning. Behind the counter were more shelves stocked with medicines and toiletries.

Geoff looked spellbound at an old, tarnished cash register that sat prominently at the end of the counter. "You like that old workhorse?" the man asked him. "It works as good today as the day it was made."

"Yeah, this is like stepping back in time," Geoff said. "It feels just like the old grocery store in our town. Hey, Pete. Take a look at this old cash register."

Peter walked over and glanced at the artifact, unimpressed.

"Remember that market in our village?"

"Nope."

"Well, this store looks almost like it. There was an old cash register just like this one."

Geoff continued to look around, reflecting and commenting on images of bygone days.

"You sound like a nostalgic person," the man said.

"A what kind of person?"

"Nostalgic. A nostalgic person is someone who is sentimental."

Peter stuck his head out from behind a shelf. "Yep, that describes him, all right. He was pretty nostalgic last night. He had a bad case of homesickness."

Geoff glared at Peter. The man said firmly, "Homesickness is a private matter."

Peter returned with bread and peanut butter. "I know what *we're* having for supper."

"Peanut butter and jelly sandwiches?" Geoff said.

"Nope. You'll never guess what I saw on the shelf over there… Chef Boyardee!"

"No fooling!"

"Yep, it's right over there."

"What's with that?" the store owner asked.

"Last year we camped on the dunes at Port Jefferson on Long Island, and it seemed like all we ate was Chef Boyardee."

"Yeah, all you need is a can opener, a fork, and an appetite," Geoff said. "Just open the can and supper's ready! Hot or cold, tastes the same. We sure like it."

The man laughed and said, "Is this all you need?"

"Yes, for now," Peter said. "We'll be back later for more."

"OK, then, your total comes to a dollar and five cents."

Geoff gave the man two dollars and watched intently as he set it on a small white marble surface above the cash register drawer. Then he pushed a few buttons, and $1.05 showed up in the price window. *Ding-g-g* came a distinctive chime, and the cash drawer popped open.

"I told you it works as well as the day it was made," said the man as he gave Geoff his change and extended his hand. "My name's Muggsy."

"I'm Geoff."

"Well, Geoff, you have a strong handshake for a young man. It shows character. I like that in a person."

Geoff pointed to Peter. "This is Pete."

Peter stood in the background and nodded.

"So, tell me, what brought you boys to Cuttyhunk?"

Geoff told him how they got to the island, and Muggsy quizzed him about his family. Geoff pulled out a piece of paper and handed it to him. "We met a man on the boat over who thought we were runaways until I showed him this."

Muggsy looked at the paper, nodded, and handed it back. "We seldom find boys your age around here without parents. They must really trust you to be on your own. What's your connection to Gladys Snow?"

"We have to check in with her. She's at the Bosworth House."

"I know where she is. Why her?"

Peter joined in. "My parents are friends with the Fairchilds, and they told us to check with Gladys Snow when we got here."

"Why are you camping up the hill?"

"We wanted to get here before you closed but didn't make it," Peter explained. "The weather was coming in fast, and we needed to make camp or get soaked. We didn't want to camp in someone's backyard, so we went up there."

"Is this your first time here?"

"For me, yes. Pete's been here before with his family."

Muggsy looked at Peter. "What's your family name?"

"Sparks."

"Sparks, hmm. And they know the Fairchilds?"

"Yes."

"Before she married, Flo Fairchild was Flo House; that's a well-respected name around here. How long are you planning to camp up the hill?"

"Just until we find a good spot down on the beach," Peter said. "We hope today."

Geoff pointed to a faded brownish photo pinned to a corkboard on the wall behind the cash register. It was a shot of a large wave smacking into a barrier and shooting spray high into the air with more wild waves behind it. The sea was frothing with white turbulence. "Where was that picture taken?"

Muggsy turned to the photo. "That's a picture of the beach by the barges, taken when Hazel hit in '54. That storm really ripped into those barges."

"So those are breakers, right?"

"Yes, those are Mother Nature's worst."

Geoff turned to Peter. "Are those the kind of breakers you're talking about? We're not surfing in *those,* are we?"

Peter stepped up to the photo. "I think they're a little dangerous for surfing."

"You'd have to be insane to go out in *that,*" Muggsy said. "Look, fellas, jumping into the breakers is one thing. Camping's another. Moving to the beach is a good plan. Plenty of driftwood to burn or to make useful tools and campsite furniture. Beachcombing is always fun, and you can find all sorts of interesting things. There's a freshwater spigot near the main dock. You'll be out of the way of folks. There's a fine beach on the other side of the jetty if you don't mind swimming across the channel.

"You boys are young and think you're immortal, but watch out for those breakers. You know why they're called breakers, don't you?" Muggsy cocked his head and squinted as he waited.

The boys hesitated a moment and shook their heads.

"Because they are breakers, that's why."

The boys chuckled nervously.

"And," Muggsy continued as he leaned toward the boys, "they will break *you* if you turn your back on them or underestimate their power. Big or small... makes no difference. They come up suddenly, turn you upside down, boil you in whatever's on the bottom—sand, rocks, and all the other debris you see cast up along the shoreline. Then there's the undertow that can drag you back out where the next one waits its turn to thrash and pummel you. The sea has no mercy—she doesn't care if you're a piece of wood or a human being. Get caught under one of those, and you may never see land again.

"When you're on the beach, look to see what they've done to the barges. Then imagine what will be left of you if a breaker throws you into the rusted, twisted, sharp iron on them. Go slow. Learn your limits. If one gets ahold of you, there's nothing anyone can do but wait and watch until it spits out what's left of you. Out there, you boys are on your own. Do I make myself clear?"

The boys stood motionless, spellbound. They nodded and simultaneously choked out, "Yes, sir."

"Nobody's going to tell you to stay out of them. You have to learn when to just stand on the beach and watch. Be smart. OK, you boys didn't come for a scary campfire story. If you'd like, I can get a knife and you can make a sandwich right here. Would you like one?"

"S-s-sure," stammered Geoff, still reeling from Muggsy's warning.

"I'll be right back." Muggsy went through a door into what looked like a kitchen. Moments later he returned with a woman following him as she dried her hands on the fringes of her apron.

"Boys, this is Mrs. Thomson, my wife. These boys are here to camp for a few weeks. They know the Fairchilds."

The boys nodded respectfully.

"Nice to meet you boys." Mrs. Thomson gave the parentless young wayfarers a smile that said, *Watch yourselves. I'm on to you.* She scanned them from head to toe as if searching for weapons. "You say you know the Fairchilds?"

"Yes, ma'am," Peter said.

"From where?"

"Our parents are friends with the Fairchilds back home."

"Where's back home?"

"Connecticut, ma'am."

"You're here to camp?"

"Yes, ma'am."

"Where?"

"Right now, we're set up by the tower, but we'll be moving to the beach."

Mrs. Thomson gave the boys another scrutinizing look and turned back to her kitchen. "Be careful camping. And mind them breakers."

The door closed behind her.

"Well, looks like the missus just approved you."

"She what?" Geoff said.

"Well, since you boys have no parents here, island folks will look after you. Looks like you passed Mrs. Thomson's test. She's a stern one, but inside she's really a softie."

Peter smiled at Muggsy and resumed wandering around the store.

"What would happen if we didn't pass her test?" Geoff asked.

"Well, then, there'd be no need for you fellas to go looking for a campsite down on the beach."

"Why not?"

"Because you'd be leaving the island today."

"As in, being kicked off?"

"Yep, as in being kicked off."

"Is that right— I mean, it's OK to do that?"

"It's the way things are done here. The island's police force consists of the chief of police and the eyes and ears of the rest of us. Nothing gets by us. There's enough trouble with day visitors and boat people during the season. There's no room here for troublesome kids. Islanders won't tolerate bad behavior. Mind yourselves and you'll do fine."

"What kind of trouble can get someone kicked off?"

"Oh, stealing, vandalism, being where you shouldn't be, looking guilty, and, if you work here, not showing up."

"Looking guilty! Why does that count?"

"If you look guilty, you probably *are*."

"Not that I'm going to test it, but how do you know when someone gets out of line?"

"News travels fast around the island. Wouldn't surprise me if folks know where you're gonna camp before you even get down there."

"Wow!"

"You'll find that folks here speak their mind. They mind their own busines and expect you to do the same. It's impolite to ask questions about someone's past. If they want you to know about it, they'll tell you. Be respectful. Learn the island culture and you'll fit in just fine."

"Muggsy, not to change the subject, but is this store part of a house?" said Geoff.

"That it is."

"I thought so."

"Home is right on the other side of that wall. Getting to work in the morning is easy. You're standing in what was once a sitting room, and that was the side entrance. Since everyone knows where we are, there's no need for special doors and signs. Ah… we got distracted. Here you go."

"Hey, Pete, Muggsy brought us a knife. Time to eat."

Peter sprang to the front counter. "I'm famished."

The boys broke open the bread and spread a thick layer of peanut butter and jelly. While still devouring the first sandwiches, they prepared seconds.

"Would you like some milk to wash that down?" Muggsy asked.

"That would be great," Peter said.

Muggsy pulled a quart of milk from the refrigerator. Peter opened it and gave it to Geoff for the first swig. When Geoff handed it back, Peter gulped down the rest of it in seconds.

"We should get going," Geoff said. "We have a camp to move. How much do we owe you for the milk?"

"Don't worry about it. This quart's on me."

"Wow! Thanks, Muggsy."

"If you'd like, I can hold on to your groceries so you don't have to carry them all around. If you're not back by the time I close, I'll leave them outside on the steps and you can pick them up as you go by."

"They'll be OK sitting out there?" said Peter.

"They'll be fine."

The three stood outside. Muggsy pointed to a footpath across Broadway. "That path over yonder is a shortcut to the main dock. It'll save you a good ten minutes."

They headed down the long and narrow concrete path—wide enough for one person. Bushes sheltered it and formed a protective floral canopy. An opening in the shrubbery revealed a house with a long, closed-in porch.

"Pete! This must be the Allen House. There's a phone booth on the other side of that screen door."

Peter looked over but said nothing.

"I like that Muggsy guy," Geoff said. "I wonder where he got a name like that."

"What'd you like about him?"

"Well, for one, he was friendly. He coulda said, 'What do you want and then get out of here,' but he didn't. He warned us about the breakers without telling us not to go in them. Now, if only I could get my pop to talk to me like that."

Peter waved his hand dismissively. "Ah, he was just using reverse psychology. My parents use it on me all the time. They're always telling me to go left when they really want me to go right. They think that whatever they tell me, I'll do exactly the opposite. That's reverse psychology."

"Reverse psychology or not, I still like him."

"Muggsy made it sound like the breakers are cunning demons that can see and think."

"That's a personification."

"A what?"

"Personification—when you give life to an inanimate object. Muggsy used a personification. Composition class, Pete. Guess who must have been sleeping that day. I saw the look on your face when he told us about the breakers."

"Geoff, trust me. We're not going to get into any trouble in the breakers. I swam in them a few years ago, and look, I'm still here. Personifications? How'd you remember *that* word? You'd better be careful, or you might end up being a writer or something."

"But didn't you feel good about him?"

"Never gave it a thought, but I can see why you would. C'mon, let's cut the chitchat and pick up the pace."

The path took the boys down the hill, around the Coast Guard station, and to the road heading to the main dock. They stood in the middle of a large three-way intersection. One road led to the main dock where the *Alert* had first stopped. The other two roads went on the list of places to explore. Small broken shells littered the center of the intersection.

"Look at all the broken clamshells. That's weird."

"They don't have clams here. They have quahogs."

"What's the diff?"

"Quahogs and clams… Same thing, only quahogs are larger."

"Maybe they fix the road with the broken shells."

"Quahog shells to fix the road? Geoff, didn't you get enough sleep last night?"

"Well, back home they spray down a layer of black tar and spread crushed gravel over it. Maybe here they cover the tar with broken shells instead of gravel."

"We have better things to do than wonder about the roads. C'mon— the beach awaits."

5

RECKONING WITH THE BREAKERS

Peter slalomed his way through the maze of thorny bushes, large rocks, and tall oat grass. Geoff followed, but when he emerged, Peter was already halfway down the beach.

Geoff climbed onto a large boulder, dazed by the speed at which his surroundings had changed. The fifty feet between the road and the shoreline defined the difference between "over there" and "right here." It was the same as being high in the jungle forest canopy with the ground fifty feet below—same geographic location, yet a world away.

A breeze pressed against Geoff. He turned into it with outstretched arms, closed his eyes, and let its freshness fill his lungs. It rumbled past his ears, dulling the sound of swirling, splashing water. A salty mist filled the air with the distinctive scent of the sea. It carried him back to his childhood days when his family had piled into their station wagon and headed for the shore. Tall cattails and sea breezes greeted and filled them with the excitement of beach sounds, sandcastles, and delicious surprises from the picnic basket. Those days were the best of times, where lifelong memories would take him back to a carefree world kept safe by his vigilant mother. He stood on the boulder—lost in good feeling.

A flock of squawking sea gulls grabbed Geoff's attention. He watched as they dropped quahogs from high above to break the shells when they hit the road. They swooped down to claim what was theirs before being robbed by other gulls and flew off with quahog guts hanging out of their beaks. Geoff grimaced. "You'll never see quahog guts near my mouth. ICK!" The mystery of the pile of shells in the intersection, however, was solved.

"Get off that rock!" A commanding voice jerked him out of his dreamy trance. He stood rigidly and gazed around. The voice carried the familiar tone of his father. Could his father be on the island? Impossible. It had to be the wind playing tricks in his ear.

"I told you to get off that rock!" Geoff searched again for the faceless voice. Perhaps a prankster was crouching behind the oat grass. It could not have been Peter. He was far down the beach, standing on a barge. Had his father followed him to the island to criticize his actions? If that were true, how had he arrived undetected, and when? Geoff realized he didn't have the freedom he'd thought. He still felt as though everything he did was being scrutinized. But, unable to find a body belonging to the voice, he finally decided that he'd just imagined it.

The water became more forceful as the shoreline turned and bore the full brunt of the Atlantic. The field of boulders gave way to smaller rocks and commingling sand. Beyond the first barge, dramatic breakers thundered ashore, sending vibrations under his feet. Spray shot high into the air and blew leeward as the smell of the sea swirled in Geoff's nose. The barges, those dark slivers seen from the top of the island, had become ominous fortresses protecting the narrow strip of sand between the beach and the channel.

Geoff faced the fleet of shoreline barges. Massive timbers, saturated with preserving creosote, interlocked and strapped together, were held in place with mounds of fist-size oval rocks and sand. A string of wind-blown barges ran along the shore, forming a four-foot-high wall. On top of the barges were immovable iron cleats that, between time and the elements, had been transformed into rust-crusted artistic tributes.

He walked next to a barge running along the shoreline until he was blocked by one that ran perpendicular to the sea. One end was high on land and well intact. The other stretched seaward, exposed to unrelenting attacks from crashing waves that gnawed at the timbers—one fiber at a time. Rust had bled into the sun-bleached timbers, turning them to chestnut red that deepened in color when soaked by waves or rain.

Mother Nature announced massive happenings on the other side of the barge that sent thunderous rumblings through the ground. In contrast, Geoff stood on the tranquil side. Offshore swells became a series of frothing waves as they stumbled toward the beach. They appeared docile and innocent, yet their force pushed small rocks around like corks. When pulled back by the receding water, thousands upon thousands of stones tumbled and tripped over one another and sounded like the clacking of horses' hooves on cobblestone streets in old New Bedford.

"Hey, Geoff! Where you been?" Peter shouted.

Geoff looked around.

"Up here!"

Peter stood atop the barge; his clothing flapped, and his hair blew across his grinning face. "Go to the corner over there and I'll hoist you up. Wait till you see what's on this side!"

Standing alongside Peter, Geoff's view was vastly different from moments before. He could see the barge separating turbulent breakers on one side from the less dramatic sea on the other. The seaward end of the barge was a dangerous lure with its character, color, and raw wounds from its war with the sea. It did not take Muggsy's warning to persuade him to admire it from a safe distance.

The boys' enormous grins told of their awe and excitement. Salt spray formed droplets on their eyebrows and dripped down their cheeks. Geoff had yet to abandon his hopes for a palm tree, but there was no doubt about Peter's promise of breakers.

Geoff turned in circles, taking it all in. Waves hammered the barge beneath them. Surging water pushed through the hull's barricade of boulders, splintered wooden beams, and twisted steel. The boys stood on the first of two barges reaching out to the sea. Other barges farther down clung to the shoreline in their fight-to-the-death battle cry to protect the land. Incessant pummeling had brutalized and mangled them until all that remained was unrecognizable rubble held in place by rusted iron.

The beach between the boys and the next seaward barge was the only one with sand. Offshore, the sea came in quietly and grew to a tall, sand-filled crest. When it reached land, it exploded, dumping megatons of water with a solid thud of raw power and white suds. The water retreated with ankle-breaking force, carrying whatever was not tied down. Air bubbled through the water-soaked sand. Sea terns raced along the water-line, pecking at the bubbles, searching for delicious morsels while daring the sea to catch them off guard with the next incoming wave.

"So, what do you think?" said Peter.

"Man, this is awesome, but I am totally confused."

"About what?"

Geoff pointed. "Look over here. Rocky shoreline. Waves rolling in way out there but no breakers. In just the width of this barge, such a change. Look at it! Why are the breakers so violent here and not over there?"

Peter pointed. "It has something to do with the bottom contour out there. But look here. See where the incoming wave and outgoing water meet? You don't want to get caught in that. You'll get boiled."

"Didn't Muggsy use that word?"

"Yep. See how the sand and rocks tumble like clothes in a washing machine? If you're there, you'll get tossed around just like that. Think about all that water coming down on your head. You can't tell up from down. Just hope you can hold your breath until you can get to the surface."

"I suppose surfing today is out of the question."

"It's way too rough. If you have to yell to be heard over the breakers, they're way too dangerous."

"How do you know all this stuff?"

"On our family boat, my dad taught me knots, navigation, charting, tides, currents, and waves. You know… all that nautical stuff. When we were here a few years ago, he showed me about breakers—the same as I'm telling you now."

"Is this the same dad that you ignore?"

"This all happened before he became a pain in the butt. Hey, I found a good place for our tent. It's right over there. C'mon, I'll show you."

The boys climbed over the timbers of a barge running along the shoreline. It was filled with sand and oval stones. They stood at its back edge as Peter pointed to a trough that dropped about four feet. "This will make a perfect place for our tent. It's plenty wide enough. When the wind comes in from the sea, we'll be protected by the barge. When it comes from the channel, we'll be protected by that sand dune. It's perfect! It's near the breakers *and* the channel. See over there? There's a sandy road that comes up a little from the main dock. It'll make it easier to get here instead of having to climb over rocks. It looks like it'll be quiet here and no one will bother us. What do you think? Your call."

"Looks good, but let me just sit here and think about it."

"What's to think about? There's nothing better around here."

"Hey! You had a chance to look it over. Now it's my turn."

Peter shrugged and pointed eastward. "I'll be exploring down that way. When and *if* you decide you're OK with this spot, feel free to flag me down."

Peter headed toward the next barge running out to sea. He climbed onto it, waved at Geoff, then vanished on the other side.

Geoff surveyed his new surroundings. This was, indeed, a good place to pitch their tent, but should he agree to do so because he liked it or because he was unwilling to engage in a conflict with Peter? Yes, Peter had said it was his call, yet the dread of being responsible for the decision hung heavily on him. What if there was lightning? After all, it was a flat area, and if Geoff stood on the barge during a lightning storm, he would be the tallest object around. Would they really be safe here?

Geoff scanned the shoreline where he'd thought he'd heard his father's angry voice telling him to keep off the boulders. He closed his eyes, listening for it, but all he heard were the sounds of swaying oat grass and the sea. Perhaps he was free from his father's criticism and interrogation, at least for now. Things would be different without his father around, Geoff realized. He wouldn't need to get his permission or approval, but he would also be taking on greater responsibilities. From this point forward, all he had to do was make good choices and obey the island rules.

Geoff sat on a nearby cleat, feeling the rhythmic breakers send growling vibrations through the barge and into his body. He collected stones from the barge and set them in the sand as he paced off locations for the tent, a table, their firepit, and other camp amenities. The wheels in his head were turning as the sun broke through the layer of clouds and quickly warmed the late morning. Yes, this was a fine place to camp.

Geoff's animated assessment ended abruptly when he saw Peter's head pop above a far-off barge. His enthusiasm gave way to anxiety, and he squatted out of sight. Should he agree or disagree with Peter about the camp's location? It was a good spot, but there were other considerations, and he was out of time.

"Well, what's your decision?"

"Damn, Pete, how'd you get here so fast?" Geoff asked, looking up. "I just saw you way down there a minute ago." A shadow towered in front of him, blocking the bright hazy sun. It was not Peter. Geoff shaded his eyes, trying to get a good look at the figure. A face came through the darkened shadow. Only a few feet away, his father stood with his hands on his hips. Geoff squinted in disbelief. How had he gotten here? When? And why?

Geoff's father hovered over him. "What's your decision?"

"My decision?"

"Yes, that's precisely what I asked."

"You mean the decision about camping here or staying up on the hill?"

"Don't play with me, boy! You've had plenty of time to think about it. He said it was your call. So just what *is* your call?"

"Well, there's a lot to consider." Geoff pointed to their campsite near the tower. "Up there—calmer winds and no sea mist. Up there we could blend in with the scrub, but it's a long way to the beach. It's close to the general store. Up there—more privacy. Down here—breakers and beaches. More driftwood for fires here, and it's close to drinking water."

"Up there, down here, over there. Your gibberish makes no sense whatsoever. I didn't ask you to give me your thinking—if that's what you call it. You're becoming intolerable. What's your decision?"

"Which campsite do *you* prefer?"

"It's not my camp. It's yours. I'm asking you what *you* want. Just give me your decision."

"Please, just tell me what *you* want."

"I want you to use your God-given brain, that's what I want. You've already gone over your reasons, so make a decision."

"But it will probably be wrong."

"How can your decision *possibly* be wrong when you have yet to make it?"

"Every time we do this, you tell me why my decisions are wrong. Why do you ask what I want when you already know we'll do things your way? Why does what I want matter? I'm tired of fighting. I'm always wrong. I think you like to make me feel stupid."

"I'm trying to teach you to *think*."

"Geoff?"

Geoff uncurled himself and looked up.

"Geoff! You OK?"

"How'd you get here? How did you find me? Why are you here?"

"Geoff! Look at me! Are you OK?"

Geoff stood and blinked, trying to clear away the blur. "Oh! Pete, it's you." He sighed and slumped against the barge.

"Of course it's me. Who else? What's going on? Who'd you think it was?"

Geoff ran his hands over his face. "I could have sworn you were my father standing over me."

"Well, it's me—Pete."

"I'm OK now."

"So, what's it gonna be? Stay here or keep camp up by the tower?"

"Here, of course."

"You're not saying that just to please me, are you?"

Geoff stood tall and brushed off the sand. "Hell, no! That would be chickenshit."

"I saw you walking around talking to yourself and pointing. What were you doing?"

"OK, here's what I thought. This is a great place, just as you said. Where you thought the tent should go—great spot. It's below the wind line from the beach and sand dunes. I can cut into that sand dune and make a fireplace. We could go beachcombing and find something for a tabletop and chairs. Who knows what the tide could bring? And that sand dune over there is tall enough to put the latrine behind it."

"You picked a spot for the latrine based on how tall a sand dune is?"

"Of course. Don't you care about privacy?"

"Geoff, look over at those cottages on the hill. Pick one out. Any one. Got it?"

"Yeah."

"See how small the windows are?"

"OK, they're hard to see."

"Exactly. If you can hardly see the windows, how can anyone see you?"

"What if they have a telescope?"

Peter shook his head. "Geoff, you're paranoid. You found a place for the latrine behind a tall dune. I should be glad you thought of *that* detail. Anything else in your master plan?"

"Yes, we can put the icebox over there."

"Icebox? Geoff, I leave you alone and you've let your imagination run amok again."

"Oh yeah? Well, try this on. Imagine washing down your favorite cookie with a nice glass of… warm… lumpy… sour milk that plops out of the bottle like cottage cheese and smells like puke."

"Eew! Gross! OK, you win."

"You're gonna thank me."

"Thank you," said Peter dismissively. "Maybe we should talk more about your dad."

"Why?"

"Just a few minutes ago when I stood in front of you, you thought I was him."

"Oh, that. Imagine my surprise when *he* showed up."

"But that was *me*, not *him*. I don't know what you were saying to yourself when I walked up, but whatever it was, it was bad. I'm telling you, Geoff, you gotta get him out of your head. Something's wrong when you hear the voice of a person who's hundreds of miles away."

"No shit!" Geoff hoisted himself up on the barge.

"So, what goes on at home? Does he beat you up?"

"As in hitting? No, he's never done that. He beats me up in different ways, though. I get lots of lectures on how something should be done and criticism about how I did it. Seems like the only time he's nice to me is when I ask for his advice, which, I've learned, is a good way to avoid making a decision that would surely be wrong. It's not that I don't make decisions, but life with him is better if I don't. Why would I want to decide things, when I know he's always going to tell me I'm wrong? You think I enjoy going through the third degree? He wants me to be thorough, but I end up thinking things to death. Jeez! I never get *any* support from him. A little encouragement would sure go a long way."

"Well, he did let you come on this trip. That's gotta count for something. But hallucinating about him on the beach? Now, that's going way too far. I'm telling you, Geoff, if you don't get him out of your head, he'll haunt you every step of the way and mess up our entire trip."

Geoff agreed. Their conversation faded off to watching breakers. "When do you think we should move camp?"

"I was thinking early tomorrow morning around six."

"You want to kill the rest of the day hanging out here?"

"Yeah, let's just hang here for a while to make sure we're good with it."

The boys climbed over to a barge running perpendicular to the beach and sat with their legs dangling over the edge, watching the waves pass by.

"'I must down to the seas again, to the lonely sea and the sky,'" said Geoff in a hypnotic monotone.

"Say what?"

Geoff sat erect and became animated. "'I must down to the seas again, to the lonely sea and the sky. And all I ask is a tall ship and a star to steer her by.'"

"What's gotten into you?"

"'Sea-Fever' by John Masefield. It's a classic. One of my favorite poems. English Lit class. C'mon, Pete."

A flock of sea terns soared over the stretch of beach. Their squawking was partially muted by the sound of the wind and sea. Geoff shaded his eyes and studied their movements. "Man, would you look at those birds." He watched as they swooped down and, without so much as a flicker of their wings, suddenly veered skyward. "You gotta respect their agility! Now, that's what I want to be when I come back in the next life."

"You mean you want to come back as a bird?"

"Not just *any* bird. *That* kind of bird."

"Remember what I told you about the size of their brains?"

"Yeah, I remember, but if you look at these birds, there's plenty of space between their eyes. Look at that guy swoop down. He's got smarts!"

"That's not smarts. That's flying skill. Won't matter, though. If you want to come back as a bird, you're already halfway there."

"Halfway?"

"Yeah, you already got bird brains. So, do you have the brains of a gull or a tern?"

They both laughed as Geoff jumped up and pulled Peter off the barge. They plopped in the sand, wrestling and rolling around.

Peter suddenly scrambled to his feet. "Look out! Here comes a breaker!"

Crash! A thundering breaker sent a swift wall of frothing water toward the boys. They jumped out of the way moments before their wrestling area became sea bottom.

Peter said, "We broke the first rule about breakers: Never, never, never turn your back on them. Before we take them on, it's important to read the wave pattern. Timing is everything in bodysurfing. Hey, I want to do a little more exploring. Wanna go?"

"Nah, I think I'll stay here and study these waves."

Geoff gazed at the waves, looking for a pattern. He saw how they would intensify, settle down, repeat. With the way they crashed, any one of them could give him a good walloping. He took small steps toward them, testing the force of the receding water on his legs and under his feet. The longer he stood in the wave action, the less threatening and frightening it became. He reasoned that developing self-confidence was as essential as experience. The sooner he found his nerve to dive through a breaker, the sooner he could get to the cool art of bodysurfing, and that alone justified taking a risk. At some point he would have to take a leap of faith. Why wait? He visualized himself on the other side of the breaker, gliding in on an incoming wave.

Geoff inched his way within a foot of a breaker and became captivated when he saw how the shoreline sharply dropped at the precise point where the wave became a breaker. There, the back-flowing water flowed like a waterfall into the sea and sounded like a giant spillway sucking water down its gullet. The clatter of tumbling rocks and sand belched from the trough. Geoff peered down the throat of the breaker. He was standing at the edge of danger, but he was ready.

He glanced over his shoulder and spotted Peter running up the beach with his hands cupped around his mouth. *"Alert's* coming! *Alert's* coming!"

Geoff gave an acknowledging wave.

Peter waved his arms wildly and pointed to the sea. "Breaker! Breaker!"

Geoff turned back to the sea and was immediately smashed by a chest-high wall of water that knocked him off his feet and tumbled him twenty feet up the beach. Then the receding water swept him back like a piece of wood. Peter arrived, grabbed his arms, and dragged him away from the strong backflow before it could sweep him into the menacing throat of the next breaker.

"You OK? You're lucky it wasn't bigger."

"Yeah, I'm OK," Geoff said while trying to catch his breath and chewing sand. "I turned my head away for only a few seconds."

"Remember rule number one. You almost had a reckoning with the breakers. Hey, let's go meet the *Alert*."

"OK, but I've got to get rid of ten pounds of sand that went up my ass."

"Wash it off in the channel. C'mon, let's see if we can beat the *Alert* to the dock."

Geoff grabbed his T-shirt, and the two leapt over the barges and darted across the sand dunes.

"Hurry!" Peter said. "It's getting close."

"Go ahead. I'll catch up." Geoff waded into the channel as the *Alert* chugged past him. He pictured himself as a passenger seeing him as an islander. And that thought gave him great comfort. His fear of being alone without the security of home was draining away. A feeling of belonging saturated his soul. Cuttyhunk was becoming his new home.

6

MEETING THE *ALERT*

Geoff washed the sand from his trunks and waded out of the channel. Only a few hundred feet ahead, the main dock was quickly filling with a crowd awaiting *Alert*'s arrival. He felt a sense of urgency to be on the dock ahead of the boat, as if being late would be disrespectful to the occasion. He quickened his pace.

He stopped abruptly on the first plank of the dock, suddenly self-conscious, and hid his disproportionately large hands behind his back. He was still dripping from his dip in the channel, and that alone made him look more out of place than he already felt. He began to itch as he imagined scrutinizing eyes crawling all over him.

Just do it, damn it, he told himself. The dock did not crumble under his feet as he slowly worked his way into the sea of greeters. No one paid attention to him beyond a passing glance.

Scattered at the fringes of the dock were pickup trucks and station wagons with lowered tailgates; both kids and adults sat swinging their legs as they waited. Conversations were mostly indiscernible quiet talk between people standing in small groups. Folks stood alone with folded arms or hands in their pockets leaning against cars, pilings, or any other "leanable" object. Children darted between people and cars as they played tag. A young boy pointed to a passenger on the boat and yelled, "Aunt Becky! It's Aunt Becky!"

Geoff stood next to a stocky woman wearing a white hat with a broad brim. She squinted as she watched the dock activity. "Excuse me, ma'am. Is something special going on? How come so many people are here?"

The woman turned and looked at him from head to toe. "You must be new here. Everybody shows up for the *Alert*."

The greeters stood with patient anticipation, but once *Alert* was secure, the dock exploded in a fury of activity with the excitement of elves on

Christmas Eve. Greeters eagerly scanned the boat for the fresh supply of people and provisions.

Boxes, packages, luggage, bicycles, plants, and children's toys came off the boat—handed from one man to the next like a bucket brigade. As they off-loaded provisions, men and boys sorted and slid the boxes across the dock with the precision of a conveyer belt. Boxes came in every size and shape, each one marked with the name of its destination—Allen House, Bosworth House, Coffee Shop, Veeder, Garfield, Wilder, Gen Store, Baldwin.

The heads of greeters bobbed and ducked around one another, searching for familiar faces waiting to disembark—friends and family coming for a visit or to deposit children intended to keep other children from going mad with boredom on this tiny island.

A slender man wearing baggy pants held up by suspenders leaned against an old panel wagon. Oxidized green paint and rust bled through the scripted words, "The Poplars," on the side panel. He watched intently, saying nothing. "Hey, Clarence!" called a man holding up a package. "You waitin' for this?" The thin man nodded and placed the package in his truck, and then resumed his watchful stance.

A short, stocky fellow wearing blue overalls scurried around the dock, retrieving and hauling boxes to his dented, rusted truck. Each box strained him, yet he moved as though he were in a race against time. From under his cocked fishing cap sweat dripped over his brows and streamed down his round face. He never stopped to talk, yet was always affable to those greeting him as he scooted past. "Hey, Potter! You makin' deliveries to the Coffee Shop today?" asked one of the men off-loading packages.

"Hadn't planned on it," Potter said as he wiped sweat from his face. "But I'll take it." The package slid across the dock and stopped by his pickup.

Other boys, Geoff's age or a little younger, played "king of the mountain" as they competed fiercely to stand alone on top of a group of tall pilings strapped together at the corner of the dock.

Gladys Snow could be on the dock. She knew they were coming to the island and might be keeping an eye out for them. Geoff made eye contact with every woman who looked his way. He reasoned that if any of them gave him more than a passing glance, it could be her. No takers. No Gladys Snow.

Clarence the boat captain leaned out the open wheelhouse window. Through his dark round sunglasses, he watched to ensure neither passengers nor cargo vanished in that dangerous narrow gap between boat and dock. His face was all business. He was not idly watching. He was working.

People streamed off the *Alert* like hungry ladybugs scampering out of a sealed cup at the nursery. Islanders and visitors hugged with smiles and bouncing excitement. Kodak Brownie cameras snapped and clicked, capturing what would become treasured memories in family albums for generations to come. Lanky preteens stood awkwardly at attention during first-time formal introductions to Aunt Mildred or Uncle Erwin. Young girls jumped like grasshoppers when reunited with their best friends from back home, eager to dash off to catch up on secrets and stories.

The wave of belongings, packages, and people flowed to a fleet of vehicles strewn along the road and around the dock entrance.

As *Alert* prepared to shove off, Bert made one last sweep through the boat, searching for a left-behind book, a forgotten child, or a misplaced package under a bench. A man released the bow line as the engine revved up and the bow swung away. Water swirled and boiled up from the stern as *Alert*'s powerful engine began driving the boat toward the fishing dock... just like the day before.

"Hey, Bert!" Geoff called.

Bert looked over. His face beamed with friendly lines. "Hey, laddie! How's the camping?"

"Going well."

"Great! See ya later." Bert gave a two-fingered salute and returned to his duties.

That was it! The greeting from Bert made him a somebody—maybe an island belonger. Geoff stood tall and proud. He looked around for an audience as he felt a strong urge to strut. Except for Bert, not a single person even glanced his way. But who cared? Geoff had gotten a two-fingered salute from Bert. What more could he want?

Pickup trucks and station wagons stuffed with people and provisions rumbled up the road. Most had broken wheel springs, loose fenders, bald tires, and rusted-out bodies. One junker had an old milk crate turned upside down for the driver's seat. Hardly a vehicle left the dock without a small gang of children and teens sitting on the tailgate, dangling their legs without a care or fear that they could bounce off.

Cars and trucks led the procession back to town, followed by ambling people who became a long thin line of color stretching along the road.

Standing at the edge of the now-quiet dock, Geoff wondered how so many people could quickly scatter and leave behind the impression that the island was a sleepy place, if not altogether deserted.

Those invigorating thirty minutes had confirmed the island's vitality. He had been lured there by the inescapable calling of *Alert*'s arrival. *Alert* was the face of the island's sense of community spirit, the umbilical cord that kept it connected to the mainland. It had brought letters, postcards, packages, news, loved ones, and visitors. Something magical had happened when the *Alert* had arrived. And it was taking hold of Geoff.

7

RIDIN' IN POTTER'S PICKUP

Geoff stood on the dock, swirling on his happy cloud from Bert's salute. Suddenly he stopped and looked around. Where was Peter? The last he'd seen him, Peter was hightailing it toward the dock just ahead of *Alert*'s arrival. Had he vanished in the pack of people heading down the road? Had he hitched a ride on a tailgate? Had he headed back to the beach? Geoff scanned the scenery and found Peter standing atop a barge, waving both hands above his head to get his attention. He raced off to join him.

"Did you recognize anybody?" Peter asked.

"Just Bert and Clarence from the boat. Bert asked me how our camping was going. He remembered! And... he gave me his two-fingered salute. How about you?"

"I met these two island boys and asked them to take a look at this place. They said it was a good spot to camp. So, let's get ready. I've been giving this some thought. We can do it in one trip, and we can do it without having to completely repack the tent and schlep our stuff. Want to hear my great idea?"

Geoff nodded.

"Earlier I walked down that way and found a lot of driftwood, rope, and fishing line. We could make a raft, or something like a stretcher, you know, and slide our tent on it with everything in it, and then we'd carry it down here. We wouldn't have to repack, just pull up stakes and slide 'er on over. What do you think?"

"Do you really think it will save us time? You know, all that work just to keep from repacking?"

"You don't think it's a good idea?"

"I didn't say that. I just can't see how it's going to save us any time."

"OK, picture us down here tomorrow after we move. Which do you think would be faster: sliding a tent off the stretcher and staking it to the ground or completely setting up camp from scratch?"

"Well, of course it would be faster your way, but look at all the time and work it would take to collect the driftwood and make the stretcher."

"True, but what's the first thing you're gonna want to do once camp is set up?"

Geoff shrugged. "Play on the beach. Watch the *Alert* come in. Swim. Hell, I don't know."

"How about… bodysurfing?"

"Bodysurfing?"

"Yep, surfing the breakers. You're right: If we make a stretcher or repack, it will probably take the same amount of time. But with a stretcher, all we have to do is slide our gear off it, and in another five minutes our camp will be completely set up."

"Why didn't you say that in the first place?"

"I just thought the benefit of the stretcher would be obvious."

Geoff winced at the jab.

They gathered driftwood, fishing line, and rope snagged in the barges, bundled and tied it up, and then headed to their camp near the tower.

Geoff walked behind Peter, talking about the returning cloud cover and fading color, the rocks, oat grass, sea gulls, and water splashing on nearby boulders. Peter occasionally looked back with impatience.

"I wonder where all the boat greeters went. They just vanished. Did they go back to those little houses on the hillside? What do they do on the island if they're not out exploring? Hey, Pete, have you been watching all the cottages?"

Peter rolled his eyes. "No, but what about them?"

"Well, we were talking about all the privacy we would have on the beach with us being so far away from civilization, but any house up there can see almost anywhere, and—"

"It's *you* who's obsessed with privacy."

"Well, I'm looking at a lot of houses that we can see from the barges. If we can see them, they can see us. What kind of privacy is that?"

"Quit being paranoid! Why would anyone want to see us? Besides, we already went over this. If the doors and windows on the cottages look like dots to us, we look like dots to them. We *won't* have a problem with privacy."

"Well, what if they have binoculars or even a powerful telescope? What if—"

"Geoff!" Peter stopped and glared. "You're getting on my nerves. We have more important things to worry about than your stupid privacy!"

Geoff looked to the hillside houses and cottages across the harbor. His eyes stopped on one that stood out prominently. "Someone could be watching us right now from that large house on the hill."

Peter's jaw tightened. "Fine. Don't pick your nose."

"OK, you win. No privacy. No problem. We're just flyspecks on the beach. Nobody can see us. Nobody is watching right now because it makes no difference, and they can't see anyway. But what if in one of those cottages there's a telescope trained on us at this very moment? I bet you'll be looking up there in the morning when you head for the latrine."

Peter shook his head and rolled his eyes as they plodded along.

An old rusted green truck came off a small hill and followed the road around toward the boys. As it passed, the driver slowed down, looked at the boys, touched the brim of his hat, and nodded.

Geoff did a double take. "Hey! I saw that guy at the dock when the boat came in. He loaded a lot of boxes onto his truck. Man, did he have sweat pouring down his face. I heard someone yell his name. Potter, I think. Yeah, that's it. Potter. Maybe we can hitch a ride with him when he heads back."

"Who'd want to give us a ride with all this driftwood? Heck, we'll be on the footpath by the Coast Guard station before he comes back, so don't get your hopes up for a ride."

A puny sounding honk came from a truck approaching from behind.

"You boys want a ride?"

Peter and Geoff looked at each other and back to the driver. "Sure," Peter said.

"Where ya goin'?"

"Up to the general store."

Geoff asked, "Are you Potter?"

"Yep, that's me, Pawtah. How'd ya know that?"

"I heard someone call your name when the boat came in."

"Good eahs. There's not enough room up heah for the both of you. One of you is gonna have to ride in the back."

"You ride inside, Pete. OK to lay this driftwood on the boxes?" Geoff asked.

"Yep, fine."

Geoff hopped onto the tailgate; his legs dangled over the edge. The truck sputtered and popped as Potter rattled along. Geoff watched the ground beneath his feet move faster and faster until it was nothing more than a blur. The truck hit a bump that joggled him. How would he ever explain bouncing off a pickup to his father? Maybe riding back there hadn't been such a hot idea after all. He put a death grip on the side of the truck as he scooted farther back on the tailgate. For the moment he felt safe. He decided to quit worrying and soak in the new experience.

Potter's truck clattered around the harbor toward the crossroad and moaned its way up Broadway. Geoff was a puppy with his head in the breeze. Potter's truck hit another pothole. The ends of the driftwood became spears, gnawing holes in his back. He knew that if they hit another, he would be rolling on the pavement. His predicament brought a swift end to his cocky confidence, and he discarded his bobble-headed giddiness. He wanted to alert Potter of his impending contact with Broadway, but reasoned that he would become known as "Geoff, the chickenshit sissy." Few labels could be worse.

He trusted Potter's good judgment that no kid would be cast off his truck. He reasoned he could survive a crash landing. He was, after all, young and still had plenty of bounce. He pictured taking a few skids on the thirty-grit pavement and spending the next few weeks removing sand and pieces of street from his ass or noseless face. Who was that island nurse? Lucille? How would she repair him—with Geoff bent over a chair or stretched belly down on a cot? Either way meant a bare ass in the face of a person of the opposite sex. Geoff tightened his death grip on a chain attached to the tailgate. *Nobody's plucking stones out of my ass.*

Potter's truck came to a squeaking stop by the tower road. "There you go, boys!" The boys thanked Potter and walked up the side road to the closed-up general store.

"It seems like whenever we've been here, the store's closed," Geoff said.

"Seems so. So, how was your ride back there?"

"It was cool! Hope I get a chance to do it again. Hey, what did you and Potter talk about?"

"Not much. In fact, if I hadn't started talking, nothing would have been said at all."

"What did you say?"

"I told him we were camping, but all he said was, 'Yeah, I know.' I asked him how he knew, and he said this was a small island and you can't take a piss without everybody knowing about it."

"He said that?"

"Yeah."

"This is what I've been telling you about privacy."

"Relax. It's an expression, Geoff. Maybe he didn't ask questions because he thought it wasn't any of his business and he was being polite."

"That could be."

"Or… maybe he knew and was just checking us out."

"Don't be so cynical. We just got our first taste of island hospitality." Peter scoffed.

"Hey! There's our bag!" Geoff pointed to a brown bag sitting on the step of the general store.

"You sure that's ours?"

Geoff opened the bag. "Well, let's see. Here's our bread, peanut butter, jelly, and… look!"

Geoff pulled out an oversized can of Chef Boyardee spaghetti and meatballs with a note taped to it that said "Enjoy!"

"He left us a can of Chef Boyardee!" Geoff said. "Tonight, we eat like kings! *Thank you*, Muggsy!"

"Thank him today. Pay him tomorrow," added Peter.

"It's a gift."

"How do you know that?"

"Who tapes a note saying 'Enjoy' on a can of food that they want you to pay for? Now, *this* is what I call island hospitality."

"Just thinking about that can of spaghetti makes my mouth water," Peter said.

Geoff waved the can in the air. "This isn't just any spaghetti; it's Chef Boyardee spaghetti and meatballs."

"Let's get up that hill, stow our stuff, and crack open that can. I'm famished."

"Pete, you're always famished. Can't you ever be just plain hungry?"

"Not now. Those peanut butter sandwiches we had this morning didn't last. My stomach clock went off hours ago."

The boys picked up the bundle of driftwood and headed toward the tower. About halfway up the road they met a man on his way down. They nodded in passing.

"Hey, you Coast Guard?" Geoff asked.

The man looked back. "Yeah."

"You coming from the tower?"

"Yeah, just got off my watch. I gotta get back to the station for some shut-eye."

"Must be a cool view from up there," said Geoff as he looked toward the tower.

"It is, but it can get cold. There's no insulation, and the wind blows through it. Only Coast Guard is allowed up there, but at night we sometimes invite islanders."

"Cool." Geoff approached the man with his hand extended. "I'm Geoff, and this here is Pete."

"Hi, guys. I'm Jacobs."

"Jacobs? Jacobs what?"

"Just Jacobs. Around here we Coasties use only last names or nicknames."

"So, what's your first name?"

"Jacobs."

"Jacobs. Never heard of a first name like that."

"I ain't neither, so you'll just have to call me Jacobs. Geoff and Pete, right?"

"Yeah," said Geoff. "We're camping up there, but we're moving down to the beach tomorrow."

"So *you're* the two guys we saw from the tower. We watched you set up your tent yesterday just before the rain and wondered what the hell you were doing up here."

"We were looking for an out-of-the-way place," Peter said.

"I'll say it is. You can't get more out of the way than there. You're moving to the beach? Which one?"

Geoff pointed. "Down there by the barges."

"Good choice. It's a great place for parties. Well, gotta go. See ya around."

The boys continued their hike up the road until they came to their jumping-off spot. "How'd you know he was Coast Guard?" Peter asked.

"Blue shirt, rolled-up shirtsleeves, blue jeans. Dead giveaway."

"I'll give you credit for observation, Geoff. Stay here—I'll be right back." Peter climbed over the wall and took the bundle of driftwood and the sack of groceries to their tent.

Geoff sat and looked around, remembering how he'd felt when they had first made camp the day before. Everything had seemed new and strange then, but that was already fading. Being on his own, away from the scrutiny of his father, was giving him a fresh sense of freedom. He sat tall and smiled. *I got to ride in Potter's pickup.*

8

DANG BOY-CRAZY GIRLS

A two-story gray house stood prominently midway on a hill below the Coast Guard tower. Its location provided a sweeping vista of the eastern side of the island. Large windows on both floors kept fresh air circulating and sunlight splashing throughout. The first floor was devoid of interior walls or partitions, and in the center of the open room was a sturdy, bare-wood, well-used split-level staircase to the second floor. It set the boundaries for a seamless family room and eating area. Two doorways led to the kitchen that frequently filled the house with a homey scent of freshly baked chocolate chip cookies. To one side of the stairs white wicker chairs surrounded a low table with a work-in-progress jigsaw puzzle. On the other side was a table with benches on each side and rush chairs at both ends.

In the corner of the dining area was a large brass telescope fastened to a wooden tripod and aimed out the window. Four giggling girls stood around it. They were in a silly mood and all talking at once. Their sentences ran into one another, making senseless cackle-talk. Their heads appeared sewed together as each of them competed for a peek through the eyepiece of the telescope before being wedged away by another. A much younger girl with more freckles than face stood among them on tiptoes. She hopped up and down in excitement, hoping for a peek. Her petite size and young age were no help to her in the battle for a look-see, but her perseverance and enthusiasm more than made up for her height deficit.

"We need to take turns. Otherwise none of us will see," said one.

"Yeah, Diana, and I suppose because you're the oldest, you get to go first," protested another.

"If we don't take turns, they'll be gone and there won't be anything for any of us to see." Diana eased the neck of the telescope away from her companions. "I'll find them again, and then we each get to look for ten seconds."

"Ten seconds? We don't have watches," the protester said.

"We'll all count," said Diana. Her lips cracked a smile as she leaned toward the eyepiece. "When it's my turn, you count slowly. When it's yours, I'll count fast."

"Becca should go first because she's a houseguest," said the protester.

"Yeah, I should go first," Becca said, jumping in to take advantage of her status.

"I'll go first. Just because," said Diana as she reclaimed the telescope.

"Why do you always get to go first?"

"Hilly, when you're the oldest, you'll get to go first," said Diana, scanning the road to relocate their distant prey.

Elbows nudged. The telescope teetered, threatening to fall from its tripod. Feet jockeying for position bumped around the floor, sounding like distant thunder. The giggling, shuffling, and excitement brought a mother out of the kitchen. She was of average height with a smooth oval face and shoulder-length, thin, straight hair. Her tan face and arms looked like she was always ready for the beach. "What's all the hubbub out here?"

The girls stood at attention, wearing big grins of innocence. Mom walked over to the window, squinted, and scanned the road from the main dock. "What's got you all in such a giddy frenzy? What are you looking at? Boys? Here, let me have a look."

Mom stepped up to the spyglass, looked over its top to the road, and found two small figures walking from the main dock. She aimed the telescope toward them. "Aha! It *is* boys! Of course. How did I know? Hmm. Not bad. Not bad at all. Anyone want to take a look?"

The girls gave in to their out-of-control giggles as they resumed their bouncing and skirmishing over who would look first. Mom stepped back, grinned as she shook her head, and returned to the kitchen.

Diana got the first look. She stood quietly, studying the boys through the telescope while the other girls continued the debate about who would be next.

"C'mon, Diana. Lemme see! It's my turn." Diana stood back, and Hilly swooped in. "The one in the front… he's mine! He's taller and has longer hair. He's definitely mine."

"Yours, eh?" said Diana.

"Yeah, mine. He's the leader!"

"How would you know that?" Diana asked.

Hilly kept a grip on the telescope as she watched. "Because he's taller and he's in front. They're carrying something. Looks like a bundle of driftwood."

Mom yelled from the kitchen. "Hilly, you've been reading too many *Teen* magazines. You're not even interested in boys yet, right?"

"I'm just practicing, Mom. I'm getting ready," Hilly said without looking away.

"Well," said Mom, "if any of you is old enough to stake a claim, it's Diana. They're handsome. Better not let *them* get away."

Diana kept looking out at the far-off silhouettes.

"Hey, Hilly," said Becca. "Your ten seconds is long over." She nudged Hilly out of the way. "Hey, someone stopped to give them a ride."

"That's Potter," Diana said, squinting.

"Lemme see, Becca," Hilly said. "Yep, that's Potter all right." She continued reporting. "They're getting in. The shorter one got in the back. The tall one is *definitely* the leader. Leaders don't ride in the back. OK, now they're moving. Now they've gone behind the hill. I can't see them anymore. Oh, my gosh! I think they're coming this way!"

Hilly and Becca let out a shriek worthy of an Elvis sighting.

Hilly looked away from the telescope. "We should go find out where they're going. OK, little sis, your turn."

The shortest girl scurried to find something to stand on. She dragged over a wooden box from under the staircase, put her eye to the lens, and scanned the road.

"Where are they? I don't see anyone."

Diana, Becca, and Hilly jabbered out a plan. Diana looked over to her little sister and chuckled. "That's because they're not there anymore, silly." Then she rejoined the planning session.

"Maybe Potter took them to the general store," Hilly said.

"Yeah, I bet that's where they went," added Becca.

"Let's try to beat them there," said Diana.

The three girls darted to the front door.

Hilly looked back toward her little sister. "Hey, Pammy! You coming?"

"Where're we going?"

"We're going up to the general store," Hilly said. "Maybe that's where Potter took them. We can get a closer look."

Mom emerged from the kitchen. "Ladies… if you're going to intercept the boys, you might want to think this out before charging off."

"We think Potter took them to the general store," Hilly said. "We're gonna take the path behind the Pink House."

"Are you sure that's where Potter took them?" Mom asked.

"Where else could they have gone?" Hilly said.

"I don't know. I'm not a mind reader, but if they didn't go to the general store, then you'll be heading one way and the boys another. You might want to think about heading over to Four Corners, where you'll have a better chance of coming across them. You'll be able to tell if they headed for the fish dock, up our way, or up Broadway. Do you have any ideas about what you're going to do if you find them?"

The girls glanced at one another, traded shrugs, and looked back to Mom. "That's what I thought. I can see you'll have them wrapped around your finger in no time. Good luck, girls."

The girls gushed out and bounded down the hill with their arms flying above them in all directions. Mom walked over and looked out the front door, only to get a fleeting glimpse of the girls before they disappeared behind the shrubbery. She shook her head and sighed. "OK, boys, with any luck they won't find you. Heaven help you if they do."

Within minutes the girls stood in the center of Four Corners looking in all directions—up Broadway, down to the fish dock, and on the road toward the main dock. Hilly dashed partway up Broadway for a glimpse around the curve and returned to the group. "They're not here."

The girls were quiet for the first time since discovering the boys. They looked at one another as if to say, *Now what?* Diana said, "Potter must have taken them up Broadway. It's the only place they could have gone."

All eyes turned at the sound of Potter's pickup rattling down Broadway. He drove in his usual posture: elbow hanging out the window, right hand draped over the steering wheel, and sweat-stained cap cocked to one side.

The girls sprinted toward him, flailing their arms. The truck clattered and squeaked to a halt. They huddled around Potter's window, jumping like popcorn in a hot kettle.

Potter leaned back. "Hi, girls. What's up?"

"Hey, Potter!" said Diana. "We saw you picking up two boys on the road from the main dock. Where'd you take them?"

"I didn't see you. Where were you?"

"At our house."

"You could see me from your house?"

"We have a telescope," said Pammy.

"Aha," Potter said, laughing with gravel in his throat. "Spying on boys, huh? No safe place for them. Why do you want to know?"

"Oh, we're just curious," Hilly said.

"Just curious? Right." Potter motioned behind him with his thumb. "I dropped them off by the general store."

"Did they say where they were going?" Diana asked.

Potter pushed his cap back on his head. "Nope. They're camping somewhere up by the tower."

"We'd better hurry if we're going to find them," Becca said.

Potter sat watching the girls through the side-view mirror. He shook his head and smiled while faintly hearing them shout their gratitude. Stepping on the clutch and jamming the truck into first gear, he looked back over his shoulder and watched the girls scamper up Broadway. "Dang boy-crazy girls. They'll chase anything with pants on. How can they be interested in boys? I just saw them five minutes ago when they were still in diapers. Where has the time gone?" Potter's foot let off the clutch. His sputtering truck rattled down the road, leaving behind bluish smoke and a rumble from the rusted-out muffler.

Broadway's steep grade soon took away the boundless energy of the four young gazelles. They huffed and puffed their way up to the general store. They stood bent over, gasping for air like winded foot racers just over the finish line.

Hilly looked up the dirt road to the Coast Guard tower and pointed. "Hey, look! Someone's coming down. And I think the boys are up there, too."

Becca and Diana quickly looked toward the tower. "Hilly, I think you're seeing things," Diana said. "There's only one person up there."

"No, really. I saw them way up there on the left."

The girls stood motionless and stared at the distant figure coming their way. Diana sighed a big breath of nervous relief, and her shoulders relaxed. "That's Jacobs coming off watch duty."

Jacobs reached them a minute later. "Hey, girls. How's it goin'?"

Diana said, "Hey, Jacobs! You didn't happen to see two boys up there, did you?"

"Yeah… as a matter of fact, I did. You know them?"

"See? I did see them. I wasn't fooling!" said Hilly.

"Where are they?" Diana asked.

"We're on a boy hunt," said Pammy, proud of her membership in the boy-chasing club.

"I shoulda known. Hilly, aren't you a little young to be chasing boys? And Pammy, I won't even ask you. You're what, eight?" Jacobs grinned good-naturedly.

"Well, Jacobs, where are they?" said Diana.

Jacobs motioned with his head. "They're up the road camping below the tower."

"I told you. I told you I saw them!" Hilly said.

Jacobs pointed. "Up there on the left, in a meadow over the wall."

"So, you passed them?" Diana asked.

"Yeah, they seem like nice guys. Pete and… uh… Pete and… Geoff. Yeah. Pete and Geoff."

"Which one was the tall one?" Hilly asked.

"Pete. He was the tall one. Didn't say much. The shorter guy, Geoff, he did the talking. Said they were camping up there but they're moving to the beach tomorrow."

"Did they say which one?" Diana asked.

"Down by the barges. Hey, I need to catch some z's. Got another watch at O-three hundred hours. Gotta go. See ya later, ladies. And you, too, Pammy."

The girls didn't pay much attention to Jacobs's exit. Their bodies turned toward the road with recharged adrenaline—cocked and ready to go.

"What are we gonna do when we find them?" Becca asked.

"I don't know," Diana said.

Pammy pointed her finger up. "I know what *I'd* do. I'd say 'Hello.'"

"*Hello*? Now, *that's* lame," Hilly said.

"Well, what would *you* say?" Pammy said.

"I don't know."

"Well, saying 'hello' is better than 'I don't know.'" Pammy bobbed her head with delight over her quick-witted response.

"Hey! Look!" Hilly pointed up the road. "I see them. Can you see them?"

The girls stood quietly, watching two barely visible boys way up the hill.

"They just jumped off the wall and they're doing something on the ground," Hilly said. "I wonder what they're doing. Let's go see."

"Maybe we should think about this," Diana said. "The worst thing we could do is find them and stand there looking at them totally speechless. Now, *that* would be lame. Let's go home and ask Mom. She has the answers to these kinds of hard questions. She can help us with a foolproof plan."

The girls agreed. Mom was, after all, a master planner. They turned to the narrow island pathway behind the church and pranced back home—Hilly in the front and Pammy as the caboose—giggling and jabbering all at once like chicks in a henhouse waiting for lights-out.

9

CHEF BOYARDEE ON THE WALL

Geoff sat studying the deep, narrow construction trenches along the old, weathered wall. Why weren't they filled back in? It left unanswered questions that his curiosity refused to ignore. He followed the wall up, collecting visual evidence as he went. At the top of the hill, it ended abruptly, as if the tradesmen who had built it had set aside their masonry trowels one day and never returned. Excess mortar, stones, and other debris had accumulated against the base of the footing. He thought, *That wall has a story. The cement is weathered… definitely not built recently. How could such a majestic structure be made so well and end so abruptly? It could not be there by accident or whim.*

Geoff returned to the wall's jumping-off place to their camp. He sat practicing the two-finger salute. He had witnessed the exchange among islanders, and he himself was the proud recipient of it from Bert. It must be a common salutation. With a little practice Geoff could become proficient. With Bert's salute, the hand began at eye level with the index and middle fingers pointed upward. The wrist was bent toward the person being saluted as the middle finger curled into the palm, converting the gesture to a one-fingered salute. It was all done with a single smooth motion.

Peter sprang out of the scrub and plopped himself on the wall, the opened Chef Boyardee in one hand and forks in the other.

"Have you looked at this wall, Pete? It has a lot of mystery to it. I mean, up there it just…"

"Forget the wall. Let's eat."

Peter curled back the lid, and they sat on the wall with forks poised for the assault on the oversized can. They looked at it lustfully. It was one of those meals only starving boys could crave. Intertwining strands of mushy spaghetti and meatballs shimmering in tomato sauce filled the can. With only peanut butter and jelly sandwiches since breakfast, this was T-bone steak and mashed potatoes. The boys licked their lips in anticipation as they wiggled their butts on the wall to settle in for a fine meal.

They attacked the contents, passing the can back and forth. Geoff stabbed a chunk of meat and held it up. "You know, these taste just like dog food."

"How would you know that?

Geoff studied the meatball and popped it into his mouth. "I tried it once. We used to have a dog."

He passed the can, but it slipped away before Peter could get a firm grip. "Shit! Shit! Shit!" yelled both boys as they watched the can tumble end over end in slow motion toward the ground. They jumped to intercept it, but it was too late. The can hit the ground and catapulted its contents skyward. Some of it splattered on the boys. Some hit the side of the wall. Some went far, far away. The boys huddled around the can chanting, "Shit! Shit! Shit!" Despondent, they crouched over the delectable dinner, assessing its state to see if any of it was salvageable.

"Look, Geoff! We only lost part of it. There's still plenty left. Man, are we lucky!"

"You know the advertising. They say this stuff really sticks to your ribs. Looks like it sticks to the can, too! The spaghetti gods are with us. If it had all flown out, I'd be crawling around eating bits and pieces off the ground. Look at the mess it made on the wall. I wonder how long that will be there before rain cleans it off. Do you think it'll stain the rocks?"

Peter shrugged. They picked up the can, handling it as though it were Grandma's delicate crystal, and repositioned themselves on the wall.

The boys carefully passed the can back and forth as they reminisced about the day. With each bite they added an item to their list of memorable moments. "We got a ride from Potter," Peter said. "How'd a guy get a name like that?"

"Maybe Potter is his last name or a nickname after a trade or hobby. I'm sure we'll be seeing him again and we can find out. For me, I'll add the ride in the back of his pickup and the salute from Bert to my list."

"Salute from Bert?"

"Yeah. He gave his two-fingered salute to some men on the dock, and then he gave one to me."

"How did *that* make your list of memorable moments? Why not that pounding you got from the breakers?"

"Well, he recognized me."

"It's been a long time since he last saw you. What? Twenty-four hours?"

"Mock me all you want. It was important to me."

"And I'm sitting here with a belly full of Chef Boyardee spaghetti and meatballs. We're losing light, and we still have to make the stretcher."

Geoff looked to the sky and over his shoulder to their tent. "Yeah, let's get it done. I'm more up to it now than waiting for the morning. You didn't know this, but I'm actually experienced at building things like this."

"Oh?"

"Yeah. I helped my brother, Peter, assemble a wooden tower for a Boy Scout project. Same thing except his had to stand up."

"How'd that work out?"

"Well, we got it up, but no matter how much twine we used, it was still pretty flimsy and Pop wouldn't let Peter climb it. I think he got the merit badge for trying."

"I'm supposed to be reassured? OK, Tower Man, show me the way."

The boys attacked the stretcher-making task. They worked on it until they had used up the driftwood. When it was done, it sagged. It moaned. It creaked. Would it work? The moment of truth would have to wait until daybreak.

"I'm not holding out a lot of hope for this," Geoff said. "It reminds me of my brother's wood tower. We might be ditching this thing somewhere between here and the beach."

"We'll find out soon enough. Right now, I'm finished. It's getting dark, and we have a big day tomorrow. It's time for some shut-eye."

Moments later they wiggled into their sleeping bags.

"Hey, Pete, do you think anyone back home is thinking about us?"

"I'm sure they are," Peter said slowly in a quiet voice.

"Do you think they miss us?"

There was no answer.

"Do you think they're wondering *how* we're doing?"

Still no response.

"Do you think they're wondering *what* we're doing?"

Nothing.

"We should check in with Gladys Snow tomorrow. You know, so they don't worry."

Peter's breathing deepened.

"Well, at least it's not raining tonight. I'm talking to myself, aren't I?"

A gentle breeze blew through the tent and quickly lured Geoff's voice to silence.

10

MUGGSY BLEW UP A BARGE

"Well, I see you moved your camp to the barges on the beach," Muggsy said when the boys went into the general store the next day. "All settled in down there?"

The boys turned to each other with raised eyebrows.

"This morning about six thirty I saw two boys walk by with their tent on a wooden stretcher. Did it hold up?"

"Driftwood makes a bad stretcher. It kept breaking," said Peter. He headed down an aisle to gather some groceries.

Geoff added, "But… we got there, and we're settled. Now we're here to stock up on provisions. Hey, we found the bag with the bread and peanut butter on the step, and we sure appreciate the can of Chef Boyardee. Thanks a lot for that!"

"You're welcome. Which barge did you camp near?"

"I don't know—there's a bunch of them. Why are they even there?"

"A big storm in '44 breached the spit between Vineyard Sound and Buzzards Bay and created a shoal that blocked the channel to large boats for almost five years. In '49, they brought in ten barges that were once used to ferry railroad freight cars across the waterways in New York City, and rebuilt the beach. It was a good use of those scrapped barges. If you're interested, I can tell you about that sometime. Anyway, four barges were laid perpendicular to the beach, and six ran along the beach. So, which barge did you camp by?"

"We're between two of the perpendicular barges near the one closer to town."

"What side are you on?"

"We're on the channel side of one running along the beach. Pete found it. So, the barges haven't been there very long."

"Well, let's see. It took two years to set the initial ten, and then in '52 they added another one at the end and one more after that in '55. Only three perpendicular barges are left."

"That was only four years ago. They didn't last long."

"The sea is persistent, but they stop waves from breaking through to the channel."

"They look pretty beat up," Geoff said. "There's not much left of the ones farther down, just a lot of twisted metal and large chunks of wood. Were you here when they went in?"

"I worked on the tug crew that brought them here," Muggsy replied. "They dug out where the barges would go and pounded in steel girders, and when there was a full moon and the tide was up, they floated the barges in. After securing them to the steel girders, they blew out the bottoms and filled them with the oval stones. I actually got to push the plunger to blow up one of the barges."

"You got to blow one up?"

"Sure did. The third perpendicular barge. I don't know if they let me do it because I was part of the crew or because they knew I was a field engineer during the war and had munitions experience."

"Wow!" Geoff exclaimed. "What did you do in the war?"

"We did a lot. We had specialized skills in construction and demolition. We facilitated moving and supporting the Allies while slowing down the enemy. My job was to get behind enemy lines and blow up bridges to keep the Germans from sending their tanks and heavy artillery our way."

"You blew up bridges?"

"That I did. It was not a pleasant time in my life."

"I was only a baby during the war—born right after D-Day."

"That's when I was there. Did your father serve?"

"He tried to enlist but they rejected him," Geoff said. "Something about his heart. He did go into the National Guard, if that counts."

"It counts. What was his job in the Guard?"

"I don't know. Once my mom told me he worked on something called the Manhattan Project."

"Your father worked on the Manhattan Project? Do you have any idea what that was?"

"Yeah, it's a road project or something like that in New York City, right?"

"A road project? Geoff, me lad, the Manhattan Project was a *very* big deal. It was a top-secret mission that made the first nuclear weapon dropped on Japan in 1945. Do you know what role your father had in it?"

"No."

"You should ask him about it sometime. He was a part of history."

"Well, my father and I don't talk to each other much. You're the first one who's ever told me about the war."

"Well, mostly we try to put it behind us. Those were bad times."

"I've never heard anyone talk about it. Not even my father. If my mother hadn't told me, I wouldn't even know he had gone into the National Guard."

Peter appeared from around the shelves with an armful of provisions and spread them all over the counter.

"Hey, Pete. Muggsy blew up a barge."

"Cool."

Muggsy looked over the sprawl of provisions. "How do you plan to keep the perishables cold?"

"Perishables?" Peter asked.

Muggsy pointed to the milk. "This is a perishable. How are you going to keep it cold?"

Peter picked up the milk and patted his stomach. "Well, I plan to store this right here. Mind if I open it now?"

"Go right ahead. And what about the butter? Why do you need butter?"

"For cooking," Geoff said.

"What on earth are you going to cook?"

"You know, supper. Chef Boyardee spaghetti and meatballs!"

"You think butter will help the taste of Chef Boyardee?"

"A meal can't get any better than Chef Boyardee unless it's Mom's meat loaf," Geoff said. "Won't butter keep it from sticking to the pot?"

"Nothing prevents Chef Boyardee from sticking."

Peter chimed in. "We're going to dig a hole in the sand and make an icebox. Don't know how we'll keep the sand from caving in, but Geoff's in charge of that one."

"So, your icebox isn't finished?"

"No," Geoff said.

"Then you don't need butter now?"

"No, not yet."

"Well, let's put this back until you do. It'll go rancid before you finish your icebox."

"Oops! I forgot the most important part: cookies," Peter said, and he dashed off.

Geoff felt the presence of someone standing behind him. He looked over his shoulder and stepped back. "Excuse me, ma'am. I didn't mean to get in your way."

"You're not in my way. I'm finding your conversation rather interesting," came the soft voice of an elderly woman. Her rounded shoulders gave her a stooped appearance. Her face was long and thin, with Grecian features that seemed to defy the usual ravages of time. It was punctuated with a nose of great distinction that seemed to say, "I am in charge." Her blue eyes were intense yet empathetic and understanding. She looked like she could read minds. Her thin silver hair was pulled into a tight bun at the back of her head, and at the hairline was a prominent widow's peak. She had an aura that commanded respect.

"Boys," said Muggsy, "this is Miss Wheeler. She lives here on the island. Miss Wheeler, this is Peter and Geoff."

The boys bowed saying, "Glad to meet you, ma'am."

"Oh, no need to be so formal, but it's nice to see boys your age still polite. You must have had a good upbringing. So, you're the two young campers I've been hearing about."

It seemed that everyone the boys encountered already knew they were there to camp. Raised in families where children were to be "seen and not heard," Peter and Geoff were captivated by Miss Wheeler's curiosity. She seemed genuinely interested as she asked numerous questions about their camp, what they had done, and how they had spent their time on the island thus far.

"Um, maybe you should come down for a visit once we get it all built," Geoff said with sheepish confidence.

"I'd like that very much."

"You mean you'd come all the way down to our camp just to see what it looks like?"

"Of course I would. I'd love to see what you boys have done."

Geoff looked inquisitively to Muggsy.

"If she said she'd come, then she'll be there."

"When we finish setting up camp, we'll invite you down, and even to supper." Geoff said.

Miss Wheeler smiled, a twinkle in her eye. "I'll hold you to that. Now, when will you come visit me at *my* cozy abode? If you boys aren't too busy this afternoon, why don't you come while it's still fresh in your mind?"

"We still have a lot to do to our camp. Would it be all right if we came tomorrow?"

"That would be fine."

Miss Wheeler gave precise instructions about heading down Broadway to Four Corners, turning left, and keeping an eye out for her small brown cottage. "Come when you can. I'm almost always there. I'll have cold milk and cookies waiting for you."

Geoff turned toward Muggsy, who nodded with a reassuring grin. "Welcome to Cuttyhunk."

The boys left and headed down the footpath alongside the Allen House. "Hey, Pete, this is our third day here, right?" Peter nodded. "We haven't checked in yet. We were supposed to do that when we first got here."

"What made you think of that?"

Geoff motioned with his chin. "The Bosworth House is right over there. That's where we find Gladys Snow. We'd better check in before our folks worry. Maybe we should do that this afternoon."

"Well, everyone on the island knows we're here. I'm sure our parents already know, too."

"Maybe, but we still need to check in."

"Yeah, well, we'll get to it. C'mon, let's keep going."

The boys wound their way down the footpath past the Coast Guard station and followed the road toward the beach. Squeaking brakes caught their attention as an old pickup truck passed them and stopped a few feet ahead. They caught up to the truck. "Hi, Mr. Potter! How are you doing?" said Geoff.

"Hop in the back, boys."

Geoff lit up. Another tailgate opportunity. Peter looked down the road and back to Potter. "Ah, no thanks. We're almost there."

Potter stuck his head out the window. "Out here it's impolite to not take a ride, no matter how short it might be."

Without a word the boys scurried to the back of Potter's pickup and sat with their legs dangling over the end and their provisions by their sides.

Potter reached the main dock and turned to back his truck onto it. "OK, boys, end of the road."

"Thanks, Mr. Potter!"

"That's Potter. Forget the *mister.*" And he backed the truck onto the dock.

Peter and Geoff ran their provisions to camp and raced back to the dock moments before *Alert*'s arrival. The crowd of greeters didn't look as ominous as the day before. Strangeness softened with familiarity.

Geoff positioned himself against a tall piling near the stern of the boat. Bert glanced at him between duties. Geoff gave him the salute and received a salute in return. Geoff beamed. He had managed to pull off the salute like a local. What a day!

With their bellies bulging with peanut butter and jelly, the boys sat lethargically on the barge, waiting for the breakers to settle down. Peter jumped down and walked the beach feeling like a caged tiger. He was eager to get into the water. Geoff looked at the barges in awe, knowing that he sat on a piece of history told to him by a man who had been there when history was being made. Perhaps Muggsy could tell him more of the story about the Manhattan Project. Then he'd be able to talk to his dad without enduring a debilitating interrogation. Who knew? Geoff thought. It might even bring them together.

11

WE NEED A BONFIRE

The boys sat on the barge as their first beach bonfire roared. Except for the ever-faithful lighthouse signal on Gay Head, over on Martha's Vineyard, and lights from town, they sat surrounded by blackness.

"That driftwood made a crappy stretcher, but it sure makes a great fire," said Geoff.

"Yep. We're burning the evidence of a good idea gone bad."

Geoff celebrated by recounting the day's activities and achievements. Peter celebrated by listing the activities for the next day—bodysurfing, meeting the *Alert*, beachcombing, and taking Miss Wheeler up on her invitation for cookies and milk.

"There's one more thing we need to add," Geoff said.

"Yeah? What?"

"Checking in with Gladys Snow."

"We talked about this earlier. Our parents probably already know we're here."

"How can you be sure of that?"

"The island has big ears. Remember?"

"The agreement with our parents was that we were to check in once we arrived, and tomorrow will be our fourth day here. Everyone may be watching and talking about us, but we still gotta check in."

Peter looked away, unmoved.

"You have no intentions of checking in, do you?" Geoff asked.

"You catch on quick, Geoff. You think our parents don't already know?"

"I'm *sure* they know."

"So, what's your problem?"

"It was part of the bargain. All we have to do is check in and it'll be done."

"If we agree they already know, there's really no need to check in. So why bother?"

"Because we promised."

"Check in or not, it won't make any difference with my dad."

"Well, it will with mine. If you don't want to go, that's fine. I'll go alone."

"Fine! We'll swing by the Bosworth House if we get up that way tomorrow."

"No ifs. Besides, it's not right to make our parents worry," Geoff said.

"Trust me, they know and they're not worried."

"Can you be sure of that?"

"*Your* parents might worry. Not mine."

"You don't think your parents worry about you?"

"Heck, my dad doesn't have anything to do with me. He's always at work. My mom takes him to the train every morning and picks him up every night. Day after day. Week after week."

"Don't you ever see him?"

"Not during the week. He's gone before I get up and doesn't come back until way after supper. He never comes up to say hello."

"Do you ever go downstairs to see him?"

"Look, if he doesn't care to see me, why should I make the effort to see him?"

"Well, he *is* your father."

"Hey, don't lecture me! You're the one hallucinating about your dad. We both have problems with our dads, even though they're different."

"Well, I suppose you're right. I see my pop most every day. That's how I get my daily dose of what I'm doing wrong, should be doing, or shoulda done. At least *you* don't have all your decisions questioned or second-guessed. Whenever Pop questions me about stuff, he turns into a trial lawyer. That's why I never want to be an attorney."

"Ah. You have it much easier than me." Peter waved his arm dismissively.

"How's that?"

"I could die in my room and they wouldn't notice for days."

"The hell. On the second day you'd start smelling like a dead rat. But tell me how you have it harder than me."

"For one, at least your dad talks to you," Peter said.

"No, he doesn't talk. He interrogates. Would it be any different for you if your dad talked to you?"

"Well, at least he'd show some interest."

"You spend time with your dad on the boat. Doesn't that count?"

"We don't spend time *together* on the boat. We both happen to be *on* it at the same time. That's why he likes it when you come along—so he doesn't have to deal with me."

"I guess we're in the same mess," said Geoff.

"I'd rather have a father who hounds me than one who ignores me. With yours, at least you exist. Have you ever thought that maybe what your dad does to you is because he cares about you? If my dad cared, seems like he'd show a little interest in me."

"If the way my father treats me is 'caring,' you can count me out. A caring father wouldn't make me feel stupid. He might even give me praise once in a while. What I wouldn't do for his approval. You know, I watched my little sister at a swim meet once. All the parents were yelling and cheering their kids on. I didn't see a single parent go up to their child and criticize them for not coming in first."

"So, what's your point? Were your parents there?"

"Yeah."

"Did they cheer your sister on?"

"Nope. They just sat at a table and watched. See what I mean?"

"Well, at least they didn't criticize her."

"Jeez, Pete. Maybe it's me. Do you think it could be me? If that had been me, my father would have waited till we got home and then told me that I didn't push myself hard enough."

"No, I don't think it's you. Maybe he did criticize your sister when they got home. Who knows?"

"With my sisters, I think he looks the other way. With me, I'm always under the microscope. Maybe it *is* me. Maybe he really does think I'm stupid. Do you think I'm stupid?"

"No, but your question is stupid. You shouldn't keep talking about being stupid. The more you talk about stupid, the faster you'll become stupid. You're not stupid, Geoff."

"Maybe if my grades were better, he'd change. Man, I try, but whenever I study, I fall asleep on my desk."

"Let's change the subject before you go wandering down some dark path. As long as we've known each other, we've spent most of our time at my house. You know my mom and two brothers, but I know nothing about yours. So, tell me about them before this fire flickers out, because when the fire dies, so do I."

"Well, my mother's always there for me. Pop's always there to decide everything for me and to constantly correct me. With him I'm just a big screw-up, and—"

"Yeah. Yeah. We already covered that. Your brother and sisters. Go on."

"Peter, the one with the brains, if he came home from school with an A-minus, he'd be punished for not 'applying himself,' as my father would say. If *I* came home with a B-minus, I'd be punished for cheating." Geoff laughed.

Then he continued. "My sisters… My oldest sister is always in love."

"Always?"

"Yep, madly."

"With who?"

"Gene Autry and Tex Ritter."

"Gene Autry, as in the singing cowboy?"

"Yep. They both sing. And some other guy named Clete. When she's in love, she gets sick."

"Like sick as in barfing?"

"Well, I haven't seen her do that, but her stomach gets upset easily. Must be those singing cowboys. She runs from the supper table a lot. I feel bad for her. It couldn't be my mother's cooking; otherwise we'd all be running. Then there's my younger sister. She's usually off doing something that could get her in big trouble. She's only thirteen and already spends a lot of time trying to snow Pop about her innocence, but he's usually on to her. If she were an actress, she'd get an Oscar. Then there's my kid sister—I sure love that kid. She's good-natured and isn't a pain in the ass to have around. I—"

Peter formed a megaphone with his hands while yelling into the sky. "Hey, kid sis! Your big brother likes you because you're not a pain in the ass!" He turned to Geoff. "Someday she might ask you why you like her, and you should have a better answer than 'Because, little sis, you're not a pain in the ass.'"

"Well, she's not. Most big brothers get assigned to haul their kid sisters around. I invite mine. She's a good kid. If I told her she was a pain in the ass, she'd probably take it as a compliment."

"You talk about always trying to get away from your house, yet you got homesick. I don't get it."

"I miss home and don't even know why. We all live in the same house, yet we hardly know anything about each other. We're afraid to talk when Pop's around. To him, everything is private. Even though he talks about privacy, he pushes us to share our feelings at the supper table. There are just some things you don't want to tell other family members. So, we all learned to not look up for fear of being called upon—just like in school. I hate being home, but I miss it now.

"So, I gotta tell you a funny story. One Saturday night we were all sitting at that round table in the kitchen. It was dead quiet. To break the silence, I slammed my napkin down on the table. It made the dishes rattle, and everyone jumped. They looked over as I picked up the napkin, and Pop scowled at me. I held up the napkin, saying, 'A bug! I just killed a huge bug!' Pop raised one eyebrow and looked at me in disbelief. I scrunched up the napkin. *CRUNCH!* My sisters screamed. Then I opened the napkin and popped one of the pieces of potato chip into my mouth. Everyone laughed. Even Pop. Imagine that. How much noise can a potato chip make when you break it? In a napkin even! That's how quiet that supper table gets. Funny, but that's one of my favorite memories. I just wish we could have more like that."

Peter put his hand on Geoff's shoulder. "You know, Geoff, I've seen a big change in you in the last few days. Want to guess what it is?"

Geoff rubbed his chin. "I need a shave?"

"No, seriously, take a guess."

Geoff looked at his arms, legs, and body and shrugged.

"You're more relaxed. You don't have that angry look on your face like you're ready to pick a fight with the world."

Geoff looked at Peter, puzzled. "Say what?"

"Yeah. You seldom tell me your thoughts unless I tick you off. Like the other night, I wasn't trying to upset you, but when I did, oh man, I couldn't believe all the crap you spit out. But here, right now, you've been telling me about what your dad does to you, but you haven't gone off in a rage. What happened in the last day that changed you? Did you finally get him out of your head?"

"Humph. I hadn't noticed. I guess when you told me I needed to get him out of my head, I thought I should give it a try. Can't say as I knew *how* to do it, but I just decided that since Pop wasn't here, he couldn't criticize me. When I did that, his voice went away. Except for that stretcher, we haven't made any bad decisions. I'm thinking that part of my problem is that I sort of expected to be criticized, and maybe that's where the voice came from. It feels good now, but I'm sure things will go back to what they were when we go home."

"Only if you let it. You want less of your dad, and I guess I want more of mine."

"I wouldn't mind being around him if he'd just stop making me feel so damned stupid. Get this… That guy Steve, on the boat over, he liked my handshake and told me I must have had a good upbringing. Muggsy said the same thing when I shook his hand. And then Miss Wheeler said she liked how we were being polite. If what Pop's doing *is* good, why do I feel so bad?"

"Search me."

Geoff jumped off the barge and picked up the last piece of driftwood. "This is it," he said as he held it up. "This is the last of that damned stretcher."

"Burn, stretcher, burn!" Peter said, laughing.

Geoff pitched the piece into the embers, and they watched the sparks shoot skyward.

"That stretcher was a disaster," Peter said. "Promise me one thing."

"What's that?"

"If your journal ever becomes a book, promise me you won't write anything about the stretcher."

"Don't worry about that. I can hardly read. Why do you think I'll ever become a writer?"

"Just in case. Promise?"

"I promise."

The flame flickered and died. Peter stood, stretched, announced he was turning in, and felt his way to the tent. Geoff sat, mesmerized by the brilliance of the Milky Way and the sound of breakers. He memorized the signal pattern on the Gay Head lighthouse. He turned toward town, making bets with himself about which cottage would be the next to go dark. He became a night cat sitting on the barge, watching everything, missing nothing. Even in darkness there was a lot to see. He bargained with himself to sit up until he saw his next shooting star, but his heavy eyes won. Geoff ducked into the tent just as a bright meteor shot across the sky.

MEETING ROBBIE

"Isn't the Bosworth House supposed to be like a boardinghouse or a hotel?" Peter asked. "Are you sure this is it?"

"It's green and we've been pointing to it for four days. I'm sure."

"I don't see any activity. Are you sure you're sure this is it?"

Geoff stood looking at the building. "Why not just walk up there and ask?"

"Good idea. Let's find the front door."

The boys walked around the house, looking for a main entrance. The large, sprawling, well-kept two-story structure stood majestically on a hill overlooking the harbor. On one side of the house were traditional wood pillars supporting a porch. On the other side was a small landing with a screen door flanked by a sun-bleached wooden chair and a gray milk crate. The growl of a fan came from inside the screen door. The boys agreed that the pillar side must mark the main entrance.

They stood at the base of the porch. Peter prodded Geoff to take the first step, but Geoff hesitated and pointed to the front door. "Look, it's wide open."

"What's wrong with a wide-open door?"

"There's no one around."

"C'mon, Geoff. Quit stalling."

"Why are you speaking so softly?"

"Because you are."

"What if this *isn't* the Bosworth House?"

"Don't worry," Peter said, nudging Geoff. "It is. I wasn't sure before, but I am now."

Geoff looked over his shoulder. "Hear that?"

"What?"

"Lawn mower. Sounds like it's coming from the Allen House."

"So what?"

"It's sputtering. That mower sure could use a new spark plug and a carburetor cleaning."

Peter wore his best look of confusion. "What the heck does that have to do with anything? And how do you know about lawn mowers?"

"That's how I make my money in the summers. If you're gonna cut grass, you need to know how to fix mowers. How do you think I earned the money for this trip?"

"Jeez, Geoff! Why are you bringing that up now? I get it, you're afraid to go in." He gave Geoff another nudge.

The boys stepped under the covered porch and inched toward the door. Geoff peeked inside. To the right he saw several tables set up for a meal, with water glasses turned upside down and silverware placed on folded napkins.

"This is it! There's a dining room over there." Geoff pointed to the tables. Unable to find a doorbell, he knocked lightly on the door and meekly said, "Hello? Hello?"

"Why are you knocking? Jeez! People don't knock on boardinghouse doors. They expect you to just walk on in."

"We're not guests here, and we need to be respectful. What if this *isn't* the Bosworth House? We could be walking into someone's private home. How would that look? If we were caught, they could come after us with a gun or waving a knife."

"Nonsense! This *is* the Bosworth House. Just go in."

"Hello? Hello?" Geoff called again timidly. They stood in the parlor of what could have been an unoccupied house. "Nobody's here. The house is wide open. Anyone can just walk in. Now what?"

"I hear something. Sounds like a fan," said Peter. "Let's check it out. Maybe we'll find someone."

The boys stepped cautiously through the dining room. Geoff stopped near a large picture window. "What a view! You can see the beach where we're camping. Wow!"

"We didn't come here to look out windows. Let's find someone."

They followed the droning sound coming from the far end of a dark corridor. The farther they went, the darker it became. The sole light source was what bled in from the dining room behind them and a doorway at the other end.

"It's like we're in a cave," Geoff said. "That humming sound is coming from the other side of that door."

They stopped at a half-closed Dutch door. Geoff peered in. "This is the kitchen, and there's the fan we heard. The fact that the bottom half of this door is closed means 'stay out.'"

"The top half is open, which means 'come in.'"

"Maybe just walking in here wasn't such a hot idea."

"You're the one who insisted we check in." Peter reached around Geoff, opened the door, and pushed him into a kitchen filled with commercial-looking cooking equipment. In the middle of the room was a large stainless-steel table that could have held enough plates to feed a small horde. Behind it were deep fryers, a black iron stove, and a huge industrial-size refrigerator with double glass doors. A steep, narrow staircase on the left led to the second floor. On the opposite wall was a large sink and sprawling counter—all stainless steel.

Geoff pointed to the stairs. "Maybe someone's up there. Maybe we can't be heard because of the fan." He crept toward the stairs and put one foot on a step, then leaned on his knee as he looked up through the opening at the top. "Hello? Hello?"

The screen door creaked open and crashed against the chair outside. The boys jerked their heads toward the back door. In walked a man with a protruding belly, wearing a white sleeveless undershirt. His thinning hair was long, jet black, and slicked down. The hair on his body was thick from his shoulders all the way down to his fingertips, and curled out from his undershirt. His face was black with beard stubble. A short apron around his waist was smeared with red streaks. He clenched a large kitchen knife in his right hand.

Geoff froze. The man's eyes locked on his, and his fierce glare pierced Geoff. Deeply grooved lines formed across his forehead, pushing his entire face into contortions. His lips pursed and his jaw tightened. "What the *hell* are you doing in my kitchen?"

The boys' eyes and mouths popped open. Fear nailed their feet to the floor and rendered them unable to respond.

"I said, what the *hell* are you doing in my kitchen! When I ask you a question, goddamn it, I expect an answer. So tell me, and be quick about it!"

The boys simultaneously stammered senseless, indiscernible explanations that succeeded only in further enraging the man. He waved his arm wildly, brandishing his long knife as if sword fighting with the wind, and pointed it directly at the boys. "Don't get cute with me. I asked you a question. What the *hell* are you doing in my kitchen?"

"Ah, we're… uh… um, we're looking for… uh, Gladys S-snow." Geoff trembled as his face turned as white as chalk dust.

"Looking for Gladys Snow, you say. Looks to me like you're snooping around. You were about to climb those stairs, weren't you, boy?" The man began walking around the table, inspecting for things out of place while suspiciously eyeing the two. "I think I caught you dead in the tracks of mischief. That'll get you in more trouble than stealing. You stealing, boy, or are you here just for the mischief? Tell me now, which is it?"

"No, really, mister, we're… we're here looking for… for G-Gladys Snow," Geoff stammered. "We're not here for any mischief. We're not stealing anything, and we're sorry for coming into your k-kitchen. We didn't mean anything, honest." As he spoke, he and Pete clutched each other's arms and edged their way around the table to keep as far from the flailing knife as possible.

"This is *my* kitchen! I'm the cook in this joint, see. Nobody comes in here without my permission. *Nobody!* You little dumb-ass shits get that?"

"Y-yes sir," Geoff replied. "We… we sure do. But like I said, we didn't mean anything."

"Robbie, it's OK." Geoff looked up the stairs as a woman's bare legs appeared on the top steps. She stooped to see the commotion. "Robbie, we know these boys. They're with the Fairchilds. They're family. They're just checking in. They just got to the island."

The woman's soothing voice eased the fiery tension. Geoff stood straight and relaxed his shoulders. Peter's eyes returned to normal size, and he closed his mouth. The crazy man lowered his arm, although the knife remained firmly affixed in his hand.

The woman took a few more steps down and came into full view. Geoff couldn't take his eyes off her. She was slender, with wavy blond hair. She was graceful and young. Her lightly tanned skin was smooth and unblemished.

Stupefied, Geoff choked out in a high-pitched voice, "Ma'am, we're sorry for causing any trouble. We're looking for Gladys Snow. We weren't sure if we were in the right place."

The woman's smile melted Geoff. "Yes, you're in the right place, and I'm Gladys Snow. Are you Geoff or Peter?"

"Wow! You know our names? Um. Yes. I'm Peter and… no, wait! I'm not Peter. I'm Geoff and *this* is Peter."

"The little shit doesn't even know his own name," the crazy man interjected.

"We were expecting you and kept an eye out," Gladys said. "Your parents know you're here safe and sound. I'm sorry you arrived in such awful weather. How are you settling in at your camp down by the barges?"

"You know where we're camping?" Geoff asked.

"Of course," Gladys said. "This is a small island. We've been watching you from the dining room window. You boys have become somewhat of a curiosity."

"You said our parents know we're here?" said Geoff.

"Yes, we got word to the Fairchilds as soon as you arrived. And that man"—Gladys pointed—"is Robbie. You've already met him. He growls a lot, but he's actually quite harmless."

Geoff looked toward Robbie and forced a nervous smile. He stepped around the table with an extended hand. Robbie looked at Geoff with annoyance and raised his right hand—knife still in it—and grunted. Geoff retreated.

"Actually, ma'am, while we're here… Our birthdays fall on the same day, and we'd like to come here for a dinner celebration. Can we do that?"

"Of course you can. Just make a reservation on the day you want to come for dinner. I've got to go back to work now. You can make your arrangements through Robbie or the girls when they come back to work." With that, Gladys Snow vanished up the stairs.

The boys, still apprehensive and once again alone with Robbie, turned to him. "Can we make reservations with you?" Geoff asked.

"Hell, no! I'm the cook, not the goddamn reservation clerk." Robbie pointed his knife toward the dining room. "You want reservations, see the girls in the dining room."

"OK, we'll do that," Geoff said. "Uh. Um… but since you're the chef…"

"Cook! Cook! Don't call me no goddamn chef! I'm the cook!"

"OK. OK. Since you're the cook, could we see a menu?"

"Menu! You smart-ass, wet-behind-the-ears little shit. You're looking at the menu. *I* am the menu. You get what *I* cook. If I say 'meat,' you get meat. If I say 'fish,' you get fish. Get it?"

"You didn't say lobster. Could we get a lobster dinner?" Geoff asked.

"Lobster? Does this place look like it could store lobster?"

"Well, we don't know," Geoff said apologetically as he cupped his hands to his chest. "We don't know anything about keeping lobsters."

"You're goddamn right you don't. If you want lobster, you have to bring lobster."

"Where do we get it?"

Robbie looked down, shaking his head in disgust. "How long are you gonna be on the island?"

"We're here till July sixth."

"Jesus, Mary, and Joseph! Do I have to put up with you for that long?" Robbie turned and headed toward the screen door but stopped and looked back. "Lobster… You get lobster down at the fish dock. See Bob Tilton."

"Does Bob Tilton sell lobster?"

"You didn't just ask me that. Does Bob Tilton sell lobster? What kind of a dumb-ass question is that? Why would I give you his name right after I told you where to get it? Jesus!"

Robbie hesitated momentarily in thought. Then he shook his head and pointed his knife at Geoff. "Look, kid, I hope you're not just being a little smart-ass, but one thing's for sure: You're as dumb as a bag of rocks." He waved his knife around the room. "And remember, this is *my* kitchen. Nobody comes in here without *my* permission. Got that?"

Both boys nodded.

"Now, get the *hell* outta here!"

Robbie left through the screen door. It slammed with distinct finality. And in the kitchen, all was quiet once again except for the drone of the fan.

The boys scurried back through the dark corridor into the dining room and out the front door where the distant popping, sputtering lawn mower was sweet music to their ears. Geoff looked back at the Bosworth House. "Phew! We're safe."

"What were you doing back there?" Peter said.

"Whadda you mean? We were checking in."

"No, I mean about Gladys Snow. Looked like you were checking her out more than you were checking us in. You had your eyes glued to her. You looked at her like she was some sort of a goddess."

"Well, isn't she? Did you see how beautiful she is and how pretty her legs are? And her voice… it sounded like… like singing, melodic singing."

"Darn, Geoff. We had a crazy man with a knife ready to carve us up and you took time to notice Gladys Snow's legs? You went off into a trance or something."

"You gotta admit…"

"Admit nothing! Look, Geoff, that lady is very old. She's probably as old as our mothers. Do you think your mom is beautiful? Do you look at her and say, 'Mom, you sure have great legs'?"

"Of course I think my mom is beautiful. And yes, I tell her. I think yours is, too, especially when she smiles. Don't you?"

"Geoff, you're deranged."

"Maybe, but we survived Robbie. God, I hope we don't have to deal with him again."

"I'm definitely staying outta his kitchen. Did you see the red streaks on his apron? With the knife in his hand, I was sure it was blood and there was about to be more."

"Hey, did you notice how Gladys Snow asked how we were settling in?" Geoff asked. "They *do* know everything, don't they?"

"Yep, Muggsy told us about that."

Peter put his arm around Geoff's shoulders and pulled him close as they walked down the driveway toward Broadway like two lazy boys strolling their way through the summer. "You have to admit, I was right," said Peter.

"About what?"

"I told you last night that our parents probably already knew we were here, and Gladys Snow confirmed it. We really didn't need to check in."

"Well, now we know where to buy lobster and that we can have our birthday celebration at the Bosworth House," said Geoff.

"That we do. And now, my friend, we're going to the general store, and the only thing I'm wondering is, what shall we get for lunch?"

In the distance, the lawn mower at the Allen House sputtered and popped its way to silence. They heard futile attempts to get it going. "I can fix that," Geoff said. "Maybe we should go over there and ask."

"No. Focus, Geoff. We're not going over there to fix anybody's lawn mower. We're going to the general store to fix the rumbling in our stomachs."

13

MISS WHEELER'S ABODE

The boys sat on an old couch that was so low, their knees were higher than their chins. They had just washed down two boxes of cookies with a quart of milk. Their bellies were full, and they no longer knew what to say to their hostess. It might have been easy talking with her at the general store, but in her home their awkwardness poured through polite smiles and darting glances. Their fidgeting feet told of two boys itching to bolt out the door.

"Those cookies were sure good, Miss Wheeler," Geoff said. "Best meal we've had in days." Miss Wheeler chuckled, obviously happy to be entertaining the young visitors—even if she had bribed them.

Geoff looked around the room for something to talk about and caught Miss Wheeler looking at him with gentle eyes. He raised his shoulders, pushed out a half smile, and sighed. A mantel clock made the only sound that broke the uncomfortable silence with its rhythmic *tick-tock, tick-tock*. He was surrounded by everything old—reminiscent of visits to his distant grandmother.

The cottage was small yet crammed with upholstered chairs and antique tables. Navigating required the agility of a cat. The room resembled a formal parlor more than a sitting room in an island cottage. Lace doilies seemed to be breeding everywhere—on the arms of chairs and the couch, on tables, under lamps, and on bookshelves. An old wool afghan, draped over the couch, waited for a chilly night. Beside the couch stood a round table that looked like a pie pan held up with four thin, dark wooden spindles. Glass table lamps with cloth shades—all different sizes, shapes, colors, and mismatched bead tassels—stood on every surface.

A plethora of small black-and-white photographs in dark wooden frames flanked the base of the lamps, crowded tabletops, and splashed across the walls. In the photos, women were gussied up in formal wear, with furs around their necks and hats with flowing feathers. The menfolk wore bow ties and tuxedos with tails. Many held walking sticks and wore top hats slightly cocked to one side. There were countless group photos of smiling women standing on bleachers as if posing for a school yearbook.

"Sure are a lot of pictures," Geoff said.

"They are people I used to work with," Miss Wheeler said. "I think of them as my family." She smiled, clearly delighted in his curiosity.

Geoff struggled to keep the conversation going. He fidgeted in the silence and was thrown off by the contrast between Miss Wheeler's cottage and what he thought an island cottage should look like. He attempted to hide his discomfort, but feared his squirming was giving him away. He looked to Peter; he was no help.

"Miss Wheeler, you have some very interesting stuff here," Geoff said. "I like the doilies and the old lamps and tassels. My grandmother's house looks much like this room, but you have a lot more pictures."

"All this is what's left over from the old days. These things hold a lot of good memories. That's what makes my little abode so comfortable for me."

Geoff wiggled out of his couch entrenchment and walked over to a large picture window facing the harbor. Outside was a wooden deck weathered with cracks and splinters and badly in need of paint. A long bench and railing ran its entire length. Retired lobster buoys huddled around a corner post, all hanging on a single rusty nail bent from all the weight. Next to it leaned a well-used lobster trap. Rocks and other beachcombing treasures lined the railing. Facing the harbor were two old chairs separated by a rickety-looking table.

"Nice deck," said Geoff.

"Yes, a lovely deck it is. I've spent many a summer day sitting in those chairs just watching the world go by. There's nothing better than sitting there at dusk. Everything settles down—the wind, the water, everything. Sometimes you can hear faint talking coming from the fish dock, but mostly you can just see people walking around. During the season, boaters walk up and down Broadway, enjoying the end of the day. When Wilfred Tilton's ducks swim out in the calm harbor, they go in a single line, and their tiny wakes are sometimes the only ripple in the water."

Geoff nodded and looked down to the deck. "Those chairs look hard to get in and out of."

"Those are Adirondack chairs. Yes, they do look difficult to get in and out of, but when you figure out how to do it, it's quite easy. Even I can still do it. And the chairs are so comfortable, you can sit in them all day long… without a seat cushion."

"Do you still sit out there?"

"Not much. Usually only when company comes. It's interesting that you mention that old wooden deck. It was only a few years ago that my summers were filled with company. Old friends came and stayed for a week. We sat on that old deck just talking and watching."

"They don't come anymore?"

Miss Wheeler bowed her head in reflection. "Oh no. Most of them are all gone now, or traveling has become too difficult. It's sad that they go, and it's hard to tell you how it feels. In about sixty years you'll know."

"Miss Wheeler, I am so sorry I asked that question. It was really very stupid of me."

Miss Wheeler walked over to Geoff's side. "Don't be silly. How could you know? I'm not entirely alone, you know. I love having you island kids over for milk and cookies, and I sure hope to see more of you. I love being around young people. You have such great hope and energy. You keep an old woman young." Miss Wheeler put her arm around Geoff and pulled him close. "I'm looking forward to coming down to see your camp and taking you up on your dinner invitation when my friend Miss Wright comes in a few days."

"Well," said Peter, "one thing's for sure, we have a lot of preparing to do. Before you know it, Miss Wright will be here, and you'll be sitting in our camp having *our* milk and cookies!"

"Well, that sounds like fun."

"By the way, how are you going to get down to our camp?" Peter asked. "It's a long way."

"Oh, that's no problem. I have a car."

"You do? We didn't see one."

Miss Wheeler chuckled. "You're standing right over it."

The boys looked down at the floor.

"The basement of my cottage is just big enough to get it in."

Peter looked toward Miss Wheeler. "Well, Miss Wheeler, we gotta go."

A few minutes later, they were out the door, around the cottage, and on the road toward their camp. Geoff lacked the spirit of brisk pace. "What's wrong, Geoff?"

"How come we had to go?"

"It was getting a little boring with all that old stuff and those pictures all over the place."

"But I would have liked to have found out more. I think she would have told us stories from her past. Did you see all those pictures of women standing for what looked like a school picture? She called them part of her family."

"Why are you so interested in that?"

"Once I found a picture of my grandma sitting on the running board of an old Packard. I was fascinated, seeing her when she was young, and wanted to know what it was like back then. My mom told me it was the family car and I should ask my grandma. When I did, she sent me away, saying I wouldn't understand. Get a load of that! What was there to not understand?"

"Maybe Miss Wheeler would have done the same. You still haven't told me what's so interesting about those pictures."

"Don't you ever wonder what old people are thinking when they look at us?"

"No."

"Well, I think if we asked her about those pictures, she'd tell us. She seems lonely and sad."

"Maybe that's what happens when you get old," Peter said.

"You know how she said some of the pictures were of her family? I couldn't tell. Could you?"

"You looked closely at them. I didn't."

"I'd sure like to know which ones were family and which were friends. Don't you wonder who the people are in pictures that you see in people's homes?"

"Not really."

"You're not very interested in her, are you?"

"It's not that I'm not interested. I'm just not as interested as you are."

"Did you feel like she was studying you?"

"No, Geoff, mostly she looked at you. Probably because you were closer and did the talking."

"Well, I could feel her eyes on me when I was looking around the room," Geoff said. "It was like she was looking inside me. I don't usually like to be around old people because I don't know what to say to them, but I like her. I think having her down for supper is going to be fun."

"Let's hope she brings some of those pictures or we'll have nothing to talk about," Peter said. "But right now, we have a lot to do. Company's coming to supper in a few days, and we'd better get crackin'."

14

WITHERING AWAY AT LAND'S END

Geoff kicked aside his sleeping bag, crawled outside, and stretched. He splashed water on his face, brushed his teeth, and plunged a spoon into a fresh jar of applesauce. He strolled around, studying a suitable location for their fireplace, table, and icebox. Miss Wheeler and her friend were coming to dinner soon, and the boys were hardly ready for them. With towels and T-shirts hanging on stretch lines and over the top edge of the tent, it looked like the home of two scruffy boys, not two young gentlemen preparing to entertain noble guests. To create a five-star camp, they needed building materials. Rocks for a fireplace were abundant and piled high in the barges. Making the icebox was a matter of digging. Geoff concerned himself with a more immediate problem: finding furniture.

He turned his eyes to the eastern end of the island. Surely the constant thundering of Atlantic breakers on the Vineyard Sound side would provide a smorgasbord for all sorts of camping needs. They hadn't seen anyone down there since moving to the beach. That meant the pickings would be primo.

The island's east end was calling. The roofless skeletal remains of a deserted, faraway building stood as a black shadow against the early morning blue-gray cloud cover. A warm wind blew in his face, teasing his curiosity and drawing his imagination deep into the enigma of the desolate structure.

Geoff followed a line of battered barges eastward. To the lee of the barges were scores of small sand dunes. Oat grass clung persistently, holding the dunes in place and contributing its own version of "swishing" to the sounds of the shore.

Once past the remnants of barges, he found himself in a flat, bleak wasteland of colorless sand, smooth rocks, and sun-bleached driftwood.

The breeze in his face stiffened. The area between Buzzards Bay and Vineyard Sound narrowed to rock-throwing distance. Large waves slammed against the rocks, spewing foam and spray high above.

A flock of terns hovered overhead and fixed their eyes on Geoff. They were not behaving as majestic creatures soaring aloft in the wind currents. Instead, they floated low and appeared agitated by his presence. They squawked as they circled and, in a seemingly planned and well-executed effort, took turns dive-bombing from behind. Geoff ducked as one swooped past and squawked in his ear.

The emboldened terns dove with greater ferocity and determination to drive him away or peck deep holes in his head. Geoff squatted close to the ground and looked back as one swooped within a foot of him. *Soon another found the courage to attack, inciting the rest of the flock to take on a mob mentality. Geoff struggled to stand, but stumbled. The birds took turns impaling his body. Geoff lay incapacitated, screaming with the excruciating terror of being eaten alive. When finished, the birds flew away, squawking with insidious glee. Geoff's face was unrecognizable, his eyes reduced to bloody holes. "I shoulda waited for Pete," he murmured. All he could do was hope to be found before the elements finished him off or crabs came to feast on his eye sockets.*

Geoff stood just as a squawking bird circled back for a victory lap, shaking him out of his horrifying daydream. He watched their pattern. Flailing his arms only provoked them. They dove close but just out of reach. As long as Geoff ignored them, all those birds could do was swoop and deliver empty threats. He continued his exploration while confounding the powerless sky beasts.

He stood in front of the old structure. It was no longer that mysterious, faraway building. Deserted and left to wither away at the merciless hands of the elements, it sat on a tall concrete foundation that made it look larger than it was. Concrete walls wore the scars of wind, rain, sand, and abandonment. Steep gables outlined the slope of the old roof. Windows and doors were long gone, yet the openings showed what his predecessors saw when standing inside. A long ramp from the Buzzards Bay side ran up to a wide opening.

Geoff stepped inside. The wind surged through the openings and sent out an eerie whining moan. He stood in the center of the structure, turning to see the changing vista. The Coast Guard boathouse near the main dock was a mere blemish of red off in the distance. Houses and cottages were indiscernible flecks that dotted the island hillside.

The rugged shoreline was just as Geoff imagined—a lumberyard of building materials. Wedged between boulders were chairs with missing legs, wooden boxes, torn clothing, bent kitchen utensils, chafed fishing nets, miles of weathered rope, an old door, and even rusted parts from outboard motors.

Geoff busied himself gathering supplies. Then he stood over his pile of booty, beaming with pride. He had come hoping for a table, but what a discovery! By himself, it would take several trips to haul his treasure back to camp, but he and Pete could easily do it in one or two. That door, though, would be the first to go back.

He rescued a wet, sandy yellow slicker snagged on debris and held it up to his shoulders. Geoff was lanky and had some growing to do, but it would have taken two of him to fill the sleeves of that slicker. He shook off loose sand and tried it on. The sleeves dangled below his hands, the shoulders sagged halfway to his elbows, and the bottom brushed his knees. It was in good condition, and best of all, it was free.

Geoff began dragging the door back to camp. Trapped sand in the sleeves scraped his skin and became unbearably itchy. He dropped the table to scratch and to shake out the annoyance. Why was there so much damn sand in those sleeves? It slid down his arm. He swatted it. Then it felt like it was crawling up his arm. He swatted again. Horror overcame him. Sand did not slide uphill. Nor did it crawl. He broke into a freakish dance that resembled a panicked, headless chicken on the run—jumping, hopping, and flapping his arms. He screamed and cursed as he ran in circles while unbuckling and scrambling out of the slicker.

He cast it aside and jumped away. He poked at it cautiously with a piece of driftwood, but whatever occupied it was not giving up its home. Geoff tentatively picked up the slicker and held it at arm's length, studying it closely. Maybe his imagination had gotten the best of him. "Maybes" walked through his head. He looked down one sleeve, fully prepared to recoil should a lobster or octopus leap at his face. He checked the other sleeve. He threw the slicker high into the air, then repeatedly and violently slammed it on the ground. He was determined to win this war of possession with the mystery creature, but could not officially claim ownership until evicting its occupant.

He stood over the garment—waiting. A small crab, not much larger than a quarter, emerged from the sleeve. It scampered a few feet and stopped in defiance. Geoff kicked the slicker out of the way just in case the crab decided to double back. It ran sideways, forward, backward. It kept its red claws high over its head, ready to clamp on anything that came close. The little creature had gumption, even though it was like Bambi facing off with Godzilla. Geoff donned the slicker and resumed dragging the door across the sand. The itching stopped.

Peter was standing tall on the barge when he spotted Geoff winding through the valleys of the sand dunes into camp.

"You found our table!"

"Well, it's still a door. When we find legs for it, it'll be perfect. It's the right size and strong, like a Hungarian bull."

The boys sat on the barge as Geoff shared his tales from the east end of the island. He talked about the diving terns, the old structure, and the abundance of driftwood and camping supplies, and told Peter he needed his help to retrieve the booty. Geoff walked around camp acting like an interior decorator elaborating on his concept of the location of the table, the fireplace, and the icebox. Peter was more interested in exploration than homemaking and quickly agreed with Geoff's ideas.

By late morning, the east end treasures had become a campsite stockpile of planks, short posts, rope, fishing nets, and wooden boxes. They even had a supply of rusted nails and small spikes.

"You know, Geoff, you're more interested in this than I am. Why don't you start setting things up while I do a little exploring of my own."

Geoff watched as Peter headed east. He gazed beyond him to the roofless skeletal remains of the deserted building. It cast a feeling of isolation and desolation, and an untold story Geoff felt determined to discover.

BEACH INVASION

Because their tent was snuggled in the lee valley of the barge, it was not visible from the beach. From the main dock, a person might spot it if they knew exactly where to look. From the town? Well, from that far away a person couldn't see anything except battered barges, sandy beaches, and breaking waves. Privacy assured. Geoff's paranoia was put to rest.

A sea breeze blew over the barge and the ridge of the tent. It fluttered and flapped, sending out the only unnatural sound. A head rubbed against the inside of the tent, creating rolling lumps against the canvas. Moments later, Geoff crawled out with toothpaste in one hand and toothbrush in the other. The morning's bright haze completely shut one of his eyes and kept the other barely open. Hair stuck out in twenty-three directions. His face wore a grumpy expression that seemed to say, "Who the hell just woke me up and why." He splashed water on his face and hair, then stretched, twisted, scratched, and looked around. He spread a blob of toothpaste on the brush and vigorously scrubbed his way into his morning routine while strolling around camp.

Peter crawled out of the tent and mimicked the same scratching, stretching, grumpy-looking ritual.

"Mornin', sleepyhead," said Geoff through a mouth full of foamy toothpaste.

Peter grunted. "You have toothpaste running down your chin."

Geoff spit out what was left. "I hear they're serving applesauce at the camp. We can try out our new table."

Peter downed the applesauce and patted his stomach. "Great breakfast. I want to do a little exploring. Wanna come?"

"I think I'll hang back here. Miss Wheeler will be coming for supper soon and we're not even ready. I'm gonna work on the camp."

"What's left? The table's done. What are you going to work on next?"

"I'll surprise you."

Peter ventured off, and Geoff busied himself carving out a spot in a sand dune for their fireplace. He was putting on the finishing touches when Peter popped over the barge. "Hey, that's coming along pretty well. Nice job! What's this? You made a raised hearth?"

"Nothin' but the best for Miss Wheeler. When this is done, we'll be ready to set a date with her. Maybe later this afternoon we could stop by her place. C'mon. Give me a hand setting these rocks down in front of the tent."

Peter joined Geoff in laying out what was left of the stones.

Geoff caught movement from the corner of his eye and stood for a better look. About a quarter of the way between camp and the main dock he spotted a dark station wagon weaving its way through the maze of sand dunes. "Hey, look, Pete. There's a car coming up the sandy path from the main dock. It's gonna get stuck."

Moments later all the doors and the tailgate opened, and out exploded five children as if fleeing a swarm of wasps. They headed toward the boys, their arms flailing with the excitement of children racing to be first in the water.

"Pete. We may be having company."

Peter stood and watched the young group. "Nah, they're probably headed to the beach. The best one is right behind us. They don't know us, and no one would come to us like *that*. It looks like a bunch of girls. No. I see a boy. Four girls and a boy."

The boys stood motionless and watched.

"Yep, they're heading to the beach," said Peter as he knelt to resume his task.

As they neared, Geoff heard them talking all at once. They were not veering off to the beach. "Um, Pete, I think we're about to be invaded."

The young gang stopped about fifty feet from camp and stood silently in a tight group. A small blond girl smiled broadly and gave a quick wave—one that seemed to say, "Can we come closer? We won't harm you."

The woman driving the vehicle made her way through the sand toward the kids. They huddled around her.

"Yep," said Geoff from the side of his mouth. "We're definitely in for an invasion."

The woman waved her arm and yelled, "Hello! Hello! Can we come in?"

Peter and Geoff looked at each other and waved back.

The visitors, still clustered around the woman, approached the camp. "Hi, I'm Nancy Baldwin, and these young people would like to meet you."

"Well, I'm Geoff and this is Pete."

"Nice to meet you, Geoff and Pete." Mrs. Baldwin turned to the kids. "This is Diana, my oldest daughter, and her friend Becca." The girls smiled with their chins shyly tilted down. "This is Hilary, my next-oldest daughter, and this is Billy Garfield, another young islander." Billy looked on with a bashful smile.

"And this last one is Pam, my youngest."

Pam cupped her hands around her mouth and bent forward. "Pammy. My name's Pammy." She then pointed back to the main part of the island. "We've been watching you through the telescope in our house ever since you got here."

Geoff's eyebrows went north.

"Yeah, and we know when you brush your teeth. We've seen *every-thing!*" said Hilary.

Geoff blushed.

"Well," said Mrs. Baldwin, "we don't want to be a bother. We just wanted to meet you. You have become quite the talk around the island. It's not every day young men like you come here by themselves." She looked at her charge of children. "Are you all ready?"

"Aw, Mom, can we stay? We can walk home," said Pammy.

"Not without being invited."

Peter leapt upon the barge and turned to the others with outstretched arms. "Who wants to play tag?" And he dashed across the barge toward the beach.

Pammy was the first to respond, scampering up the barge and racing after Peter. Hilary and Billy gave each other a quick look, and then they, too, darted beachward.

"Well, that sounds like an invitation to me," Mrs. Baldwin said, and she looked to Diana and Becca. "You girls staying or going back with me?"

"We'll stay to make sure the others get back OK," said Diana.

"Well, Geoff, it was certainly nice to meet you. I'm sure we'll be seeing more of you," Mrs. Baldwin said.

"Hey, you didn't get caught in the sand, did you?"

"No, I don't think so."

"You stopped right about where it gets soft, so I thought maybe you did. I'll give you a push if you're stuck."

"How considerate. But don't worry, I'm not stuck. See you later!"

With Mrs. Baldwin gone, things instantly got quiet among Geoff, Diana, and Becca. Geoff stood looking at the girls. He was dumbstruck. When he saw Diana's eyes looking directly at him, he stepped back with his arms stiffly glued to his side and gave her a half smile.

"So… this is your camp," Diana said.

Geoff looked over his shoulder. "Yep, this is it."

"Nice table. Where'd you get it?"

Geoff pointed toward the east end of the island. "It was wedged in the rocks out by that old farmhouse down there. It used to be a door."

Diana chuckled. "That's not a farmhouse, silly. It's the old Coast Guard boathouse."

"Old Coast Guard boathouse, eh? Yeah, well, we found the rest of this stuff down there, too."

"Beachcombing is pretty good along this part of the island, especially after a storm," Diana said. "Everyone likes to beachcomb, so if you don't go early, all the good stuff will have already been picked over."

"We haven't seen anyone out here since we set up camp. You're the first ones."

"Wait till the season starts. There'll be plenty of beachcombers. That's a favorite island pastime. I bet you don't know how these barges got here."

"Bet I do. Muggsy told us."

"Do you know about shoaling?"

Geoff looked away and scratched his head. "Yeah, of course I know what it is. It's something my grandma wears when it's cold."

Diana chuckled. "No, silly. That's a shawl. A shoal is—"

"Just kidding," Geoff interrupted. "Muggsy told us about the shoals. At first, I thought he said 'shawl,' and I wondered why there'd be shawls in the channel when the sea broke through."

Diana laughed. Then the conversation went cold for what seemed like hours.

"Um. How long are you here?" Diana asked.

"Until July sixth."

"Well, I can teach you about the island."

"You know a lot about this place?"

"This is my home."

"You live here all year?"

"No, just summers."

"All summer?"

"No, not all summer. Sometimes we go back to Concord for a week or two."

"Where's that?"

"It's about twenty miles from Boston. You?"

"We're from Connecticut—way down in the corner by New York."

"Is your town part of the city or out in the country?"

"It's out in the country about forty-five miles from New York. There used to be a lot of dairy farms, then one day they were all gone except for one behind our property."

"What happened to the cows?"

Geoff chuckled. "They all had to mo-o-o-o-ve away."

Diana laughed and bumped Geoff's shoulder with hers. An electric shock shot through Geoff. He had never been bumped by a girl.

"Sounds like country to me. Are you a farm boy?"

"Well, more farm than city. Like I said, most of the dairies are gone, so I'm not a farm boy anymore. So, what's it like in… what town did you say?"

"Concord. It's a suburb of Boston. Most of the people who live there go into the city to work. We don't have farm animals like you."

Geoff looked at Becca. "Are you here for the summer, too?"

"No, I'll be going back at the end of the week."

Diana looked over to the fireplace. "You make this?"

"Yeah, just finished it this morning."

"Looks good," said Diana, with Becca nodding in agreement.

"We're having Miss Wheeler over for supper."

"Piney! She's coming here to your camp?"

"Piney? Is that what you call her?"

"It's her nickname. How'd you get her to come for supper?"

"Well, we met her in the general store. She asked about our camp and we invited her. But how did she get a nickname like that?"

Diana shrugged and said, "I don't know—we've always called her Piney. She's always inviting the island kids in for milk and cookies. When's she coming?"

"We haven't made a date yet. Gonna do that this afternoon. We wanted to get camp ready first with this table and that fireplace. Check out that table. Pretty sturdy, eh?"

Diana tried to wiggle the table. "Yep, pretty sturdy." She pointed to the rocks in front of the tent. "What are you making here?"

"That's our bedroom patio."

The girls nodded and laughed nervously.

"Yeah, we get a lot of sand in the tent and in our sleeping bags. We're hoping this will help."

"Can we see inside your tent?" Becca said.

"Um, sure, but it's a mess."

The girls stooped over and poked their heads inside the tent. "Oh, look! It's got a little window in the back," Becca said.

"That's for air circulation," Geoff said.

"So, when you get your patio done, your camp's ready for Piney?" Diana asked.

"Well, we have to build an icebox."

"Icebox? How are you going to do that?"

"We're gonna dig a hole in the sand, line the bottom and sides with rocks, find a board for a lid, and then put in a small block of ice. We'll be able to keep milk and butter."

"An icebox in the sand... Well... that's neat. I'll have to see it when it's finished."

"Is that a promise? If it is, I'll make sure it's well made."

Diana's eyes darted all over the planet. But whenever she looked at Geoff, their eyes held each other's gaze. Geoff's heart pounded so hard, he felt like it could be seen all the way through his shirt.

"So... is your name Geoff all the time or do you have a nickname?" said Diana.

"My mother calls me Geoffrey whenever I'm in trouble. Otherwise I'm Geoff. Peter is Pete. How about you?

"Well, most islanders have a nickname. We just chop off some letters and add an ee-sound to the ending. Pam is Pammy. Hilary is Hilly. Billy is… Billy. Becca is Becca because she hates to be called Becky. And Pete—I think we'll just stick to Pete. Me? I'm just plain Diana."

"What, not Diany?"

"Only if *you* want me to call you Geoffy."

"Argh! Diana it is."

Geoff, Diana, and Becca lined up along the barge and watched Peter playing tag with the others. "They're never going to catch him," said Becca. "He's way too fast for them."

Diana stood on her toes looking over the sand piled on top of the barge. Geoff crouched down to the same eye level as Diana and looked toward the beach. Diana chuckled. "What are you doing?"

Geoff stood up quickly. "Me? Nothing. Why?"

"You squatted down to my height."

"I just wanted to see the world from your eye level."

"I know I'm a little small. We come from a short family, so this is as tall as I'm probably going to get."

"It's a great height. When I was getting ready for First Communion, the nuns lined us up by our heights—short ones in the front. Girls on one side. Boys on the other. I was first in line, right next to Kathy Gardner. Six or seven years later for Confirmation, Kathy Gardner and I were still in front. I only began growing like a weed two years ago."

"Are you still growing?"

"It's slowed down, but I'm hoping to reach six feet."

"Well, you're on your way."

Diana leaned toward Becca and began a soft conversation with her. Geoff looked in the opposite direction, gritted his teeth, and murmured, "You idiot! Kathy Gardner? Jeez! What the hell is wrong with you?"

Geoff turned back to Diana, who was still making small talk with Becca. For the first time, he was able to take a good long look at her without being caught. Freckles populated her round face—even over her slightly curved-up nose. Her small mouth did not hinder her broad and generous smile. Her eyes squinted with the bright haze, making upside-down happy faces. Her thin, short brown hair blew in her face with the slightest breeze. She wore a gray sweater with its sleeves pushed up to her elbows. Her laugh was mild and soft like her voice. She moved with grace and purpose. She looked confident and very much in control of herself. As she spoke to Becca, she often glanced over at Geoff and then back out toward the beach. When she stopped talking midsentence, Becca turned to see Diana's distraction—her eyes locked on Geoff's like a magnet.

"You were saying…" said Becca as she tapped Diana's arm to pull her back from her spell.

Peter and his young followers ran toward them, red-faced from the beach workout. They all jumped off the barge and stood in a large circle in the camp. "That was fun!" said Pammy. "Let's do that again!"

"No, no," said Diana. "We should get going." She looked over to Geoff. "Hey, why don't you guys come over later?"

Peter and Geoff looked at each other. "Sure," said Peter. "When?"

"After supper? We'll be done by about six. Do you have a watch?"

"Yeah, somewhere around here," Geoff said. "Where do you live?"

Diana turned toward the island and pointed. "See that two-story gray house on the hill away from the others, all by itself? It's the one with the chimneys on both ends."

Geoff stepped close to Diana and looked up her arm as she pointed. "Yeah, I think I got it."

"That's our house. It's just up the road from Piney's."

"We'll be there by six."

Diana clapped her hands to pry the three children away from Peter and head home. They bounded off like gazelles—still filled with never-ending energy. Diana stopped, looked back, smiled, and waved, then rejoined Billy and the others. A hush veiled their camp. As suddenly as they had appeared, they were gone.

"You like her, don't you," Peter said.

"What's not to like?"

"I mean you *like* her."

"As in, was my heart pounding?"

"Yeah."

"Hell, no. How could it? We only talked for a few minutes."

The afternoon wore on as the boys finished preparing their camp for

Miss Wheeler. When they were finished, Geoff searched for his watch and set it out on the table. They scarfed down a can of Chef Boyardee while Geoff kept one eye on the watch. "Diana said we should come about six. I say we leave about five thirty at the latest. Don't you think? I should probably wear shoes. Do you think my hair is combed OK? Should we take a flashlight? Do you think thirty minutes is enough time, or should we leave a little earlier? Did you notice how Hilly didn't say, 'We can see everything'; she said, 'We can see *everything*'? What do you think she meant?"

"You're acting weird on me, Geoff. I think you lied when you said you didn't like her. Did she look at you?"

"Of course we looked at each other."

"No, I mean did she look into your eyes?"

"How would I know *that*?"

"Easy. You look at her and you can tell. So, did she?"

"She looked at my mouth."

"Your mouth? Not your eyes?"

"Well, we looked into each other's eyes once, but it was an accident."

"Accident, my foot."

"It was only an accident!"

"Right. I see a romance blossoming here."

"Pete, we didn't come here for that. We came to camp and explore."

"We'll still do that, but I see I'm gonna have to get you two together."

"If I want to get together with her, I can do it on my own."

"Yeah, well, you might falter, and we're only here for three weeks. Time's a-wastin'. Have you ever been kissed?"

"That's private."

"Right. I take that as a no. Man, I can see I have a lot of work to do here."

"There's not gonna be any kissin', so get your mind off that. You sound like some sort of authority on the subject. What do you know? Hell, you're about as interested in girls as the man in the moon."

"I just haven't had time for them. C'mon, lover boy, you ready?"

Geoff stood and ran his hands through his hair.

"OK, put your watch away and let's go," Pete said.

As they left camp, Geoff looked back. All was quiet. The beach invasion was over.

16

ADOPTED

The boys heard trampling feet, laughing, and screaming inside the Baldwins' house. The high-energy, smiling, freckle-faced Pammy appeared in an open window. She cupped her hands to her mouth and yelled, "We've been watching for you. Go around back!"

The boys stood in the kitchen, enveloped by their hosts, bright lights, and the mouthwatering aroma of freshly baked chocolate chip cookies. Pammy, Hilly, and Billy quickly surrounded Peter with rapid-fire questions, from "What did you do when we left?" to "What did you eat for supper?" Before he could answer one question, they had asked another.

Mrs. Baldwin walked into the kitchen. "Girls! Girls! Let them in. One question at a time." There was a momentary silence while her commands sank in.

"Hello, Mrs. Baldwin. It's nice to see you again," said Geoff as he bowed his head.

"Geoff, it's nice to see you, too. Billy, show our guests around," said Mrs. Baldwin.

Pammy, Hilly, and Billy latched on to Peter's arms and pulled him out of the kitchen, pushing their way past Diana, Becca, and Geoff.

Mountains of attention went to Peter, who clearly had become their hero. Geoff and Diana looked on, then at each other, and chuckled nervously. Becca put her hand on Diana's arm and said, "I think I'll go in there with the others."

Mrs. Baldwin leaned into Diana and Geoff and whispered, "You two... out of the kitchen."

They left the kitchen and joined the others. "Wow! This is one big open room!" said Geoff, turning in a circle.

"It used to be an army barracks," Diana said. "My parents bought it after the war and moved it from the other side of the Coast Guard tower."

"The whole house? In one piece?"

"Yep, in one piece."

"That would have been fun to watch."

"Well, they added the kitchen, but everything else you see used to be the barracks."

Geoff heard voices in the kitchen, and moments later Mr. Baldwin, whose shoulder was Geoff's pillow on the *Alert*, walked into the room. "Geoff!"

"Mr. Baldwin, nice to see you again." Geoff stepped toward him with an outstretched hand.

"How's camping on the beach?"

"It's going well."

Mr. Baldwin, Diana, and Geoff stood together as Mr. Baldwin asked about their camp and their impressions of the island. Then he said, "Well, Geoff, I have some things to do. I hope we'll be seeing a lot more of you," before stepping back into the kitchen.

Diana leaned toward Geoff. "My dad told us about meeting you on the boat. That's how we knew to look for you through the telescope."

"We didn't start off on the beach."

"Yeah, I know. Jacobs, a Coastie, told us you were camping up near the tower. We saw you crouched over something on the road up there."

Geoff looked skyward and laughed. "We dropped our can of Chef Boyardee and thought we'd lost all our spaghetti and meatballs. We were afraid we'd be sacking out that night without chow."

Geoff spotted a telescope mounted on a tripod aimed out the window. "So, this is how you've been watching us."

"Uh-huh."

Pammy jumped out of a chair and sprang over to Diana and Geoff. "We've been watching you through that telescope. We can see *everything* you do. *Everything.*"

Diana pointed Pammy in the direction of the others. "Pammy, go on, now. Shoo!"

Geoff nodded toward the telescope. "Mind if I take a look?"

"Go ahead."

Geoff aimed the telescope in the direction of their camp. He looked through the lens and then over the top. Relieved, he said, "I can't find it."

"Just keep looking. It's down there. Your camp is between the first and second barge, mostly hidden behind a sand dune. We can't see much of it, but it's easy to find when you're moving around."

Geoff moved the telescope slightly as he scanned the beach. "Oh, my. You *can* see everything. We'd better be careful. You know, we bundled up some driftwood and used it to move our camp down to the beach. While we were walking with it, I looked over to this very house and told Pete I felt eyes on us. He just laughed at me."

"Well, we *were* watching."

"You were? Wow! That's scary."

"We wondered what you were doing with all that driftwood, and saw Potter giving you a ride. But don't worry, we don't spend much time looking. It's just fun to see if we can see what you're doing. How did you use the driftwood to move?"

"Pete thought we could save time moving if we made a stretcher and slid the tent onto it."

"Did it work?"

"Not well. It wasn't such a hot idea, but it gave us a lot of firewood."

"I looked last night and could see that you had a fire going on the beach. Who's the bonfire maker?"

"Oh, we both are."

"Hey, you guys!" Hilly called from the other side of the room. "Mom just brought out the cookies. You'd better come get some before they're gone!" She was right—the cookies vanished within minutes.

Geoff stood back and watched Peter with the others, noticing how relaxed he seemed among them and how he was quick to smile and laugh. He treated each one the same, never paying more attention to one over the other. With Peter, they all got equal time, and he remained in the spotlight and seemed to enjoy being the center of attention.

The feeling of the Baldwin House saturated Geoff. The sounds of excitement from the others hopping around Peter faded into the distance. In this wide-open room, running was permitted. The furniture was childproof. Things seemed to be in place by accident. Order was unimportant. Happy children mattered. They laughed often and got along well. There was an addictive, magical quality about it. *Why couldn't my home be like this?* he thought. Was what he was seeing in

Peter the same sense of acceptance and safety that had swept over Geoff? He realized he was in the home he'd always wanted.

Geoff and Diana slid into an old couch and watched Peter play board games with the others, content with the conviviality and interaction. Hours passed, and another day faded away.

A cool breeze swept across Geoff's shoulder. He turned toward it and found a bright moon rising over Martha's Vineyard shining through the open front door. He walked over for a better look. The moon was always good magic. He motioned to Diana to join him. "There's something about the moon. I could watch it all night."

"Have you ever noticed how everything seems better when the moon's out?" Diana asked.

She's a moon lover! Yes!

They stood close in the doorway, soaking in its warm yellow glow. Their arms touched as they stood quietly enjoying the accidental contact.

Peter came up behind them. "Hey, Geoff. We should be going. It's getting late."

The children regrouped and made plans for the next day and the days that followed. The boys were on the fringes of receiving an exhaustive orientation to the island.

They stood outside the back door, letting their eyes acclimate to the night sky.

"I think they adopted us," said Peter.

"I'll say. One thing's for sure: They like you. I think they adopted *you*."

"We shoulda brought a flashlight."

"Nah, we have all the light we need. We've got the moon."

"You sure put a lot of stock in that moon."

"So?"

"It's just a dead rock circling the earth. You make like it's got life on it. If it wasn't for the sun reflecting off it, you'd never even know it was there."

Geoff waved his arms toward the sky. "Well, tonight it's shining a light on us more powerful than any flashlight we have.

That lifeless rock affects the tides, currents, temperature, and wind. All life depends upon it. Without the moon, our planet would probably be uninhabitable."

"Jeez, Geoff, where'd you get all that?"

"From that science project on the moon we did in school, remember?"

"Oh, yeah. That project."

"It was my best grade ever in science. Sometimes I don't think I learn much in school, but since that project, I look at the moon a whole lot differently. I've always liked it—even as a small boy. But here on this island it's brighter than I've ever seen it. I bet you could read a newspaper."

Peter put his arm around Geoff's shoulder as they walked down the moon-flooded road. Peter chattered about the kids, and Geoff was warmed by the good feeling in the Baldwin House. They had, indeed, been adopted.

17

ISLAND LIFE

Geoff awoke with a jolt. Miss Wheeler and her friend were to be supper guests, and the boys were far from ready to receive them. They needed provisions and, more importantly, a way to keep perishables from turning into distasteful lumps or experiments with colorful fuzz. Geoff had spoken numerous times about building an icebox in the sand, yet all he had to show for it was talk.

The time for pondering was over. He pinpointed a suitable location, dropped to his knees, and began scooping sand with the vigor of a dog looking for a buried bone. When satisfied with its depth and width, he commandeered the flat rocks from their "patio" at the tent entrance and repurposed them as a wall liner. Working fast was critical; air would dry out the moist sand, and the walls could cave in with the slightest vibration. With rocks lining the bottom and walls of the hole, Geoff sat at their table admiring his work. Icebox finished.

Peter crawled out of the tent and stood like he did on most bright, hazy days—with one eye squinting and the other completely shut.

"C'mon, Pete, get some breakfast. We've got to get camp ready, go for provisions, get ice, confirm the time with Miss Wheeler, and do a whole bunch of other stuff."

Peter sank his spoon into the applesauce and walked around camp. He spotted the icebox and stared at it like a Pointer dog on a pheasant. "When did you make *that*?"

"This morning. It needs a lid. I figure we can pick up a small chunk of ice on our way back from the general store."

The boys worked frantically to put the finishing touches on their camp. They made a beachcombing run for firewood and found a suitable lid for the icebox. They sat at their table, inspecting the camp for anything out of place. Except for food, they were ready.

Alert rounded the jetty and chugged up the channel. They sprinted toward the dock. The island was abuzz with life.

The boys dodged through the crowd of greeters—familiar faces everywhere. Geoff spotted Gladys Snow, gasped, and stopped dead in his tracks. Peter came up behind him and spoke quietly in his ear. "Geoff. She's old, very old."

Suddenly, Pammy appeared in front of Peter, jumping up and down with excitement. "Can we play tag on the beach?"

"Not today, Pammy. We have a lot to do."

Pammy frowned and slumped.

"Pammy, don't be a whiny," said Peter.

Geoff looked around, sending his eyes on a scouting mission. Where there was Pammy, there would be Diana.

"I saw Diana over there," said Pammy.

Geoff slalomed his way through the people, but collided with an old woman who zigged right in front of where he was about to zag.

"Why, look here! It's young Geoff. How are you?"

"Miss Wheeler! I'm OK. How about you?"

"I'm doing well, thank you. I'm here to pick up Miss Wright. We'll be down for supper at four."

"You just saved us a trip to your cottage to confirm everything."

"Miss Wright doesn't know about it, so if you meet her here, don't say anything. I want it to be a surprise."

Geoff excused himself and resumed his search for Diana. Peter popped in front of him. "C'mon, Geoff. Potter offered us a ride to the general store."

"You didn't see Diana, did you?"

"Yeah, she came looking for you. I don't know where she is now, but I think she left the dock. Let's go or we'll miss Potter's ride."

"You go ahead. I'll catch up."

"No, the shopping list is in your head and you have the money. C'mon."

The boys hurried over to Potter's truck as he loaded the last box. "Hop on," Potter said as he wiped his forehead and climbed into the truck.

"This is uptown!" said Geoff as he waved to people.

"We don't know those people," Peter said. "Why are you waving?"

"If we don't wave, we'll never get to know them. When you wave, they wave back."

The truck slowed. Peter looked over his shoulder and turned back to Geoff. "Geoff, trust me, you're gonna like this!"

Geoff turned to look just as Potter stopped the truck. His eyes widened, his brows went up, and his heart pounded. Diana, Becca, and Pammy scrambled around to the tailgate. It was wide enough for four and tight for five. Pammy took charge of the seating arrangements, pushing Diana toward Geoff and making a space for herself between Becca and Peter.

Geoff and Diana were joined from shoulder to ankle. He did all he could not to look at her. Wow! Tingling all over and tailgating with Diana… what could be better? A broad smile spread across his face.

Potter let the girls off at Four Corners. As he headed off, Diana waved. "Come see us after Piney leaves."

At the general store, Potter yelled, "OK, boys, end of the line."

"Hey, can we help you unload this stuff?" said Geoff.

"Sure, but just the boxes that say 'General Store' or 'Muggsy.'"

Potter gave the boys a smile and pulled on the brim of his hat—his gesture of thanks for the extra hands. He climbed back into the truck, wiggled the gear shift into first, and sputtered off.

Instead of turning his attention to the store, Peter seemed preoccupied with something down the path by the Allen House. "What's up? Aren't we going to the general store?" said Geoff.

"Yeah, but I was thinking about calling home."

Geoff, confused, looked at Peter. "Where'd *that* come from? A few days ago you insisted we didn't need to check in, and now you want to call home? I don't get it."

"Well, I'm close to my mom. It'll be good to hear her voice."

"So, you're a little homesick, huh?"

"Just a slight case of it."

"Are you thinking about calling her *now*?"

"Yeah. We're here, and it won't take long."

"OK. You don't mind if I tag along, do you? I'd like to see how that crank phone works."

The boys huddled around the phone booth. There was no rotary dialer. Instead, below the phone was a black box with a crank on the side.

"Do you know how to use that phone?" The boys turned toward the voice of a man watching them. They both shook their heads.

"It's a party line, so you first have to listen to make sure no one else is talking. If no one's there, hang up the phone, give the crank about four or five good turns, and wait for the operator."

"Thanks, mister," said Peter as he picked up the receiver. "It's clear. Quick! Let's crank it before someone else does." Peter vigorously turned the crank and waited.

"Hello? Operator? Yes, I'd like to make a collect phone call, please."

The boys looked at each other in surprise, and Peter covered the phone with his hand. "It worked!" he said.

"I'm going up to the store," said Geoff.

Peter nodded and gave his home phone number to the operator.

Geoff stepped into the store and was immediately greeted by Muggsy. "Well, you just made a friend there when you helped Potter. How's the camping?"

"Doing OK."

"Everyone's talking about the two boys camping on the beach. They see you every day when the *Alert* comes in. You've gotten to know some of the island kids. And now you're helping Potter. You're beginning to fit in quite well around here. And I hear you have the eye of the oldest Baldwin girl."

"Jeez. How would you know *that*?"

"I told you this is a small island with big ears. I also heard that Miss Wheeler and her friend will be your dinner guests later this afternoon."

"Wow! Word *does* travel fast. Actually, we're here for dinner provisions."

"What's on your menu?" Muggsy asked.

"Mashed potatoes and corn, and milk and cookies for dessert."

"Mashed potatoes and corn? You can't call that supper. There's no meat!"

"Meat?"

"Yes, meat."

"Meat as in hamburgers? That kind of meat?"

"What other kind is there?" quipped Muggsy.

"You have hamburger meat?"

"Of course we have it. Forty-five cents a pound. You can make four hamburgers for the price of your Chef Boyardee spaghetti and meatballs."

A few minutes later with his call finished, Peter joined Geoff.

"That was fast. How'd it go?"

"I'll tell you later. Did you get everything we need?"

"We were just talking about our menu for Miss Wheeler. He has hamburger. We gotta have meat."

"Sounds good, but we don't have the pots for that kind of cooking," Peter said.

"Meat!" said Geoff as he pointed his finger in the air. "Chef Boyardee! Why not that?"

"No, we can't feed them *that*," said Peter. "Let me find something. There's got to be some other canned meat around here." Peter dashed off and returned with a can of Dinty Moore Beef Stew. He put it on the counter. "This has meat in it."

Muggsy laughed. "You can't feed Dinty Moore to your guests."

"Why not?"

"That's stew. Look, maybe you should just stick with your original menu."

"Chef Boyardee looks like dog food—hot or cold—but it sure tastes good," Geoff said.

"Chef Boyardee, Dinty Moore stew: same slop," Muggsy said. "Don't serve it to Miss Wheeler. She has class. She deserves better."

"Wow! This is harder than I thought."

"Preparing an elegant meal for two fine ladies is no easy feat," said Muggsy. "Best to keep it simple."

The boys scoured the store shelves and returned to the cash register with a box of instant potatoes, milk, bread, butter, salt and pepper, creamed corn, cookies, and plates and utensils.

Muggsy looked over the provisions and picked up the butter, opened it, and removed a stick. "There you go again with the butter. It will add flavor, but you'll only need one stick, not four. Do you know how to cook instant potatoes?"

"Of course!" said Geoff. "Just add milk, butter, salt, and pepper, and stir."

"Just seeing if you knew. How do you plan to keep these perishables cool?"

"We made an icebox," Geoff said.

"An icebox? Really?

"Yeah, I dug a hole in the sand, lined it with stones and found a piece of driftwood for a lid. We'll get ice from the fish dock on our way back."

"That's pretty ingenious! Watch your milk, though. It'll turn quickly in this heat."

"It won't last past cookies," said Peter.

Muggsy sorted through the provisions. "Well, boys, that comes to four dollars and sixty-nine cents."

Geoff sent Peter a worried look. "This is gonna blow our food budget."

"We'll be fine. It's OK to splurge once in a while."

Muggsy bagged everything and handed Geoff another box of cookies. "Take these. They're Miss Wheeler's favorites."

Geoff looked at the package. "Nabisco Sugar Wafers?"

"Miss Wheeler knows the favorites of all the island kids, and I know hers. This may be a little pricey for your budget, so it's my gift to you."

"Hey, Geoff. We're running out of time. We gotta go."

The boys thanked Muggsy and scurried toward the fish dock. "So tell me how your phone call went."

"It went fine, but my mom said she got a call from your parents."

"Is something wrong?" Geoff stopped abruptly.

"Your mom said you didn't check in with them and they were worried."

"Didn't Gladys Snow tell us she contacted them?"

"She did, but she only called the Fairchilds, and they contacted my mom. The Fairchilds probably thought my mom would contact your parents."

"Oh, man, that's bad. Maybe I should call home. My father is gonna be all over me for that. The agreement I had with him is that we would check in with Gladys Snow when we arrived, and we did that. I don't remember him telling me to call home."

"You're right, but don't worry. My mom got it all straightened out. There was just a little mix-up. Your folks know we're here and we're OK."

"I'm sure that one's gonna come back to bite me. I just know it."

"My mom asked how you were doing. I told her you were a little homesick at first, but you've made friends all over the island and now you don't want to go home."

"You told her *that*?"

"Yeah. Why?"

"If that gets back to my mother, she could take it personally. Right now I'm more concerned about my father." Geoff looked down, pondering the consequences.

"C'mon. Think about that later," Peter said. "Right now we're burning daylight and we need ice. Our guests will be at our camp before we know it."

The boys walked on the dock and up to the row of fishermen's shacks. A thin man who was working on his boat stopped when he saw them. He stood up straight and gave the boys a stern look. His eyes locked on Geoff's and dissected him with a laser-cutting, lead-melting glare.

"Pete," said Geoff softly, "don't look now, but there's a guy over there and he's glaring at us. He looks like he's going to attack. Are we not supposed to be here?"

"I don't know." Peter nonchalantly glanced over as if scanning the entire dock. "He looks scary all right. Let's just get what we came for and pretend we don't see him."

"Maybe we should look for ice somewhere else. That guy really scares me."

"Ignore him. The worst thing he can do is throw us off. C'mon."

They walked over to the first open shack, which had a sign over the door that read, "Coot." Shielding their eyes with their hands, they looked into the darkness.

"Can I help you?" came a booming baritone voice from behind them.

They turned slowly toward the voice expecting to find the thin man with the lead-melting glare. Instead, they were met by a monster with glowing red eyes and a tyrannosaurus mouth with thousands of teeth. They froze, petrified, and their hair stood on end. Their feet stammered and they fled off the dock flailing their arms with Godzilla hot on their heels scorching them with its blowtorch breath.

"Uh, yes," said Peter. "Ice. We need ice."

The man stepped past them and peered into the shack, then down the row of sheds. "Joey!" he snapped. A head popped out of another shack. "Ice!"

The man returned to his work. Looking up at the boys was a small black dog standing firmly nearby, growling and baring its teeth.

"Hey!" came the baritone voice. The dog cowered and ran back toward the man.

Joey darted toward the boys. "You need ice? We got plenty. How much?"

The boys looked at him blankly. "We have an icebox about this big," said Geoff, forming the dimensions with his hands.

"That's about one-foot square. I can get you a piece that size."

"We need it smaller so our provisions will fit."

"What's going in the icebox?"

Geoff lifted and opened one of the bags. Joey looked in. "Milk and butter. That's it? Fifteen pounds should be enough."

Joey swung a scale from around the doorway, reached for an ice pick, and began stabbing at an ice block in the freezer. Moments later he reappeared in the doorway holding a chunk of clear ice.

"That's fifteen pounds? Seems like it should be larger than that!" said Geoff.

Joey placed it in the metal basket on the scale and slid a weight over until a balancing needle stayed in the middle of the scale. "Ha! Fifteen pounds. Right on the money," he said with a grin.

"How'd you do that?" Geoff asked, astonished.

"Practice. Some guys come around here and make bets on whether I can get within a pound. Never bet against me."

"Don't worry about that. We won't. What do I owe you?"

"Fifteen pounds at a nickel a pound. Got seventy-five cents?"

Geoff paid Joey and picked up the piece of slippery ice.

"Where's your cooler?"

"We don't have a cooler, just an icebox."

"No problem. My hands are used to the cold. I'll bring it to your boat."

"We don't have a boat."

"Didn't you come off a boat?"

"No, we're camping here, over on the beach by the barges."

"So, *you're* the guys camping down there! Man, there's been a lot of talk about you."

"Good or bad?" said Peter.

"Neither. Just folks talking. We don't get campers around here very often, and when we do, everyone wants to know about 'em. So, you don't have anything to carry that ice?"

"No. My shirt, maybe," said Geoff.

"Stay here." Joey ran down the dock to one of the sheds and reappeared waving a towel. "Let's wrap it in this towel so you won't freeze your hands off."

"Thanks! We'll get it back to you tomorrow."

"Don't bother. Some boater left it. Keep it."

Geoff moved closer to Joey and said softly, "Say, who's that thin guy over there?"

"Him? That's Coot, my boss." Joey pointed to the sign over the door.

"Coot?" said Geoff.

"Yeah, Coot. It's his nickname. I don't know what his real name is. Just Coot."

"How'd a person get a name like that?"

"Coot? It's a bird. The story is that one of his friends called him an old coot one day and it stuck. Everyone knows him. He's a fishing guide. Rich folks come from the mainland for the striped bass, and he takes them out. The bay is full of rocky shoals. Very dangerous. There's Sow and Pigs Reef off the West End that extends a mile out. Every now and then some old fool tries to take a shortcut. Most run hard aground, but Coot knows where and how to get across—even at night when there's a sea. And he knows the best places for bass. He also watches the island kids, likes to keep 'em on their toes."

"I wonder if he knows who we are."

"Oh, wonder no more. He knows. Ole Coot knows everything."

"Is that little black dog his?"

"Yep, that's Cutty. Wherever you see Coot, you know the dog's nearby. Good dog. Feisty, though. Very protective. Terriers are like that."

"Feisty, right. He's looking at me as if he wants a piece of my ankle. Anyway, we'd better get back before this thing melts down to an ice cube."

The boys headed back to camp. "Coot, eh?" said Geoff. "He looks scary. We should steer clear of him."

"Aw, he was just sizing us up," said Peter.

Back at camp, with sore arms and a slightly smaller chunk of ice, Geoff whacked it with the flat side of the hatchet and dropped the broken pieces into the hole. "Ta-da! We have a working icebox!" he said.

The *Alert* belched out its usual departing *WHO-O-O-OP!* The boys stood watching as it passed in the channel. Geoff waved.

"*Alert*'s leaving. That means it's three o'clock," said Peter. "Miss Wheeler will be here in an hour. There's still lots to do. We'd better hustle up!"

Geoff prepared the wood for the fire and then ran off to the main dock to refill canteens and clean up. By the time he returned, Peter had their camp in ship-shape condition. They were ready for their dinner guests.

"OK," said Geoff. "We'll light the fire as soon as we see Miss Wheeler's car."

"How will we know it's hers? We've never seen it."

"We'll know."

The boys were ready.

"I'm still worried that my parents didn't know when we got here," Geoff said.

"I told you, my mom got it all straightened out. You need to get over it."

Geoff nodded and sighed. They hitched themselves up on the barge and waited. All they needed now were their dinner guests.

18

DINNER ON THE BEACH

Four o'clock came. No Miss Wheeler. Four fifteen.

"You don't think they forgot, do you?" said Peter.

"I spoke to Miss Wheeler on the dock. They'll be here."

Four thirty.

Geoff stood on a cleat to give him more height as he looked toward the road, hoping to see a car coming their way.

The boys looked at each other, and it was clear that both of them were losing hope. Their shoulders sagged as they sat on the edge of the barge, looking down at the sand. The late afternoon breeze swayed the oat grass and attempted to dislodge the napkins and paper plates from under the stones.

"Maybe something happened," said Geoff.

"She did say four, didn't she?"

"Yeah, four. Let's wait another fifteen minutes and then go see if they're OK."

Four forty-five.

"OK, let's go see," Peter said.

Beep! Beep! A faded dark-blue car stopped in the sand over by the main dock. The doors opened, and out stepped Miss Wheeler and Miss Wright. Miss Wheeler waved a handkerchief over her head.

"Don't say anything about being late," Peter said. "Light the fire."

Peter ran to greet their dinner guests. By the time they arrived in camp, Geoff had a fire crackling.

Miss Wheeler extended her arms and embraced Geoff, then introduced him to Miss Wright. Both wore midcalf dresses with splashes of small pastel flowers. They were clad in black laced shoes with thick stubby heels and tan stockings. Each carried a small purse looped around her arm. Small black hats clung to their heads, held in place with long pins. Miss Wright wore a pair of short white gloves as if she were attending an afternoon tea.

Miss Wheeler looked around the camp. "Why, this is very nice. Very nice indeed. I'm a little tired from the walk. Would you mind if I sit?"

"Please, sit here," said Peter, offering her a seat on the most stable of the two benches.

"It looks like you've been busy," Miss Wheeler said. "Show us what you've done."

Geoff busied himself with cooking while Peter gave their guests a tour of their camp. With each explanation, the women commented, "How nice," or "How pleasant," and then leaned shoulder to shoulder and giggled. They giggled a lot. They giggled when they had nothing to say and just glanced at each other. They must have had a long history of giggling, Geoff thought.

Flames from the fire crackled and danced. Geoff shielded his face from the heat as he added more kindling and wood, beating it down with a stick until there was a generous bed of red-hot coals.

"Geoff, you really know how to build a fire, don't you?" said Miss Wheeler.

"I learned this in the Boy Scouts. The fire's hot enough for cooking. We have a fine meal planned for you."

The women giggled in anticipation.

Geoff retrieved the milk and butter from the icebox. Milk went into one pot and the corn into another. When the milk began to froth and form tiny popping bubbles, he pulled it off the coals and placed it on the table. He dumped instant potatoes into the hot milk and stirred as though he had done it a dozen times before. He was a regular chef. He cut the butter into small chunks and stirred them in. The mix was too thick. He poured in more milk. Too thin. More potatoes. Too thick. More milk. Too thin. He looked in the box. Empty.

"Well, Geoff," Miss Wheeler said. "Why don't you put your pot back on the fire? The heat will thicken the potatoes. Make peaks with the spoon, and when they start to stand up, they'll be cooked just right."

Geoff placed the potato pot back on the coals. The corn pot began to bubble. Geoff jumped around, attempting to attend to both, but the faster he moved, the more he lost control. He came close to overturning the corn. He hit the hearth with his foot, and part of it crumbled around his ankle. The entire fireplace sat on the brink of collapsing—dinner and all. Disaster was imminent.

Peter stepped over to Geoff and said softly, "Need help?"

"Everything's falling apart."

"Don't worry about it. It looks hot enough. Let's serve."

"Could you get the bread?"

The boys sat across from the women and pushed the pots of potatoes and corn their way. "Dinner's ready," Peter said. "Please, serve yourselves."

"This looks *so* good!" said Miss Wright. "I had no idea what to expect when Miss Wheeler told me we were dining with you. I pictured us sitting around a campfire on a log, and all I could think about was how I was going to get back up." Her comment brought on giggles from the women and nervous chuckles from the boys.

"Well, you inspired us," said Peter. "We made all this because of you."

"I apologize for not having butter for the bread. I used it all up," said Geoff.

"Don't worry," said Miss Wheeler. "There's plenty of butter in the potatoes."

They sat quietly eating the fine meal of corn and potatoes. The women gave approving nods. Finally, what little was left in the pots began looking unsavory. There would be neither seconds nor leftovers. The potatoes became a thick sticky paste, and the corn shriveled and pruned.

Peter stood. "We have a surprise for you. Close your eyes."

He retrieved the Nabisco Sugar Wafers hidden in the tent and slid them toward their guests.

"You can open your eyes now. Surprise!" Peter said.

The women opened their eyes and looked at Peter. He nodded toward the cookies. Miss Wheeler exclaimed, "Oh, my! Look what you've done! My favorite. How did you know?"

"Muggsy," said Geoff. "He gave them to us. He wouldn't let us pay for them."

"This was very sweet of you. I'll have to be sure to thank Muggsy for the cookies. Do you like these?"

"Never tried them," said Geoff.

Miss Wheeler pushed the plate toward the boys. Peter picked up two and took a gulp of milk. "Boy! These are good. They practically melt in your mouth! Move over, Oreos!"

Geoff tried one and nodded. "Not bad, but I'm a Fig Newton kind of cookie eater."

The boys relaxed and were freer with their smiles and laughs, and the women continued to smile and giggle at every opportunity. The conversation, however, needed more than giggling to keep it alive. Geoff searched for something to say that they hadn't talked about already. "Miss Wheeler, do you live here all year?"

"Oh, no. I only stay for half the year. In the winter, I head to Virginia and South Carolina to be with my brothers."

"When did you first come here?" Geoff asked.

"Well, let's see. I first visited Cuttyhunk in 1940. I fell in love with the island, bought my small cottage and began coming here on extended visits about eleven years ago."

"How'd you find *this* place? You know, Cuttyhunk."

"It was happenstance. I met a gentleman on the train. We started talking and found we both had a passion for music. One topic led to another, and he told me about this island and how his family owned most of it at one time. Have you heard of Cornelius Wood?"

"No," Geoff said.

"See that big house up there over my shoulder? That's Winter House. It's the largest on the island. It belongs to the Wood family."

"When we first got here, we camped up by the tower and passed that house," Geoff said. "It sure is big. Why did you buy the cottage where you live? I mean, how did you choose that particular cottage?"

"It was available. It had a good view, and it was a perfect size for me."

"I know it's not polite to ask, but would you mind telling me what you do, like how you spend your time on the mainland?" Geoff said.

"Don't worry about being polite. It's OK to ask. I worked for years, but I'm retired now. Women of my time were supposed to stay home and tend to a family, but my family was actually the women at a junior college near Boston."

"Really? What did you do?" Geoff asked.

"I held several positions there. When I retired, I was the academic dean at Pine Manor College."

"I'm sorry, I've never heard of it," Geoff said.

"Well, you're a little too young to know about it. It's a women's liberal arts college now. I began there in 1916 and retired in 1948. Thirty-two years."

Miss Wright leaned into Miss Wheeler. "Thirty-two *wonderful* years," she said with a fond look.

"Wow! Thirty-two years is a very long time," Geoff said.

"She was one of the cornerstone women at the college. She was the associate principal and academic dean—very high up. Right next to the president. She took care of all the administrative tasks. Whenever the president came up with a new idea, she'd share it with her staff, and Miss Wheeler was responsible for implementing it."

"Now, Carolyn."

"Now Carolyn nothing! No one knows anything about you, Hetty, because you're so modest. It's time people knew about you." Miss Wright looked again at the boys and leaned over the table. "Pine Manor began as a junior college for women. Back at the turn of the century, it was difficult for women to get into college. We were supposed to stay home and take care of the house. Until women received higher education, no one realized the value they brought to the world outside the home. Miss Wheeler was a true pioneer who gave opportunities to thousands of women who may never have had it without her. She was way ahead of her time."

"Carolyn, please," Miss Wheeler said sternly.

"All right. All right." Miss Wright leaned toward the boys and cupped her hands around her mouth as if she were revealing a secret. "She was the most loved of anyone there. She never forgot any girl and kept up with their interests in later life. She was the only one to do that. When the women returned for reunions, they all sought out Miss Wheeler just to be near her and proudly introduce her to their families. To Miss Wheeler, the college was her home and the girls were her children."

Miss Wright put her hand on Miss Wheeler's arm and patted her gently.

"How I miss those girls," said Miss Wheeler, looking down at the table. A tear rolled down her cheek.

"So, all those pictures on the walls of your cottage are the girls at Pine Manor?" Geoff asked.

Miss Wheeler looked into Geoff's eyes and nodded slowly. Geoff's face stiffened and his brow furrowed. He had inadvertently tapped into part of Miss Wheeler's trunk of treasured memories. Perhaps, he thought, this was why it was part of the island's culture to never ask anyone about their past. The boys sat wordless. A silence fell over the table like a dark veil of sadness. Miss Wheeler's blue eyes were disarmingly gentle and told of an inner peace and caring.

"You know, Carolyn, you did a lot at Pine Manor yourself," said Miss Wheeler.

"Ha! We've known each other too long for *that*. Deflecting attention won't change the facts about you," said Miss Wright. She looked at the boys. "You see, I told you she was modest. Did you know that she has a PhD? Yes, she does. She earned a doctorate in music back in the day when it was unheard of for women to continue beyond what's now known as eighth grade."

Miss Wheeler pulled out a small white handkerchief and wiped her eyes and smiled. "I'll bet you never suspected this would happen, did you?"

Geoff pursed his lips and shook his head slowly. His eyes began to well up with tears.

"Well, boys, you can't go through life putting everything you have—your devotion, your commitment, your passion, everything—into bringing a dream to life without looking back in nostalgia when it's time to turn the reins over to someone else," Miss Wheeler said. "Now… we're here for supper with two fine young men. Let's talk about more pleasant topics." She folded her hands in front of her.

"Let's talk about your nickname!" said Miss Wright.

The two women returned to their usual giggling.

"Nickname?" said Geoff.

"Yes," said Miss Wheeler with a deep sigh. "I have a nickname."

"You do? What is it?" said Geoff, pretending he didn't already know.

"Piney."

"How'd you get *that* nickname?" Geoff asked.

"Well, thirty-two years at Pine Manor," said Miss Wheeler. "That's what started it. It's really a silly story, but it's fun to tell." She smiled as she reflected. "You remember I told you how I met Mr. Wood. Well, he invited me to the island and I was a guest at Winter House where he introduced me to his friends and associates. When asked what I did, I replied, 'I'm the pine of Dean Manor.' Everyone looked at me and I realized that in my nervousness I got the words backwards. Everyone thought it was silly and we all laughed over it, and that was the beginning of my island nickname."

"Is that really true?" said Geoff.

"As true as I'm sitting here," Miss Wheeler said, chuckling over the memory. "One thing about the island is that everyone gets a nickname, so you'd better be careful with what you do or say, or you'll earn a nickname from it. Somewhere along the way my little story turned into my nickname, and I suspect the island kids don't think I know that's what they call me behind my back."

"How do you know they call you Piney?" Geoff asked.

"You can't spend your life in a women's college without knowing every little thing that's going on." She leaned back and giggled. "Haven't you been told that you can't do anything on this island without everyone knowing about it?"

"Oh, we're discovering that," Peter said.

"Yeah," Geoff said. "We've been hearing that a lot. I don't know if they're telling us something or warning us. Anyway, I would never call you Piney."

"Why is that?" said Miss Wheeler.

"I think it's disrespectful."

"Actually, I like it. It's a term of endearment. It identifies me with the best years of my life."

"Endearment?" said Geoff.

"Yes, it's a compliment."

"Well, *I'm* not going to call you Piney," Geoff said. "To me, you'll always be Miss Wheeler."

"How many people do you know with a name like Piney?" Miss Wheeler asked, smiling.

Geoff hesitantly reached across the table and touched Miss Wheeler's hand. "I'm sorry I made you sad. I shouldn't have asked you about your past."

"And why not?"

"I've been told not to ask about anyone's past because it's prying. It's impolite."

"Oh, my dear sweet boy, don't apologize for reminding people of the great joys in their life. We all need those reminders. These are not tears of sadness, but of the joy of those good memories. They comfort me as this old body moves more and more slowly." Miss Wheeler wrapped her hands around Geoff's. "You seem like a very caring and sensitive boy. Hold on to those traits. They will take you far."

Miss Wright looked over her shoulder toward the waning sun. She pulled up her white knitted shawl. "Br-r-r. It's beginning to get a bit chilly."

"Well, maybe it's time for us to go," said Miss Wheeler. "Sundown's a-comin', and we like to be in my cottage before it gets dark. It's harder to see at night these days, and we didn't bring a flashlight. You boys have been delightful."

The boys scrambled to assist. Each held an arm and escorted them to their car. "You boys must come from good homes," said Miss Wheeler as she pushed a button to start the car. The car made a grinding noise from under the hood. Her entire body moved rhythmically as she pumped the gas. "Come on, you old jalopy! Just one more time." After a few more groans, the car started, sending out deep growls through the salt-eaten muffler.

"What, no key?" said Geoff.

"Oh, it has a key. I haven't been able to find it in years. It's back there in the cottage somewhere. I just push this button."

"You push a *button* to start it?" Geoff asked.

"Yes, that's how most cars are. Well, the older ones."

"So, *anyone* can start it?" said Geoff.

"Yes, anyone. The story about keys in cars is a long one, and if you're interested, come on over for milk and cookies and I'll give you a little history lesson." Miss Wheeler traded glances with Miss Wright and giggled.

The boys stepped back from the old car's running board as Miss Wheeler muscled the gear shift into reverse and winced whenever grinding noises came from underneath the car. "I hope this ole banger lasts longer than me!" she said as she backed up. She zigzagged her way toward the paved road.

They smiled and waved. The car turned and sent out more grinding noises as Miss Wheeler jammed it into first gear. Her left hand, holding her white hankie, waved wildly, and her old car sputtered and spit its way down the road.

19

THE OLD TATTOOED LADY

A new day came, bringing with it new adventures. Pammy exploded with enthusiasm, clapping her hands while trying to contain her "let's go" legs. Normally, a walk to the West End was not particularly exciting. Peter, however, with his flamboyant flair, was about to transform an otherwise ordinary hike into a first-class adventure. He crouched as if telling a gripping, nail-biting ghost story around a campfire and pantomimed the trek as he described what they would encounter. At the car dump, they would race in what had been, in the 1940s, the pride of Detroit. The old salt-eaten chassis would leap off its masonry blocks and clutch the dirt road as it sharply snaked up, down, and sideways. When rocks and grass made the road impassable, they would swing their machetes to hack their way through jungle foliage whose branches would attempt to snag and carry them off. At the abandoned World War II shed clinging precariously to an eroding cliff, they would become commandos casting rock grenades to clank off its corrugated metal skins.

Diana and Geoff listened to the plan, amused with what Peter painted in the young minds. Diana leaned toward Geoff and said softly, "Sounds exciting. Do you want to join them or go sailing with me?"

Geoff looked ahead and kept a straight face. "Oh, I don't know. His excursion sounds mighty interesting."

He felt an elbow in his ribs.

"We gotta go to the general store before we go sailing." Diana waved a short grocery list.

They all scooted out the back door and headed up the path behind a small pink cottage. Everyone talked at once, a good omen for the West End escapade.

They emerged by the church. "Hey, there's Mousey!" Diana pointed to an old woman standing outside the general store. The others ran ahead.

"Why is she called Mousey?" Geoff asked.

"Because she has a tattoo of a mouse on her foot."

"A tattoo on an old woman? This I gotta see!"

Mousey was an elderly woman with a gaunt face, thin gray hair, and wire-rim glasses. A limp, worn dress hung on her thin body as though it were hanging lifelessly on a hook. She draped a sweater over her shoulders.

As the chattering, jumping clan surrounded her, Mousey turned in a circle. "What are you all so excited about? What kind of adventure are you on today?" Everybody responded at once. "One at a time. One at a time," she said as she laughed and waved her arms.

Geoff kept his eye focused on her foot. Suddenly it appeared, just as Diana had said. He stooped slightly to get a closer look. It was a faded navy-blue mouse with a long tail fashioned like the letter "S" that wound around her ankle. Alongside the mouse was tattooed "R.A.T."

Mousey looked at the stupefied Geoff. "And who's this young man?"

Geoff stood to attention. "I'm Geoff."

Pammy chimed in, "And that's Pete. They're camping on the beach."

Mousey gave Geoff a thorough head-to-toe once-over like a dermatologist on the hunt for warts. "I'm guessin' that you ain't never seen a tattoo before."

"Well, yeah. On sailors."

"Ha! So, I'm the first lady you've ever seen with one?"

"Yeah, the first one. That's absolutely amazing!" Geoff fought the urge to keep gawking.

"I smoke, too."

Smoking? No big deal. Most women smoked. The tattoo, however— now, that was worth writing home about.

Mousey leaned toward Geoff and slapped his arm. "Not only do I smoke, but I roll 'em, too."

"No foolin'! I've never seen smokes rolled."

"Well, young Geoff, you're in for a treat!" Mousey reached inside her dress pocket and pulled out a soiled pouch and a small blue package with "Zig-Zag" on the cover.

"Watch this," she said, holding the pouch between her teeth. She opened the Zig-Zag package and retrieved a thin white piece of paper, cradled it in her fingers, and made a U-shaped bed. She tapped tobacco from the pouch, spreading it across the paper without dropping so much as a single snippet. Her precision and dexterity captivated Geoff.

"You do that so easily, and with only two hands."

"That's all God gave us, but you ain't seen nuthin' yet." She carefully rolled the cigarette and licked the edge. Then she twisted the ends and put the entire cigarette in her mouth to apply just enough spit to hold it together. She rolled it with the finesse and experience of an accomplished artist, but it was the most pathetic-looking cigarette Geoff had ever seen.

"How do you like that?" Mousey pointed to the fragile cigarette dangling from the side of her mouth. It threatened to open and spray tobacco in every direction.

"That was… *wow*!" said Geoff. "But it's pretty short."

"A smoke is a smoke! A soul can't spend all day smokin'! Besides, they say smokin's bad for you. Got a match?"

Geoff patted his pockets. Mousey reached into her pocket, retrieved a stick match, and scraped her thumbnail across the top. Flames hissed in every direction while she put the match to the cigarette and puffed.

Mousey held the cigarette between the tips of her thumb and index finger, sucked deeply, exhaled, and watched the smoke dissipate. She gave the cigarette an approving look. "Want a drag?" she said, holding it out to Geoff.

"Thanks for offering, but I don't smoke yet. Boy, you sure made that look easy."

"What? Smokin' or rollin'?" Mousey laughed and slapped Geoff's arm. "Just funnin' ya. It's easy with a little practice. Why, I can even roll and light a smoke in a nor'easter." Geoff's face revealed his wonder.

"What! Don't believe me? Any fool can roll and light a smoke on days like today. Real skill's tested in a nor'easter. Come see me then and I'll show ya. I can see from the look on your face that you've never heard of a nor'easter. Hang around here a while and you'll see one firsthand." Mousey raised her head high, took another puff, and waved the cigarette around appreciatively.

"How come you don't just buy a pack? Wouldn't it be easier?"

"Damn things cost seventeen cents a pack! I'll be damned before I pay that much for 'em! Besides, they take up too much room in my pocket."

"Hey, guys!" Hilly interjected. "We need to get going on our adventure." She looked at Mousey. "We should be going."

Mousey smiled as they parted. The three children followed Peter up Broadway and disappeared over the rolling pathway toward the West End road. Mousey took a few more puffs on her smoke and crushed it under her foot as she spit out pieces of tobacco. "Well, I'd best be on my way. See you later." She resumed her walk toward Broadway, and Geoff watched until she rounded the corner of the building. Diana and Geoff stood outside the general store—Diana smiling with amusement over Geoff's fascination with Mousey.

"Who is she? She's amazing."

"Mousey? She's Muggsy's mom. You know, Muggsy, from the…"

"Yeah, yeah, I know Muggsy. *She's* his mother?"

"Yep. Everyone likes Mousey."

"I can see why."

"She's not like many of the other old people here. She gets out. She likes the island kids and likes to talk to us. She treats us like real people."

"Where'd she get that tattoo?"

"I don't know. If we're gonna go sailing, we'd better get to it before they come back from their hike, but first we have to pick up a few things for my mom."

Diana darted around the store collecting items while Geoff chatted with Muggsy. "I have a question," Geoff said. "Whenever we meet the boat, I see a thin man standing next to a truck with the faded name 'The Poplars' on it. Who is he?"

"That's Clarence Allen. He and Lucille own the Allen House. Used to be called The Poplars. Why do you ask?"

"I just see him standing there, leaning against his truck with his arms folded. He's always in the same place. He never says anything. Just watches and nods. I catch him glaring at me every now and again. So, *he* owns the Allen House."

"Like I told you before, everyone has their eyes on you two. When something's amiss, they look suspiciously at newcomers. Island kids know not to make mischief. When you notice folks not looking at you, that's a good sign."

"I'll keep that in mind." Geoff pointed out the door. "I just met Mousey. She's your mother?"

"That she is. She's a pistol! Gets around very well for her age. Likes to be around island kids. Says it keeps her young."

"Where'd she get her tattoo?"

"You should ask her. She loves telling that story. No, maybe I should. You won't believe it if she tells you. Ready for this? My mom used to be a bouncer in a New Bedford waterfront bar. Didn't put up with anyone's guff. When someone had too much to drink and got rowdy, she'd grab them by the ear and toss 'em out. Nobody messed with her when she got riled. She got the tattoo on a dare. She can tell you the rest of the story. Close your mouth, Geoff."

Geoff leaned over the counter. "Muggsy, I have another question."

"And that is?"

"Well, Pete and I have been wondering about how you got the name 'Muggsy.' Would it be impolite to ask?"

Muggsy laughed and sighed as he gazed off into a piece of his past. "Well, I've had that name for about as long as I can remember. When I was four, my older brother, Vinny, came home with some friends and found me playing in the dirt. He rubbed some of it on my face and made quite a mess. He stood over me saying, 'My, what a mug.' From that day on I was known as Muggsy."

"Wow! What is your real name? I mean, your first name?"

"Hah! We'll save that for another time."

Diana approached the counter with an armful of provisions. Muggsy tallied and sacked them. They walked briskly back toward her house. "I still can't believe that Mousey," Geoff said. "Both my grandmothers are still alive, but they're not like *her*."

"What are they like?"

"Well, when one of them comes for a visit, she sits at the end of the couch with her hands folded in her lap and spends all her time scowling. When the other one comes, all she does is nap. Now, Mousey... making cigarettes in the wind and showing off a tattoo! She's incredible!"

"Most people would have bad things to say about tattoos on women."

"My father says tattoos desecrate our bodies. He would definitely dis-approve."

"And you?"

"Oh, I'm cool with it."

"Would you say the same thing if *I* had a tattoo?"

"A tattoo on *you*?"

"You wouldn't say bad things?"

"Me? Heck no. It's not my place, but if you did have one, I'd be cool with that, too. I should tell you what Muggsy just told me."

Diana wrapped her arm around Geoff's. "Later. C'mon, you. Let's drop off these groceries and go sailing."

20

SAILING WITH DIANA

"See that pink house?"

"You mean *that* pink house?"

"Yeah, *that* pink house."

"What about it?"

"It's called the Pink House."

"Because it's pink?"

"It's sort of a landmark around here."

"Allen House. Bosworth House. So, do the Pinks live there?"

"Smarty-pants. Well, it doesn't look like much, but when there's a party—like almost every Saturday—there are cars, jeeps, and pickup trucks parked all around here. There's a lot of laughing, drinking, and happy people coming and going. Everyone's welcome. Plumes of cigarette smoke pour out the front door. Sometimes you'd think the place was on fire. The Pink House is a happy place. We pass it all the time, and I wasn't sure if you knew what we call it. Now you know."

With groceries delivered, Diana picked up the pace as they headed to the Cuttyhunk Yacht Club. Her bare feet were undaunted by the rough, hot pavement. Geoff grunted with every step. His feet were still in training. "Walk on the side of the road in the sandy part. It's not as hard, but watch out for thistle."

They rounded a curve, and the Cuttyhunk Yacht Club gear shed appeared on their left. Clearly it had been built for function and utility; it had no windows, and only a wide wobbly barn door. Diana extended her palm to the shed. "This is it. This is the Cuttyhunk Yacht Club— the good old CYC."

"What's in there?"

"Gear… Sails, tillers, centerboards, life vests. Everything. C'mon. I think we can do this in one trip."

Diana pulled open the large barn door and revealed a smorgasbord of shelves and racks of boat gear. Tillers, centerboards, sail bags, and oars were neatly lined up. Masts hung overhead with lines and pulleys dangling down like cobwebs. The only light coming into the musty shed was through the open door and through cracks between the siding.

Diana walked around the shed gathering gear. She handed Geoff a sail bag and reached for a tiller and centerboard. "Grab a couple of those oars and life jackets. I think we're set. Let's go sailing."

Geoff followed Diana across the road through an opening between tall clumps of oat grass that exposed a panoramic view of the Cuttyhunk harbor and the yacht club pier. The makeshift pier was made from tree limbs stuck in the mud. At the far end, two planks attached the pier to a rectangular floating dock. A lone skiff tied to the float quietly slapped the water as it bobbed and gently tugged on its painter.

"Are we sailing in *this?*"

"No, silly." Diana pointed to a huddle of small boats moored about a hundred feet away. "We're sailing in one of those."

"Oh. Of course." A flush of ignorance swept across Geoff's cheeks.

"With all the time we've talked about sailing, I never asked if you've done this before."

"Pete helped me salvage a flat-bottom rowboat. I made a sail from an old bedsheet and a broomstick. All it did was blow sideways."

"Bet you didn't have a centerboard."

"A what?"

Diana pointed to the centerboard lying on the float. "That. You'll see how it works. Let's go pick out a boat. You row."

They climbed into the boat and headed out to the small sailing fleet. "Put yer back into it, matie!" said Geoff as he plunged the oars deep into the water, encouraged by Diana's amusement. "Come on, you sea dogs!" he continued, leaning back and pulling hard on the oars. An oar slipped out of the oarlock, sending Geoff backward and plopping him into several inches of water in the bottom of the boat.

"Good going, mister. You're going to be sopping wet before we even start." Diana laughed as she helped pull Geoff back to the seat.

"What a klutz," Geoff said, laughing too.

"I like that you're not afraid to laugh at yourself."

In his efforts to make a good impression, it seemed all Geoff did was make himself look foolish, yet he was actually scoring points.

They rowed to the moored flotilla. "Let's take that one. It has a mast."

They towed it back to the float. Diana began issuing orders. "Hand me the tiller. Hand me the sail bag. Hand me the life vests." She quickly attached the tiller to the transom, locked down the centerboard, and stuffed the life vests under the front seat. Geoff tossed in the sail bag. She resumed her flow of orders. "Hand me that halyard line. Feed this part into the mast track. Connect the shackle at the end of the boom to the clew cringe, and do the same with the tack. Make sure you run the Cunningham through the cringe and attach it to the cleat. Secure that sheet. Ease the line to the traveler."

Geoff's head jerked from one side to the other as he attempted to keep up with her directives and foreign boat talk. It was hard to follow one set of instructions and watch Diana as she issued new orders. By the time he looked to where she pointed, she was pointing somewhere else. The firmness in her voice showed self-assuredness that commanded unfettered compliance.

"You said to slide these metal thingies into that slot when we raise the sail, right?"

"There are no 'thingies' on sailboats! Everything has a name. Otherwise you wouldn't know one thingy from the next, but yes, you slide those thingies into that whatchamacallit when we hoist the whosiewhat."

"How do we stop this boat if we have to?"

"I don't know. I've never had to do that. We just yell at everyone to get out of the way. That's why we have crew. Just kidding. See how we have the bow, the pointy end, heading into the wind? Boats can't sail into the wind. That's why we're not moving. When we need to stop, we just point the boat into the wind."

Geoff put his hands on his head, swimming in a tsunami of detail and newness. Diana laughed. "Don't worry. You'll see. It's easy. You should see your face! OK, you fit the guides into the mast track as I hoist the sail. You ready?"

"Ready."

"Set the mainsul!" bellowed Diana as she hoisted the sail. It went up quickly. She put her back into making it taut. The breeze slammed the boom to the left and right as the sail luffed and snapped. She pulled on another line, and the frenzied boom settled down.

"You see, we're head to wind. We can sit here like this all day and this boat will never sail. Untie the bow line and shove us sideways."

When Geoff released the line and pushed away, the wind filled the sails and the boat heeled to leeward. He gripped the gunwales and looked to Diana for reassurance. None came. Only a hearty laugh. "Don't worry. We're not going to tip over, but just in case… you can swim, can't you?"

Diana steered the boat toward the middle of the harbor and shot through the moored armada of CYC sailboats. She came close to another boat, and Geoff flattened his body against the opposite side of theirs as if it would help them avert a collision. Wind gusts pressed against the sail, bringing broad smiles to Diana and panic to Geoff.

The terrified Geoff was trapped in a boat while being tortured by a pretty girl whose body had been taken over by an evil alien.

"OK, let me make it easier for you." Diana let out a line. The boat immediately responded by righting itself. "There, better?"

"Aah. Better. What did you do?"

"I eased the traveler to spill some of the wind, so a gust has less effect on performance." Diana bent over to look under the sail. "Relax and enjoy the ride."

"You're not gonna let us turn over, are you?"

Diana pulled on her clothing. "Why would I want to do that? I'm wearing a sweater. Ever swim in a wet sweater? But you can never tell what the wind will do. So, no promises. You never answered my question. You can swim, can't you?"

"Sure, I can swim."

Diana nodded, smiled, and turned her eyes out into the harbor.

"What happens when we get to the other side?"

"We turn around, silly."

"Is that hard?"

"I don't know. We're about to figure it out. See how calm the water is over there? There's less wind, and we can't sail without it. Let's find wind. Ready about!"

"Ready about? What does *that* mean?"

"Hard a lee!" The boom flew to the opposite side of the boat and sent out a crisp snap when it traveled as far as the mainsheet permitted. Diana ducked under the swinging boom and shifted her weight to the windward side. Geoff, well, he just tumbled ass over teakettle with legs a-flyin'. When done rolling around, his head was in the water on the bottom of the boat and his leg dangled over the side. He righted himself and tried to figure out exactly what Diana had meant by "hardly," except it must have been a warning that she was about to turn.

The two were bound together in a ten-foot boat where one was in her element and the other was experiencing the most terrifying event of his life.

"You're afraid we're gonna turn over, aren't you? Don't worry. I won't let that happen. You're safe with me. It's fun watching you. You'll get over it after a few more sailing days. It's hard to get in trouble with these turnabouts."

"Is that what they call these boats?"

"Yep. Turnabouts. Watch." Diana's grin widened. "Hard a lee." She pushed the tiller to one side and the boat turned sharply. Geoff, once again, found himself face down on the sole. "That's why! Because they turn about very quickly. Turn… about. Get it?"

The more they sailed, the less Geoff overreacted to shifts in the boat's performance or what happened every time Diana yelled, "Hardly." He was learning that the boat could turn fast, sail fast, heel hard, and not tip over, but could not figure out what yelling "hardly" had to do with turning.

"What does 'hardly' mean?"

"Hardly?"

"Yeah, when you turn the boat, you yell 'hardly'."

"You silly. I yell 'hard a lee' which tells you I'm about to turn. You thought I was yelling 'hardly'? Well, there's something else I should tell you. These boats are for beginner sailors. They're very responsive and safe. Before they tip over from too much wind, they'll round up."

"Argh! Another nautical term. What does that mean?"

"The boat will only heel over so far, and if the wind pushes it past a certain point, you'll lose control of the boat and it will turn itself into the wind. It's considered novice sailing if that happens, and it's awful in a race, because you can crash into other boats or suddenly find yourself in the back of the pack."

"So, all this time you let me think we were gonna tip over?"

Diana smiled and looked out over the harbor.

"You did, didn't you?"

Diana did not respond. She sat tall, squinted, and focused. Her face told of a distraction somewhere out there in the harbor. He looked out to find what she was looking at. "What's out there? What do you see?"

There was no response. Then, "We're going over there to catch that boat. We're going racing. Ready about! Hard a lee!" Diana pulled in the sheet, tightened the sail, and centered the traveler.

The boat sailed in the "groove" and cut through the water like a razor-sharp knife, heeling over hard with the breeze. "Sit on the gunwale and hike out! It'll move weight to windward and we'll go faster. Put your feet under the seat to hold yourself in!" She sat on the gunwale next to Geoff. The shift in weight brought the boat higher, and it picked up speed. She looked up at the sail and tightened the mainsheet to get more power. They quickly narrowed the gap between the two boats.

As they closed in on the competition, Geoff watched the solo sailor in the other boat respond by pulling on lines and adjusting the sail on her boat. She hoisted herself up on the gunwale and hovered low to reduce wind drag. The girls mirrored each other in their postures, their actions, and how they played out their competitive attitudes in this unannounced race to who knows where.

"How did this become a race?"

"It's always a race," Diana said, keeping her focus on the other boat.

As they closed the gap, Geoff could see the face of Diana's competitor. "Who's that?"

Diana tweaked the sail and adjusted the mainsheet. "That's Bev Snow."

"Bev Snow? As in Gladys Snow?"

"You got it." As the race continued, Diana's responses became terser. She scanned her surroundings. "Ready about!"

Geoff clutched the gunwale.

"Say 'ready' when you're ready."

"Oh—ready!"

"Hard a lee!"

"Why did we turn?"

"Low tide."

"What does low tide have to do with turning?"

Diana pointed over her shoulder without allowing their conversation to distract her. "The pond over there… very shallow muck. Boat will run aground. She would win. Can't have that!"

"Why is it so important to beat her?"

"Because she's the best."

"Do you ever win?"

"Sometimes. Mostly she does."

The competitors sailed side by side, vying to outmaneuver one another by using their sail to block the wind to the other boat. They read each other well. Even with the boats only inches apart, they pretended not to notice or acknowledge the other. They kept their heads forward, only looking at each other out of the corners of their eyes. It was as much a game of wits, positioning, and dogged competitiveness as it was about sailing skill. Or maybe that was what true sailing was about.

Geoff became a quick study as the race cast him into the sailing world of instant decisions and rapidly changing conditions. Through sheer repetition, he began anticipating how the boat would react whenever Diana trimmed the sails, eased the mainsheet, or turned with only the warning "Hard a lee!" As he adjusted to the rigors of racing, his fears morphed into exhilaration.

When racing, Diana was competitive, focused, intense. Geoff felt like he was looking at the "real" Diana.

As if the boat instinctively knew the race was over, it slowed down and sat upright. Geoff could feel a change in how the water flowed past the hull. Diana emerged from her different world and sat up straight. She looked at Geoff and sighed. Her shoulders relaxed, and her girlish smile returned. She watched as Bev Snow tacked away. The two exchanged salutes, and both went about casual sailing as quickly as they had engaged in battle.

"What's happening?"

"The race is over."

"Who won?"

"We both did."

"How could you tell?"

"A start and finish line are only a small part of racing."

Geoff looked puzzled.

"Racing is not about who can sail the fastest, but about using your skills and experience to take advantage of the wind, anticipate what's coming, reading the competition, and good teamwork. If you want to become a good sailor, you should race."

"Wow! I thought it was just a matter of hoisting the sail and blowing with the wind. Where'd you learn all this stuff?"

Diana motioned with her head. "From her. She's the club instructor."

Diana continued to look over at Bev in a long silence.

"You have a lot of respect for her, don't you?"

"Oh, yes, we're good friends, but we only hang out together when we're sailing. What I really like about her is that she's competitive. She never takes racing personally like some of the guys do. With them, the losers sometimes wear a big chip on their shoulders, and the winners strut around like roosters. If it wasn't for her, I wouldn't be much of a sailor."

"Do you ever race together, like as a team?"

"As in the same boat? Never. If we're in the same boat, we can't race each other. I think she likes racing me because I give her a good run. I'm one of the few who can beat her at times."

Diana gazed in Bev's direction. "I remember one time after a race where Bev just squeaked in front of me and I was racing to get my boat to bed first. We both jumped into the water and swam to see who would be the first one to touch the dock."

Geoff looked over toward Bev's boat, which was shrinking as it headed to the opposite side of the harbor. "So, she's Gladys Snow's daughter."

"How do you know Gladys Snow?"

"I met her at the Bosworth House. We were supposed to check in with her once we got here."

"So, how do you like sailing? I know this isn't what you expected, and I hope I didn't scare you away."

"Not hardly! You sure made it exciting. You're exciting. I can see why you like it. Do you think we could do this again?"

"Thought you'd never ask. But what do you mean, I'm exciting?"

"Um. Well, I saw a different side of you. And you're fun to be with," Geoff said, carefully avoiding eye contact.

"You know you don't need to sail with me all the time." Diana looked down, blushing from the compliment. "I mean, if you were a member of the club, you could come down to the dock and sail anytime."

"But why would I want to sail without you?"

Smiling, Diana looked away.

Diana sailed the boat toward the float and turned only seconds before it made contact. The boat drifted sideways and gently kissed the float. They removed the gear and towed the sailboat back to its mooring. Back at the float, Geoff started to remove the oars. "Leave those for Bev," Diana said. "She'll be in soon, and that will save her a trip to the shed."

With gear stowed, they stood by the oat grass and looked back to ensure they hadn't left anything unattended or behind. Geoff sighed happily as he looked out over the harbor. "Thanks! That was fun."

Diana leaned into Geoff and pulled him by the arm. "C'mon, sailor man, let's go find the others."

21

DON'T WORRY ABOUT OTHER BOYS

Diana and Geoff arrived at the Baldwin House to find Peter and the West End Gang engaged in a rousing game of Candyland. They were eager to exchange stories. Peter's excursion had definitely been a hit. Pammy exuded the most excitement and could hardly contain herself when describing her favorite parts of their trip: rock throwing at the corrugated military building perched on the cliff and racing the rusted-out cars at the dump.

Geoff watched Peter as he interacted with the kids. He saw an animation and exuberance in him he hadn't seen before. Peter had more spirit, more life in his eyes. He smiled broadly. He looked happy. He looked… at home. Had the same "family" magic of the Baldwin House grabbed Peter like it had Geoff?

The lazy afternoon around the game table drifted into evening. Geoff and Peter accepted the invitation to stay for supper, since hot dogs and the company at the Baldwins' sounded far better than cold Chef Boyardee at the beach. When supper ended, everyone was eager to clear the table and get back to the board games. Geoff and Diana volunteered for kitchen cleanup, an offer that was immediately accepted. They discovered that the kitchen was the most private room in the house—especially when there were dishes to be washed.

After a while, the commotion of vigorous game playing ended. "Hey Geoff!" Peter called from the other room. "See ya back at camp." Bare feet pounded the stairs to the bedrooms. Everyone was turning in for the night.

Diana and Geoff stood in the shadows of the kitchen. They faced each other without saying a word. The silence lasted an eternity. Geoff's heart raced. Something immense was taking place. All systems in his body were going haywire: intense heat in some places and coldness in others. Blood boiled in his head, and he could feel his heart pounding in his ankles. His breathing picked up as though he had just run the hundred-yard dash. The overpowering magnetic force pulling him to Diana was both exciting and frightening.

Geoff jumped back and cleared his throat. "Uh, er-r, I, uh, I, um, I have something for you."

Diana let out a deep sigh as if she'd been holding her breath. "Yeah, what?" came a whisper.

Geoff reached into his pocket and pulled out a photo Peter had taken the day before. Diana took the photo and held it up to a small band of light. "It's you!"

"Yeah, that's me all right."

"Thanks!" She stepped closer to Geoff, stood on her tiptoes and put her hand on one cheek, and gently kissed him on the other. She leaned close and whispered, "You don't have to worry about other boys."

Geoff stood back with a satisfied grin. He had just won the Irish Sweepstakes! He wrapped his arms around Diana and pulled her close. Her small frame got lost in his arms. She was slighter than Geoff had imagined, but that small girl sure knew how to hug back. They stood, embracing: no intruders, no interruptions, and no distractions. Diana's kiss and hug were unexpected bonuses at the end of the day. This was like sailing for the first time.

Creaking floorboards from little feet moving about upstairs brought them back to earth. Geoff said softly, "Guess I should go." Diana shook her head.

They walked to the back door and looked at each other as if something very sexy had just happened. Her eyes remained locked on his, sending messages he had not known before. This was all very new and confusing. The numbing, flushing, dumbfounding sensation returned, and his body burst into flames. Diana's soft words rang in Geoff's head with the clarity of a distant church bell on a winter morning. He could feel her breath lingering in his ear. His cheek still tingled from her kiss. An inner voice told him to pull her back into his arms and kiss her again and again, but he didn't have the nerve to go that far.

"This has been my best day on the island. Thank you for taking me sailing. Hey, do you think you can stay up for another half hour?"

"I may be awake all night. Why? What are you thinking?"

"Look through that telescope in about thirty minutes."

Geoff turned to the back door and was pulled back by Diana. "I had a great day, too. "I'll see you tomorrow, OK?"

Camp was dark and still. Geoff climbed over the barge and felt his way to the bonfire pit. He broke up small pieces of driftwood and crushed a handful of shavings. The damp shavings smoked and struggled to ignite. He knelt and blew gently. An unannounced *whomph* belched through the smoke as the shavings burst into flames.

Peter appeared on the barge. "Hey! You're back! What are you doing?"

"Makin' a bonfire." Geoff continued to coax the fire.

"It's kinda late. Don't you think you should hit the sack?"

"I told Diana to look through the telescope and let me know tomorrow if she could see me." He stood behind the bonfire to illuminate his body. He jumped and waved wildly. "Do you think she can see this?"

"I don't think you need a telescope to see *that*. OK, I'm wide awake now. Tell me everything. All of it—word for word. What happened in the kitchen? Did you give her your picture?"

"Yes, I gave her the picture."

"It was my idea, you know."

"Yes, and it was a good one—thank you. It was in my pocket all day. I don't know how it survived sailing. Sheer luck, I guess."

Peter pried for details, and Geoff frustrated him with vague responses. Those moments with Diana would remain his secret lest the magic of it vanish in cheap embellishments and distorted fantasies.

"Since it was my idea to take the picture, I should think you'd show a little gratitude by at least filling me in on the details. But it doesn't look like you want to tell me, so-o-o-o I'm sacking out."

Geoff sat alone in a reverie. He recounted the pleasures of his day with Diana as if he were Uncle Scrooge McDuck counting his gold in his secret money room. Sitting under the stars with the warmth of a fire increased his euphoria. Diana had changed his perception of sailing—she had made it electric. The thought of her tender kiss brought chills as he wondered whether it might have been more than innocence. Maybe it was.

When she'd whispered, "You don't have to worry about other boys," Geoff knew he would walk through fire to sustain her admiration.

"You don't have to worry about other boys." Her lingering words roamed through his heart and made it sing.

He sat quietly in the enormity of the darkness. He pondered the feat of being where he was—physically and mentally—and the "who" of the self-reliant person he was becoming.

I wonder if my family knows where I am, he thought. *I wonder if they know* who *I am.*

THE ENCOUNTER

Greeters stood on the dock with their eyes fixed on the arriving *Alert*. Geoff glanced around, trying to count the number of people he recognized. He was feeling more comfortable and at home with each passing day. He felt the bump of the *Alert* against the dock that signaled "dock fury" was about to begin. Boxes, cargo, and provisions flowed off the boat, and people poured over the gangplank. Geoff and Diana stood together, his heart pounding as he pressed his arm against the girl who had told him not to worry about other boys.

The crowd had begun to thin out when Geoff's eye caught sight of a man standing near the *Alert*. Startled, he tried intently to get a better look at the man's face as people wove in and out of his line of vision.

"What's wrong?" said Diana.

"I thought I saw my father."

"Your father? Where?"

"I'm not sure it's him. I keep losing him. Wait! There he is!"

"Which one?"

Geoff pointed. "I'm not sure it's him. He keeps turning away. I can't see his face. Wait here. I'm going to get a closer look."

Geoff slowly made his way toward the man who was facing away from him. He trembled as his heart pounded and his mouth became dry. Unlike his father, this man was slightly stooped over and appeared wobbly and disoriented. Geoff stopped about ten feet behind him and tilted his body to the left and then to the right, attempting to see his face.

Diana came to Geoff's side and softly said, "Is that your dad?"

"It looks like him, but what's he doing *here*? I need to see his face."

Geoff stepped cautiously toward the man. When he was at arm's length, the man slowly turned around. Geoff stiffened and stumbled backward with shock. "Pop? What are you doing here?"

The man's face, squinting from the bright haze, quickly morphed into anger. He took a step toward Geoff and grabbed his shoulder. Geoff jerked away. The man lost his grip and fell back, landing on his butt with legs up. A thin metal flask shot out of his pants pocket and spun across the dock. He sat looking confused. With great effort, he stood, wobbling as he looked at the crowd. Another man picked up the errant flask and handed it back to him. He snatched the flask and stuffed it back into his pocket. When he refocused on Geoff, he lunged at him again but was intercepted by Mr. Baldwin, Clarence from the Allen House, and another man Geoff did not know.

Geoff's heart continued to pound, terrified by what he was seeing. His ears began to ring, and he felt dizzy. Color vanished. Everything looked like an out-of-focus black-and-white movie. He wanted to flee, but his body refused to respond to his commands.

"That's my son and he's coming back with me, so get out of the way!" shouted the man as he pointed.

Mr. Baldwin turned to Geoff. "Is this man your father?"

Geoff nodded without taking his eyes off him.

The man resumed his rant. "What's wrong with the home I made for you? Isn't that good enough? How is this place any better? Why are you hiding behind those people? Can't you stand up for yourself?"

Geoff took a step toward his father and felt Mr. Baldwin's arm across his chest. Mr. Baldwin looked at his wife. "Nance, quickly, take the boys up to the house."

Mrs. Baldwin put her hand on Geoff's arm and tried to nudge him off the dock, but Geoff resisted and kept his eyes on his father. Diana put her hand on him. "We should do what my dad says. Come on, Geoff, please."

Geoff turned to leave the dock but kept his head turned toward his father, who shouted over the heads of the crowd. "We had an agreement. You promised to call home when you got here, and you didn't. What is wrong with you? Why can't you keep your promises? You made your mother and me worry. You didn't live up to your end of our agreement. Your trip is over. You're coming back with me. Do you hear me, boy?"

Geoff stood by the Baldwins' car, looking back at the dock. His father remained surrounded by the three men, his yelling fading in the distance. "We had an agreement. We had an agreement." And then his father dropped to his knees and hung his head. Mr. Baldwin knelt and put his arm around his shoulder. Several other islanders moved in closer.

Geoff started walking back to the dock. "This can't be happening," he whispered.

Mrs. Baldwin ran after Geoff who appeared to be in shock about the encounter.

"This is a bad dream. It's just a bad dream," Geoff repeated softly.

"Please, trust us. Come with me. Everything's going to be all right."

Mrs. Baldwin led him back to the car. He and Diana climbed in and sat quietly. With a distant look in his eyes, he said, "How can I ever face him again?"

"It's not your fault," Mrs. Baldwin said reassuringly. "Everything's going to be all right."

"Where's Pete?" Geoff asked.

"He and the girls went ahead. They're back at the house," said Mrs. Baldwin.

The drive back to the Baldwin House was normally festive, but that day it was the longest five-minute silent ride Geoff had ever experienced.

Once there, Geoff stood looking out the window by the telescope as Peter kept his young gang entertained around the game table. Hot dogs and tuna fish sandwiches appeared and vanished within minutes. Geoff and Diana were cleaning the kitchen when Mr. Baldwin came through the back door. Geoff looked at him expectantly.

"Come out back."

Geoff followed Mr. Baldwin to a circle of lawn chairs behind the house. "Well, young man, you certainly have had an exciting morning."

Geoff sighed deeply. "I'll say."

"Have you ever seen your father like this before?"

"What do you mean?"

"Do you know your father had been drinking?"

"Is that why he was so different?"

"You've never seen him like this before?"

"Never."

"What did he mean when he said you didn't keep your end of the agreement?"

Geoff described his agreement about checking in with Gladys Snow – which he did four days late, and how he later learned his father expected him to call home upon his arrival on the island. Geoff didn't think it was a big enough deal to call home to resolve the misunderstanding, yet he knew the matter would be troublesome when he returned home. It had never occurred to him that his father might show up.

"Apparently it was a big enough deal to him," said Mr. Baldwin.

"Why did he come now? This all happened two weeks ago. If it was so important to him, why did he wait so long?"

Mr. Baldwin shrugged slightly.

"It killed me to see him fall. He's never yelled at me like that. At home, yelling is forbidden. I don't understand what happened. What did I do?"

Mr. Baldwin put his hand on Geoff's arm. "There are some things you probably should know so you won't blame yourself."

"But it was my fault."

"You can take the blame for the mess-up with communications, but not for what you saw on the dock. I don't expect you to understand this now, but someday it will make sense. Geoff, your father's actions were driven by alcohol. He was drunk. That was not your father on the dock. It was the bottle doing the talking. People can do and say some terrible things when they've had too much to drink—things they would never do and say when they're sober."

Mr. Baldwin asked Geoff several questions about life at home, his father's work, his reactions to his father at home, and what he had witnessed on the dock. Geoff opened up and poured out his feelings. Then he said, "I feel like I'm betraying him by telling you these things."

"So, you keep them bottled up inside and let them fester and make a mess of you. There's no good in that and there's no betrayal in sharing your feelings. I think the best thing for you to do is get your head back to the island. You can't do anything about the situation with your father right now. It's easy for me to tell you not to think about it, but try not to let it consume you. You'll be dealing with it soon enough."

"Where is he now?"

"Clarence Allen and a few others took him to the Allen House for lunch. Then they're going to take him back to the boat. You're not leaving today, not with your father in his condition. I want your telephone number so we can call your mother."

"Can I go see him?"

"As much as you feel bad about all this, I don't think that would be wise. He's already hurting enough inside. He's calmed down, and as long as you stay away from him, we'll all feel better."

"I can't see him off when *Alert* leaves?"

"It would be better if you didn't, but I think it would be all right if you waited until the boat left and then waved to him."

"I could wait near the channel by our camp."

"That would be OK."

"Can Diana come with me?"

"I think she'd be hurt if you didn't ask her."

Mr. Baldwin drove Geoff and Diana down to the main dock and up the sandy patch toward Geoff's camp. After he left, Geoff and Diana stood at the edge of the channel, watching from a distance as people climbed aboard *Alert*. A few minutes later the *Alert* let out its afternoon *WHO-O-O-OP*, pulled away from the dock, turned, and headed up the channel toward them. As she passed, Geoff waved, and some passengers waved back.

"Can you see your dad?"

"No. Maybe he's on the other side or even in the cabin. Wait! There he is."

"Where?"

"He's under the cover near the stern. Can you see him? He's standing up. He's looking this way. He sees us."

Geoff jumped, flailed his arms, and yelled as loudly as he could. "Pop! Goodbye, Pop. I love you. I love you, Pop. Goodbye." There was no response. His father became a shrinking silhouette under the canopy of the boat as *Alert* chugged down the channel. Geoff's arms fell limp at his side as he watched the shadow figure sit down and lower his head in his hands.

Geoff's mind swirled with thoughts and visions of his father. He felt a mix of sadness for what he had witnessed, confusion over what he didn't understand, trepidation about facing his father, and guilt for believing he was responsible for what had happened.

* * *

On the barge behind the tent, Geoff and Diana leaned back to back for a long time without saying a word. They watched the angle of the sun change the color of the landscape. "Thanks for being with me," Geoff said.

"I wouldn't want it any other way. Thanks for asking me."

"And thanks for just sitting here with me."

"Sometimes the best thing to say is nothing at all, but I have an idea. Let's go up to the tower."

They sat on the wall just below the tower, watching the day vanish. Diana pointed. "Look at how the Sound calms down and Gay Head looks like you can reach out and touch it. And when it gets dark, and if it's really clear, you can see the red glow of the Hathaway sign in New Bedford."

Another hour passed without a word, and then Diana broke the silence. "C'mon. There's one more thing I want to show you."

They jumped off the wall and headed down the road. Near Broadway, she steered him through an opening in the wall and on to a large sea of grass surrounding the Woods' house. Diana found the highest spot, and they sat watching dusk give way to the star-studded night sky. Geoff had spent many nights pondering the heavens from his camp, yet the view from the hill brought a different perspective and sense of peace to soothe the pain from his encounter with his father.

23

A NEW FRIEND IN THE KITCHEN

The boys stood stiff, motionless, and shoulder to shoulder as they looked up at the Bosworth House. Their eyes locked on the open front door that led to the cavern of horrors.

"You sure we have to do this?" said Geoff.

"We don't have to do anything,"

"All we have to do is talk to him."

"Talk? All he does is spit, yell, and curse," Pete said. "You call that talking?"

"He's deranged."

"He's a disembodied evil spirit."

"He's a lunatic."

"Maybe we could do this over at the Allen House."

"Can't. You have to be a guest there."

"I guess the Allen House is out then."

"Yep, it's out."

"This was all *your* idea. Why don't *you* go in and talk to him?"

"Don't be a chickenshit."

"No, really. I can't go in there."

"Fine, Pete. I'll go. Would you at least come into the dining room?"

Geoff sucked in a deep breath. He took a timid step toward the porch, his eyes darting around as though fearful something would leap out at him. *CRACK!* Geoff jumped like a cat shaken out of a deep sleep.

"Jeez, Geoff! What?"

He pointed to the ground and looked over to Peter. "Stick," he said, rolling his eyes.

Geoff nervously looked back to the steps, took another deep breath, and inched cautiously toward the door. He poked his head inside. The coast was clear.

Peter cupped his hands around his mouth and whispered loudly, "Don't worry. Gladys Snow will save you."

Once inside, Geoff rounded the corner and heard clattering dishes in the dining room. The sound was welcoming, for it meant he would not be alone. If Robbie went wild, at least there would be a witness. Geoff tiptoed inside the dining room where a thin blond girl scurried around tables, dealing plates from the stack in her arm. She paused in her tasks. "Hey. Can I help you?"

"Yes, ma'am. My friend and I were here two weeks ago asking about coming here for a lobster dinner."

"OK, I'm sorry, but we don't serve lobster here."

"Yeah, I know. We talked to Robbie, and he said we had to bring them. Gladys Snow said we should come back on the day we want to have dinner here and let you know. So that's why we're here."

The girl leaned to look around Geoff. "We?"

"Yeah, Pete and me." Geoff looked over his shoulder expecting to find Peter. "Um. Yeah. I guess Pete decided to wait outside."

The girl gave a cursory smile.

"Would tonight be OK?"

"Yes, that shouldn't be a problem. We expect a light dinner crowd. What time do you want to come?"

Geoff shrugged. "Oh, how's five?"

"That'll be great. That's when we begin serving."

"We're celebrating our birthdays."

"Happy birthday."

"Well, it's not actually today. We're just celebrating it."

"Happy birthday anyway! You'd better let Robbie know about bringing the lobster. He's in the kitchen down that hall."

"Right. Uh, I know the way."

"Don't pass the Dutch door."

"Yeah, already found that out. You know, you look familiar. Have I seen you before?"

The girl shrugged. "Maybe. My name's Bev."

"Bev? Bev Snow?"

"The one and only."

"I went sailing with Diana Baldwin, and she raced you."

"So, it was *you* in the boat with her. I was wondering who that was."

"Wow! You sure are a good sailor. You both got into it. Do you race often?"

"We like racing each other. She's very good. She's an intense competitor, and when we race, we both get better."

"She really respects you."

"We respect each other."

"Well, I guess I'd better go talk to Robbie."

"Don't forget about the Dutch door."

The kitchen fan drowned out all other noise. Geoff obeyed the ban of the half-open Dutch door. He leaned over the opening.

"Hello?" he said meekly while looking for kitchen life. "Hello?" he repeated a bit more loudly. Nothing.

Geoff cleared his throat, stuck his chin out, and turned his face in a stretching motion. "Ahem. HELLO!" He stepped back from the doorway.

The screen door creaked. In walked Robbie. He wiped his hands and glared.

"Hi, it's me… Geoff."

"I know who the hell you are," Robbie said gruffly. "I see you learned to keep the hell out of my kitchen."

"Oh, I'm never coming into your kitchen again without permission."

"You're goddamned right you're not. Well, kid, you didn't come here to tell me that. I'm busy. What's on your mind?"

"My friend Peter and I plan to have dinner here tonight. We're celebrating our birthdays. We were born on the same—"

"I don't give a shit about your birthday. What the hell do you want?" Robbie's impatience filled his glass and overflowed.

"We want a lobster dinner, and Bev in the dining room said I needed to talk to you."

"Well, nothing's changed since the last time you were here. We still got no goddamn lobster."

"I know that. I know we have to buy it. Bob Tilton, you told us. We're going to buy it from him, but that's all we know."

"What else is there to know?"

"Um. What do we do next?"

Robbie looked down and shook his head. "You're not too bright, are you, kid?"

"Well, I don't know."

"You don't know if you're not too bright or how it works? Which is it?"

"I don't know how it works."

"You buy it. You bring the goddamn things to me. That's how it works, you dumb shit. How hard is that? Jesus, Mary, and Joseph!"

"How soon should we bring them?"

"Right after you buy them. Jeez! Can't anything intelligent come out of your mouth? Look, kid, go down to the dock, buy lobsters, bring them back here to me right away. They spoil fast, so unless you don't care about having a real bad night, you'd better get them to me right quick. When are you gonna be here?"

"For supper or with the lobster?"

"You're amazing, kid, just amazing. For supper, you dumb shit."

"Oh, supper… five."

"Then get 'em to me no later than three."

"Will do. Do we need to tell you what else we want besides the lobster?"

"Hell, no. Nothing's changed since the last time you were here. *I'm* the menu, remember? I'm out back peeling potatoes, so that's what you'll be getting. They may be mashed, baked, or boiled. You get what I put on the plate."

"OK, we'll get the lobsters and be back here before three." Geoff turned to leave.

"Bring them to the back door. And stay the hell out of my kitchen!"

Geoff murmured, "I'm not in your goddamned kitchen."

Robbie cocked his head, squinted, and walked briskly toward Geoff with his long knife pointed at him. "What did you just say?"

"Nothing."

"Don't get smart with me, kid. I heard you."

Geoff stared at the point of the brandished knife and fought the urge to flee. "No, sir, not getting smart."

"What then? You said something. What was it?"

"I was just talking to myself."

"Maybe, but you were cussing at me, weren't you, you little bastard?"

Geoff shifted his eyes to the top of the stairs.

"She's not here to rescue you this time. It's just you and me, boy."

The fire in Robbie's eyes burned holes in Geoff. He knew that when cornered, the best defense was to stand one's ground and attack. Knock your opponent off balance, then run. He took a deep breath and gave Robbie his best version of an angry look.

"Ha! Look at the tough guy trying to stare me down. Tell me, what did you say?"

"I obeyed your rules, and you still jumped down my throat. I'm tired of being afraid of you. You're standing there waving that knife at me trying to scare me, but I don't think you're going to hurt me."

"Tell me what you said, you little shit."

"I said I wasn't in your goddamn kitchen."

Robbie stepped closer to Geoff. He waved his knife in his face, grabbed his shirt, and pulled him close. "Say that again, you little chickenshit."

"I said I wasn't in your goddamn kitchen."

"I can't hear you, boy."

Geoff tried to wiggle away, but Robbie's grip kept him inches from his face. "I said I wasn't in your goddamn kitchen, you son of a bitch."

"Did you just call me a son of a bitch?"

"You're a goddamn son of a bitch!"

"Well, look at what we have here. The kid's growing a dick."

Robbie loosened his grip on Geoff's shirt. "Nobody's ever had the balls to stand up to me." He grabbed Geoff's chin and leaned close as he turned it from side to side. "You're standing up to me, and all you got on your face is fuzz."

Robbie put his hand close to Geoff's cheek and patted it a few times. "I had you pegged as a wimpy little chickenshit, but goddamn it, you have spunk. I'll give you that. I like that in a person." He stood back and relaxed his demeanor. "When's your birthday?"

"In a few days."

"How old will you be?"

"Fifteen."

"Fifteen, you say." Robbie nodded and looked away.

"Yes, sir."

"And you want to celebrate it here."

"Yes, sir."

"So, tell me, boy, what are you going to do?"

"About what?"

"About your lobster."

"Going to the dock to buy lobster from Bob Tilton and get it back to you by three."

"Those instructions easy enough?"

"Yes, sir. Easy enough."

"Then get to it and keep the hell out of my kitchen and don't give me any more of your goddamn smart-ass lip!" Robbie slapped Geoff on the shoulder, turned, and left out the back door.

Geoff found Peter and Bev talking and laughing when he emerged from the dark tunnel to hell. "Well, I see you survived," said Peter. "Ready to go?"

Bev added, "I heard part of your conversation. He must like you. He only cussed at you maybe four or five times. Usually every other word that comes out of his mouth would make the preacher cringe. I would have come to help, but when Robbie's in a rage, we all go into hiding. Besides, it sounded like you were holding your own. I heard Robbie tell you to be back by three. You guys better get going."

The boys headed down Broadway. "What happened back there?" Peter asked.

"He yelled at me for being in his kitchen, and I told him I wasn't in his goddamn kitchen."

"You actually said *goddamn*? How'd he react to that?"

"Not well. He got close and was spitting in my face while he yelled, and he practically tore my shirt off. I told him he was a son of a bitch."

"You told him *that*?"

"Yeah, I yelled it at him. You didn't hear me?"

"I walked in just a few minutes before you came out of the kitchen. I didn't hear anything except that fan."

"Well, it got pretty hot in there. It was downright scary."

"Aah, that's what he likes to do. He just likes to scare people. No big deal."

"Well, you weren't there, so you don't know how bad it got. When I called him a son of a bitch, his tone changed. He actually started acting human."

"All of this because you called his kitchen a goddamn kitchen?"

Geoff shrugged. "Maybe. All I know is he stopped cussing and yelling at me and started talking normal. I can tell you one thing, though: I'm not going to back down from him ever again."

"You know, if you want, we can forget eating at the Bosworth House and just take the lobster back to camp."

"We have no idea how to cook a lobster."

"Well, then, Geoff, let's get the lobster and take it back to your new friend in the kitchen, and later today we'll set your taste buds loose on an epic journey."

Peter put one arm around Geoff and waved the other as he told tales of lobster and shared his grandiose ideas for their new adventures in the days ahead.

24

LOBSTERS IN THE GUNNYSACK

"Look! There's that Coot guy."

"So?"

"He's scowling."

"Geoff, there's no law against scowling."

"Well, he almost scared me to death when we got ice."

"You're the one who said we wouldn't get thrown off the dock if we were here for good reason, and buying lobster is a good reason. Quit worrying! No one's going to throw us off."

"He's a dock troll, I tell you." Geoff looked ahead as they walked, but his eyes kept darting over to Coot. "Pete, he's looking at us. He's glaring!"

"Maybe that's how he looks all the time. It could be the sun in his eyes."

"Maybe, but he's still glaring at us. A quarter says he'll ask us what we want."

"I'm not taking that one."

"Can I help you?" Coot's booming voice thundered across the dock.

The boys became rigid. Geoff looked over to Coot. "Lobster. We're here for lobster."

"Speak up, boy, I can't hear you."

Geoff cupped his hands around his mouth and leaned forward. "Lobster. We're here to buy lobster from Bob Tilton."

Coot pointed to Bob Tilton's shed and returned to his task.

"Phew! We got past him. He *is* a troll," said Geoff.

Peter stood at the threshold of Bob Tilton's shed, shading his eyes. Nobody's here."

Geoff stepped inside. The wall of pinup pictures came into view as his eyes adjusted to the low light. "Am I wrong or are there more pictures up now than the day we arrived?" Geoff leaned over a freezer for a

171

closer view. He scanned each one, his nose only inches from the gallery. Some were pinned over others. Some had curled edges. Some were a little torn. A few had mustaches drawn on them. Some breasts were large, some small, some long, some round, some perky, some pointy.

"Gettin' a boner on ya, kid? Ha!" A scrappy voice came from a dark corner. Geoff reeled back and almost fell over Peter.

"Came back to see my gals, did ya?"

Geoff searched for the voice.

"Tell me quick. What do you want besides seein' my gals?"

"Lobster. We came here to buy lobster."

"Well, you're in luck. I happen to have some today." Bob Tilton groaned and wiggled out of his chair. He shooed the boys out of the way as he stepped outside.

Bob went to the edge of the dock, reached down, and pulled up a submerged gunnysack tied to a piling. He swung it onto the dock, untied it, and rolled back the open end. "Go ahead, boys, pick out your lobsters."

Geoff stood over the gunnysack and looked in. "Those are lobsters?"

"Last time I checked." Bob looked into the sack. "Yep, they're lobsters aw-right. Ain't you ever seen a lobster befaw?"

"Yeah, but those are brown with spots."

"What'd you expect?"

"Aren't they supposed to be red?"

Bob laughed. "Yeah, afta you steam 'em. You've never seen a live lobster befaw, have you, boy?"

"Well, no, not a live one."

"Well, reach on in and pick out the ones you want."

"Put my hands in there? Are you kidding? They'll come out looking like yours. Can't I just dump them out on the dock?"

"They don't dump, but you can try. If you lose any, you'll be paying for them on top of what you take."

Geoff picked up the weighty gunnysack and turned it over. None of the lobsters fell out. He shook it. Still nothing. "How do you get them out?"

"Didn't believe me, did you? I told you—they don't dump out. You have to reach in and pick out the ones you want."

Geoff set the sack upright on the dock and rolled back the opening to get a better look. The creatures were intertwined. It was difficult to see which body belonged to which claw. He cautiously put his hand part way into the sack and looked nervously at Bob.

"Don't look at me! Look at them! They'll take a finga."

Geoff pursed his lips and looked at Peter and back at Bob. He knelt and inched closer to the opening of the sack as if it contained poisonous snakes. He peered in and studied the mishmash of lobster parts. He moved his hand ever so slowly toward a lobster, hoping to grab it by the body and avoid claws.

As he touched an arm of one, another locked onto his finger. He tried to pull his hand away, but then another lobster joined the fray. Geoff tugged, but a dozen lobsters grabbed his fingers, then his hand, then his arm. "Help!" he yelled, but all he got was an old lobsterman's belly laugh. He felt the claw crush his bones and blood spurting out his fingers. Filled with adrenaline-giving strength, Geoff picked up the gunnysack and slammed it down on the dock, then flung his arm from one side to the other. Finally, he freed himself. His hand was badly scored, and several of his fingers were missing. He couldn't believe Bob Tilton had allowed his hand to venture into such a dangerous place.

"Hey! Boy! Quit your daydreamin'. You're nevah gonna get lobster just by looking at 'em."

"I can't just stick my arm in there. Those lobsters will take it off."

"The hell you say! Outta my way, kid. We can't keep these lobsters out in the heat all day. Heah, lemme show you."

Without looking, Bob plunged both arms deep into the sack. He wiggled them around and pulled out five or six lobsters clinging to his fingers, his hands, his arms, part of his sleeves, and even to one another. "Which ones do you want?"

The boys watched with disbelief and horror as Bob cackled.

Geoff jumped around, panic-stricken. "How do I get them off? What do I do? Tell me what to do!"

Bob kept his arms up, and one by one they all let go. Some tried to make a run for it under a lobster trap. Others headed for the edge of the dock. Bob corralled and set them side by side. "A lobster can't hold its own weight very long. If you get pinched, just hold your arm up and don't move. If it's got you with its pincer, you'll get quite the tear if you try to pull or shake it off, and then you get the nasty infection that comes soon afta. So, which ones do you want?"

Geoff pointed to two that looked about the same size. "How about those guys?" He looked to Peter. "What do you think?"

Peter kept a safe distance. "Yeah, they're fine."

Bob set the selected two aside, returned the others to the gunnysack, and lowered it back into the water. He walked toward his shed. The boys stood watching, still in shock. Bob looked back. "Well, bring 'em heah."

The boys looked at the lobsters. Peter took a step back. Geoff would have to do the "bringing." When he approached the lobsters, they raised their arms over their heads with claws open, ready to clamp and mangle.

"Well, boy, get to it."

"They've got their claws up."

"Grab them from behind. I don't have all day."

Geoff moved toward the lobsters, never taking his eyes off them. They were poised for revenge. He grabbed their bodies and walked toward Bob, holding them far from his side.

"Man, those guys are feisty."

"Ha! You should see the small ones. Now, those little bastards are feisty!"

Inside the shed, Bob pulled out four heavy-duty rubber bands from a small box and wrapped them around the claws. The beasts were now powerless.

"How come you didn't have those rubber bands on them while they were in the gunnysack?"

"Just brought these in this mawning. Haven't had time to band 'em yet."

"I thought you kept lobster on ice."

"Could, but that's cruel. Bad enough we throw 'em into a steam kettle. Keep 'em in a sack in the water and they'll stay alive and fresh." Bob put the lobsters in the metal cradle of his scale. "You got three pounds heah. Three dollas."

Geoff pulled out three dollars and gave them to Bob, who dug into his pocket and retrieved a large roll of bills held together with a rubber band. He meticulously removed the rubber band and folded Geoff's money over the top, and then stuffed it back in his pocket. He reached back into the semi-darkness of his shed and pulled out an oversized paper bag—much heavier than those from grocery stores—dropped in the lobsters, curled the open end, and gave the sack to Geoff.

"How are you cookin 'em?"

"Robbie, from the Bosworth House. He's fixing us supper."

"Don't linger getting 'em to him. You gotta keep these guys outta heat or you can kill 'em. If you eat a lobster that dies before you cook it, you'll be wishin' it was you who died."

"Thanks, Mr. Tilton," said Geoff. Bob nodded and faded into the darkness of his shed.

Two fisherman, who were watching from nearby, chuckled as the boys walked by.

Peter pointed across the harbor. "Look! People are heading to the main dock. That means it's getting close to three. Didn't Robbie tell you to have the lobster to him by then? If he said three, he meant three. Race you up the hill."

They ran around the Bosworth House to a knoll near the flagpole. "Since Robbie's your friend, *you* can take the lobsters to him," Pete said. "I'll stay here and see if I can spot our camp."

Geoff apprehensively approached the landing outside the kitchen door. Next to the lone chair was a bucket of potatoes. He hesitated and looked nervously at the screen door. He gulped, stepped up to the landing, and looked for movement in the kitchen.

"You're not planning to go into my kitchen, are you, boy?"

Geoff snapped to attention. He slowly looked over his shoulder toward the gravelly voice. "I'm, um, I'm just standing here on the landing."

"I can see that. The landing is part of my kitchen. See that chair? That's where I peel potatoes and carrots and such. That puts you in my kitchen! What did I tell you about coming into my kitchen?"

"I was about to knock on the door and couldn't reach it without being up here. You told me to bring the lobster by three, so here I am."

Robbie stepped up to the landing and growled as if to say, "Get out of my way." Geoff stepped aside; Robbie went in and held the door open. "Coming?"

Geoff took a small step forward.

"Well?" Robbie motioned with his head.

Geoff set the bag of lobsters on the stainless-steel worktable. Robbie shook out the lobsters and slid them side by side with his knife. "You got some good ones here. These will cook up fine. I think I'll make you something special. You said you'd be here by five?"

"Yes, five."

"You'd better be, or I'll feed these to my dog."

Thoughts swirled through Geoff's head. *Robbie has a dog? All dogs on Cuttyhunk bark. I haven't heard any dog barking around here. Besides, if he had one, it would be chasing me. Robbie doesn't have a dog. He can't have a dog.*

As gruff as he was, Robbie seemed to respect honest, straight talk and abhor wishy-washy people. Perhaps, Geoff thought, all he had to do was pay attention to Robbie's rules, be decisive with what he wanted, and speak plainly. That was it. There was nothing more to figure out.

A distant *WHO-O-O-OP* announced *Alert*'s departure. Geoff darted around the Bosworth House to find Peter and head back to their camp.

"You know, I think Robbie's bark is bigger than his bite."

"Why? What did he say?"

"Well, the usual for Robbie. You know, I think he called me a smart-ass kid a few times. Or maybe he said I was a goddamn smart-ass kid. I don't know. He actually held the screen door open and said, 'Coming?,' which I took as an invitation, and he didn't cuss me out when I stepped in. Hey—get this. He stood beside me with his knife in his hand and didn't even point it at me."

Geoff spread his hands about a foot apart. "He was this close. He may look scary, but at least he doesn't smell. Still, he's fierce. I bet if he grew a beard, the only thing we'd see on his face would be his eyes. I wanted to leave, and I wanted to stay longer. It feels kinda weird."

"I don't know why you'd want to spend *any* time with Robbie, but enough talk about him. We have less than two hours. Let's get back to camp and clean up. My mouth is already watering for lobster and hot butter."

25

DINNER AT THE BOSWORTH HOUSE

Geoff emerged from the tent wearing long pants and a button-down shirt with a collar. He rolled his shoulders, attempting to get his shirt to sit in the right places. He jiggled one leg, then the other.

"What are you doing?" Peter asked. "Is that a new kind of dance?"

"It feels funny wearing something other than a T-shirt and shorts. I'm trying to shake the sand out of my pants."

"Why didn't you just do that out here first and then get dressed?"

Geoff pointed to the Baldwin House. "Telescope. They could be watching at this very moment."

"Hmm. Good point. How do you like *my* duds?"

"Khaki pants and a blue shirt… You're wearing your school clothes to dinner?"

"Very funny. We haven't had sneakers on in almost three weeks."

"Don't we look yachty?" Geoff attempted to mimic a snooty British accent.

"You look pretty snappy." Peter lifted his Polaroid Land camera. Geoff stood stiffly, his eyebrows drawn together as he squinted and forced out a smile. After capturing the Kodak moment, Peter pulled out the exposed film, and they hovered over it, watching the magic of Polaroid chemistry come to life. The boys waited for a very long minute as the picture was transformed from a cloudy nothing to a keepsake.

"This picture looks better than the one we took for Diana," Geoff said. "Shoulda waited. How about one of you?"

"Later. It's coming up on five. Didn't Robbie tell you to be there at five or he'd give our lobster dinner to his dog?"

"Yeah, but that's just a bunch of crap. Robbie isn't as bad as he seems."

"You've certainly changed your tune. Wasn't that Robbie who was waving a knife in your face just this morning?"

"Well, you weren't with me when I asked him about our dinner and brought him the lobsters. He was in a pretty good mood."

We'll see just how long his good mood lasts," Peter said. "I think he's permanently grouchy and what you experienced was him taking a break from his nasty disposition."

"I think it's all show."

"You're not going to convince me. Like him if you want, but don't get your hopes up. Tomorrow he'll be right back to his old ways. I'm just telling you this because I don't want you to be disappointed when you see his true side. C'mon, we'd better get going."

The boys walked briskly to the Bosworth House. They stood in the small foyer waiting to be noticed. Bev Snow approached with a smile. "Hey, guys. You're right on time. Your table is over here by the window. They're the best seats in the house. Robbie insisted."

"Robbie insisted?" said Geoff.

"He sure did. After you left this afternoon, he told me to make sure to put you by the window. Whatever you did, you sure got on his good side."

The boys looked at each other as if to say, *How about that?*

All around them, other diners were engaged in quiet conversation. Some looked over to the boys, nodded, and smiled politely. The boys sat in uncomfortable silence.

Geoff leaned over to Peter and whispered, "Can you hear that?"

"Hear what?"

"Nothing."

"Are you talking in riddles again?"

"No. That's what you can hear—nothing. You can't even hear that noisy kitchen fan. Maybe that's why it's so quiet in here. This is my first formal dinner *anywhere* without parents."

"It's mine, too," Peter said.

"I'm a little nervous. We eat spaghetti out of the same can with plastic forks. What could be more uncouth than that? We've picked up some bad habits. I may have forgotten everything my father beat into me."

"I doubt that. Besides, who's gonna correct you?"

"Look at all the utensils, Pete. How come there are so many?"

"Who knows? Who cares? I know… It's part of the fancy factor so they can charge more." Both boys laughed loudly, which brought disapproving glances from around the room.

Geoff sank into his chair. "Oh jeez!"

"What?"

"I laughed out loud. No laughing out loud at the supper table. It might bother others."

"You can't laugh out loud? What a bunch of malarkey. Is that what you're taught at home?"

"Yeah, you should be there sometime. No, come to think of it, I wouldn't want you to be. Too many rules. Very embarrassing."

"So... what are some of the rules?"

"Got all night? Where should I begin? New rules come up all the time, depending on what's for supper. But there's basically two categories. There are standard rules for all occasions and then ones specific to food. Let's start with the standard rules. First, elbows. Definitely no elbows or arms on the table. Major offense. Instant tongue lashing. Second, no talking with your mouth full. Third, the cutting rule."

"The cutting rule?"

"Yes, the cutting rule. OK, free demonstration. Just for you. I'm right-handed. Start with fork in right hand. Aha! Look, food needs cutting. Shift fork to left hand. Pick up knife with right hand. Stab food with fork—still in left hand. Cut food with knife. Push food off fork with knife. Set knife down. Move fork from left to right hand. Stab cut food. Eat. Got all that?"

"Man, you could starve to death before you get one bite."

"I'll say. But guess what? I learned how to eat with my left hand, European-style. I'm as good with my left as my right."

"You're ambidextrous?"

"Only when it comes to eating."

Geoff's face lost its liveliness. He grew silent and stared through the table.

Peter sat straight and serious. "I guess we shouldn't be talking about home after your dad's surprise visit a few days ago, huh?"

"Yeah, it was kinda scary. Let's not ruin our dinner with that."

The floor creaked as Bev approached with an aluminum pitcher dripping with condensation. "Would you look at that, Pete! Ice water! We haven't had cold water since we got here."

Bev stepped back and cradled the pitcher in her hands. "How'd you guys decide to camp on Cuttyhunk?"

"My parents have friends who grew up here," Peter said. "The Fairchilds. Do you know them?"

"Oh yes, of course. They come every year. Flo Fairchild is the daughter of Mamie House. Have you been up to Household yet?"

"Household?" Geoff asked.

"Household is what the Houses call their cottage. It's right across the road from the Avalon—the inn."

Peter looked at Geoff. "We should go by there so we can tell the Fairchilds when we go back that we saw their place."

"Hey, I better get to work here," Bev said. "I'll get your soup. It's quahog chowder tonight."

Geoff looked around the dining room. The dark, shiny plank floor was dustless and free of tracked-in sand, with not a dropped crumb to be found. A round table in the middle of the room was set for large parties. Surrounding it were smaller square pine-board tables that sported an array of stress marks from age, dropped objects, and forgotten cigarettes. The wooden walls were replete with old pictures, decoratively draped fishnets, glass floats, and a stuffed striped bass mounted over a doorway. Tarnished brass nautical instruments tempted guests to fondle pieces of history. The entire room smacked of Cape Cod. As the room filled with diners, everyone spoke quietly out of respect for others and in reverence of its quaint charm.

Bev returned with soup and salad and quickly left to tend to others.

Peter leaned over the steaming soup cup for a smell. "This looks good, but it smells a little fishy."

"Did she say quahogs?"

"That she did."

"Those are the same things that the sea gulls drop on that three-way corner down to the beach."

"Yep. Same thing. Try it, Geoff. You might like it."

"So, this is bird food made into soup? That doesn't sound very appetizing. I'm picturing sea gulls dropping clams on that road and swooping down to eat the jumbled guts. Or maybe Robbie standing under them with a cup. I think I'll doctor this up a little. Something about eating clams just doesn't appeal to me, but it would be impolite not to eat it."

"They're not clams, Geoff. They're quahogs. Besides, they're cooked."

"Cooked or raw, guts is guts."

Geoff sprinkled pepper into the soup and threw in a pad of butter. He opened several little bags of oyster crackers, dumped them in, and stirred. He held the spoon in one hand and the glass of water in the other. "Just in case it needs help going down."

Geoff leaned over the soup. "OK, soup, here I come. I sure hope you taste good. Once you start going down, there's no changing your mind partway." He dipped the spoon into the soup and licked it. "Hmm. Not bad. This is pretty good. Nice and creamy." Geoff held up the spoon. "Licking spoons, by the way... not permitted."

Empty soup cups, salad bowls, and crumpled oyster cracker bags cluttered the table when Bev came to gather the dishes. "Are you ready for your lobster dinner?"

Geoff rubbed his hands together. "We're ready."

"I can't wait to sink my teeth into a hot buttered lobster claw," Peter said.

"This will be my first lobster dinner! When they bring it, it's still in the shell, right?"

"Yep, it's still in the shell and red as can be. They bring nut crackers to break the shell and little metal picks to pry the meat out of the claws. Don't worry. I'll show you. Just so you know... eating lobster can be messy. They'll bring a bowl for the shells and a wet towel for your hands. Sometimes they bring a finger bowl with lemon in it to wash off lobster goo. It gets sticky and all over everything. I don't know if this is against your dad's rules or not, but it's best to tuck our napkins into our shirts. Oh, look, here it comes!"

Geoff sat tall, trying to see the plates heading his way. "Here you go. Enjoy. Anything else you need right now?"

The boys looked in disbelief at the lobster and then at Bev. They were as speechless as stones. "Hey, guys, what's the matter?"

The boys stared at their meals. The lobster tails were cut in half—right down the middle. It looked as if the meat had been removed, chopped, mixed with a thick sauce, put back into the open tail, and covered with golden brown bread crumbs. The meat from the claws and knuckles lay nearby—already removed from the hard shell. Lemon wedges bordered a small dish of a thick, creamy green sauce. The entire lobster lay on a bed of greens with small cut, browned potatoes on the side.

"Is this *our* order?" Peter asked.

"Sure is."

"But they're not red," Peter said. "Lobsters are supposed to be red when they're cooked."

"Yes, if they're steamed."

"What is that stuff in the tail?" Peter asked, his voice rising. "Where's its antennae? Where are the legs? The claws are supposed to be in shells. And there's no hot butter."

Geoff frowned. "Pete! Settle down."

"This is *not* what we ordered."

Geoff's eyes burned holes in Peter as he tilted his head slightly toward the room and pointed with his eyes. Peter looked around to find that his angry outburst had violated one of the most important rules of respect. The hum of quiet conversation swerved to silence as heads turned and disapproving eyes settled on Peter.

Bev glanced around the room and then pointed to his plate. "Do you know what you're about to eat?"

"I'm not about to eat anything! Whatever it is, it's *not* what we ordered."

"Pete, drop it!"

"No, he *ruined* our lobster. Your pal, Robbie, he ruined it."

Bev stepped closer to the table and spoke with a disarmingly soft, calming voice. "Guys, that's lobster thermidor. Robbie made you a special treat. He hardly *ever* makes this kind of meal. You must have really gotten on his good side. Lobster thermidor is *miles* better than steamed lobster. Wait till you taste it. You'll see. So, you were expecting steamed lobster, huh?"

"Yeah, I was. I really was," said Peter.

"Well, take a bite and then tell me if you still think steamed lobster is better."

"When we talked to Robbie about a lobster dinner, he didn't say anything about making it like *this*. Lobster's expensive, and he should have given us an option."

"Pete, would you settle down. Please."

"Settle down? We asked for lobster, and Robbie changed everything. He's just getting even with us for going into his kitchen without permission."

"Pete, people are watching."

"I don't care. This is wrong."

Geoff looked around the room. All the guests' heads were turned their way. Bev looked around too, obviously at a loss.

Geoff leaned across the table. "Pete, you gotta stop or leave. Settle down and try it."

Peter sat back in his chair, crossed his arms, and sighed. Geoff picked up a fork and plunged it into the lobster. Bev took advantage of the distraction. "Now, before you take a bite, dip it into that sauce. It's called lobster butter. Makes my mouth water just looking at it."

Geoff took a bite. "*Wow!* My, my, my! Pete, take a bite, but try to eat it slowly. Try to avoid the temptation to scarf it down."

Peter appeared to have quieted down, and sat looking at his dinner.

"I'll be back to check on you," said Bev as she slowly backed away.

Geoff picked up a piece of the claw and held it up. "Is this what you were expecting?"

"Yeah, that is what we were *supposed* to get."

"Well, take a bite of that lobster and dip it into that green stuff. It's absolutely scrumptious. You thought the soup was good. Wait till you taste this!"

Peter begrudgingly picked up his fork and poked at the lobster.

"When I brought the lobsters to Robbie this afternoon, he said he was going to cook us something special. The only picture I had of cooked lobster is what you described. But here we are, and we can't undo what Robbie did. All this does is show that what I said about him is true. He *does* have a soft heart."

"The heck it does. What does this have to do with Robbie having a soft heart?"

"Well, it's obvious that making lobster thermidor is much harder than tossing a lobster into steaming water. He didn't have to do this, but I know one thing… This is delicious and it's getting cold. So, let's enjoy our meal and be glad Robbie did what he did."

"What if I don't like it?"

"Gosh, Pete. I hope you don't. I'd be glad to trade my lobster claws for your lobster tail. Bev can bring some hot butter and you can still have it the way you wanted it. Whadda ya say?"

Peter hesitated, but once he tasted it, the delectable meal ensnared his taste buds, and he surrendered to lobster thermidor.

In minutes, his ill-tempered mood morphed into culinary enchantment. He joined Geoff in the celebration, and soon they were bouncing in their chairs like children eating their favorite pudding. They bobbled their heads. They moaned in enjoyment as they slowly pulled their forks from their mouths, sucking the flavor off each tine. The small bowl that had once held the green sauce was clean enough to put back in the cupboard. The tail was devoid of any evidence that Robbie had made lobster thermidor.

"I sure was disappointed when I saw how Robbie prepared this," Peter said. "I thought he was teaching us a lesson or something, but I don't think I'll ever be able to eat plain old steamed lobster again!"

"Man, you got that right. Too bad we can't have seconds."

Peter sat back in his chair and patted his stomach. "Now, *this* was a celebration. Look at us, sitting in here looking out this huge window and enjoying a lobster dinner and we're not even fifteen yet. Did you ever imagine we'd be in a place like this?"

Geoff gazed out the window with fleeting thoughts about the encounter with his father, thinking, *No, I never imagined this at all.* Chairs chattered across the floor as the last of the other dinner guests left. "I hope they're not leaving because of us. Maybe we should go so they can close up."

Peter waved and got Bev's attention. "Wow! Look at your plates!" she said. "You sure cleaned them off. I take it you liked it."

"Boy, howdy, did we!" said Geoff.

Peter looked out the window. "It's dusk. We gotta go. Got a bonfire to catch. Hey, Bev, we need to square up."

The bill sat upside down between the boys. Geoff curled the edge up for a peek. "Hey, Pete," he said quietly. "This was an expensive dinner. It's three bucks apiece."

"Three bucks each? Jeez! That's as much as our entire food budget for a day."

"It's more like four fifty each when you count the cost of the lobster," Geoff said. "We'll just have to eat more peanut butter and jelly. This was the most expensive meal I've ever had. We should add a tip. I think ten percent should be enough, and that brings the bill to six dollars and sixty cents. Let's just give her seven."

"Can we afford it?"

"Isn't it a little late to be asking that now?"

"No, I mean about the big tip."

"Better to give it to Bev than lose the change in the sand," Geoff said. "Oh, don't forget, we have to thank Robbie. And I think we should apologize to Bev for the ruckus."

"I caused it. I'll apologize. You go thank Robbie."

Peter spotted Bev and handed her the money. "No change needed. Thanks."

She waved it in the air. "Thanks for the tip, guys. It means a lot to me."

"Is it OK to go down to the kitchen to thank Robbie?"

"Remember about the Dutch door."

Geoff stopped at the forbidding door and looked in. The lights were on, a pot stood steaming on the stove, the kitchen was spotless, and the noisy fan was on, but Robbie wasn't there.

Geoff rapped authoritatively on the narrow counter of the Dutch door. "Robbie?" He stood listening for any sound that was not the fan. No movement. "Robbie? You here?"

"OK, OK! I'm coming." Robbie's grating voice came through the back door. Once inside, he took his usual stance—legs apart and long knife in right hand, ready for a scrape like a man suddenly awakened from a deep sleep by a grizzly. "What the hell do you want?"

"Robbie, that was the best lobster we've ever had. I came back here to…"

"It was probably your *first*."

"Well, that's true, but we were expecting steamed lobster, and you prepared lobster thermidor instead."

"So, what's your point?"

"Thank you."

"OK, you thanked me. Now get the hell out of my kitchen." Robbie turned and started for the door.

"Robbie, could you wait a minute? Please."

Robbie looked over his shoulder, turned, and set his knife down on the stainless-steel table. "All right, boy, what do you want?"

"I know you don't like to be thanked, but I'm here to thank you anyway."

"How would you know what I like and don't like?"

Geoff put his hands up. "I'm just here to say thanks for making that lobster thermidor. Bev told us how much more work it takes, and we know that all you really had to do was plop those lobsters into a steam kettle. We appreciate it, that's all."

Robbie tilted his head down, squinted one eye, and wiped sweat off his forehead. "Well, are you gonna stand out there all night with bad manners or step into my kitchen and thank me proper?"

Geoff grinned and boldly stepped in. "Thank you for the lobster dinner. It tasted great from the first bite to the last. Now I wish we would've sprung for larger lobsters."

"How'd you like that lobster butter?"

"That green stuff? It was delicious! I wish I had had more. I was expecting melted butter, but that green stuff was much better. What's lobster butter, anyway?"

"Well, it's not butter like you think. Inside the carcass there's a layer of green fatty shit called tomalley. It's their liver. Most people won't eat it. Some think it's the best part of the lobster—a delicacy. I scooped it out and mixed in a little mayonnaise, spicey mustard, and paprika."

"You mean that green stuff came from the guts of the lobster?"

"No, not guts. Tomalley. You're lucky I didn't just scoop it out and save it for myself."

Geoff gulped. "Well, it was delicious."

"You done thanking me?"

"Well, for now."

"OK then, get the hell out of my kitchen." Robbie retrieved his knife. Geoff left through the Dutch door. "One more thing..." Robbie said.

"Sir?"

"You're welcome." The screen door slammed behind Robbie, abruptly announcing that their conversation was over.

Geoff joined Peter at the front door, and the two bounded down the hill back toward their camp. Their day was far from over. A bonfire, marshmallows, and sitting with Diana would be a good ending for Geoff's day.

"That was the best lobster I ever had!" said Peter. "Lobster thermidor… I'll have to remember that. What part of our dinner did you like the best?"

Geoff thought for a while as they walked down the hill. "I'd have to say being invited into Robbie's kitchen."

"That was this afternoon. I mean our dinner. What did you like best?"

"Like I said, being invited into Robbie's kitchen."

"What, he invited you in there again?"

"Uh-huh."

"What for this time?"

"When I thanked him for the lobster, he invited me into his kitchen to 'thank him proper,' as he put it."

"Well, you sure have taken a liking to him. I don't know what the attraction is, but trust me, you're in for a disappointment."

"I'll take my chances."

"Don't say I didn't warn you. I'm your friend, and I just don't want you to get your hopes up on a hopeless thing. Besides, once we leave here, you're never gonna see him again."

"I'm a big boy."

"Suit yourself."

"What about your outburst? That wasn't too swift."

"I already apologized for that. It's behind us. C'mon, we're gonna be late."

They picked up their pace and were met in camp by the girls and Billy. The long dusk made a colorful backdrop for a bonfire and fun on the beach. When the fire died down and the marshmallows were gone, it was time to walk their friends home. Geoff and Diana lagged behind, hiding in the dark to lose themselves in the new and inexplicable ecstasy of holding hands and the thrill of young love.

Peter talked as they returned to camp, but Geoff, still intoxicated from being with Diana, heard nothing. When they arrived, Peter announced he was bushed and dove into the tent.

Geoff climbed over the barge and sat in the sand. He pulled his legs up, rested his chin on his knees, and became mesmerized with the soft embers of the fading bonfire. He sat quietly, confused and lost in thought. His feelings for Diana grew stronger just by being around her.

He could neither define nor understand them. He feared they were intensifying, even though he would be leaving soon and she would be hundreds of miles away and he would probably never see her again.

He thought, too, about what Peter had said about Robbie—that he was bound to disappoint Geoff. Perhaps that was true, but Geoff struggled with a more complicated possibility that his being drawn to Robbie was a betrayal of his father.

Perhaps life was not as simple as a tent pitched on a beach and a bonfire to tantalize the poetic imagination of a boy.

26

THE DOCK TROLL

"Can I help you?"

Coot's thunderous voice perforated the air and continued to haunt Geoff, reminding him of farmer Tyler's "Can I help you?" when he'd discovered Geoff and his brother, Peter, slinking through his pumpkin patch back home. The fish dock was a major social center, attracting islanders and boaters alike. It enticed Geoff, too, but Coot's scrutiny overwhelmed Geoff's tolerance for paranoia. He hesitated to step on that dock, even for legitimate reasons. Whatever Coot's intention, his tone said, "Get the hell off my dock." If Coot's demeanor was meant to keep Geoff on edge, it was effective.

"Well? Can I help you?" came the demanding voice, sounding immensely impatient.

"Um. I'm… I'm looking for Johnny Curran."

"Speak up! I can't hear you."

Geoff walked cautiously toward Coot and cleared his throat. "Johnny Curran. I'm looking for Johnny Curran."

Coot appeared to lose interest and returned his attention to his task. He stood in front of a thick plank fastened to the railing on the dock. In one hand he held a thin curved knife, and in the other he had what looked like a long, dead, limp sea creature. He positioned it on the plank, made a precision cut, held it tightly, and, with pliers, swiftly ripped the skin off. With a flick of his wrist, the skinless dead thing went flying over his shoulder, plunked into the water, and was immediately targeted by a dozen sea gulls. One gull outmaneuvered the others, plucked it from the surface, and flew off with the rest of the flock following and squawking in protest.

Coot set the greenish-blue skin aside and looked up at Geoff. "He's not here. Have you checked the Pink House?"

"Not yet. Muggsy said I should check here first."

"What's your business with him?" Coot asked in a less ferocious voice without taking his eyes off his work.

"I hear he goes over to church on Sundays. I'd like to go with him."

Coot resumed his task and ignored Geoff. His inattention told Geoff he was free to leave, but he was fascinated with what Coot was doing. "Coot, may I ask you something?"

Coot hesitated momentarily and nodded.

Geoff's eyes darted around as he scraped his hand through his hair. "Uh..."

"Yes, what is it?"

"What are you doing?"

"Come close and see for yourself."

Cutty growled and showed his teeth when Geoff came within a few feet. Coot scowled. "Hey!" he snapped at the dog. The dog's ears drooped, the fierceness in his eyes was quickly transformed into a look of humility, and he scooted behind a lobster trap.

Coot reached into a bucket filled with ice and retrieved another dead, slimy creature. He flaunted the limp beast within a foot of Geoff's face. "Eels. Good eatin'. We use 'em for bait."

"Good eating?" Geoff's mouth curved down and his forehead wrinkled.

"Here, I'll show you." With speed and agility, Coot pulled the skin from the eel and flung the body into the water. Another swarm of squawking sea gulls dove for the morsel. Coot pointed at them with his knife. "See there? Good eating."

"How come you throw the eel into the water instead of the skin?"

"I need the skin, not the meat." Coot rolled the inside-out skin over a fishing lure with a business-like hook protruding from the skin. He reached into a coffee can, pulled out a cork, and stuck it on the end of the hook.

"Those for fishing?"

"Yep. Lures. Gotta watch out for the hook. It's a bitch to get out if the barb goes below the skin. It hurts like hell, and it'll make you pissin' mad."

Geoff stood silently and watched, trying to figure out how to back away and resume his search for Johnny Curran.

"Want to try making one?"

Geoff stood at attention. "Sure."

"Well, then step on over here, son."

Geoff had never seen a dead eel before, let alone touched one, but Coot's command left no room for wimpy hesitation. Geoff stood at the cutting plank, plunged his hand into the bucket, and pulled out a slimy, limp eel as if he were a slimy-eel-touching veteran. "Set it down here. Put the tail on this side. Make a cut here. Put your hand there. Hold the pliers this way. Pull quickly and with authority. Put the skin here. Fling the eel into the water. Skin another. And another. There you go. You're getting the hang of it. Better let me pull the skin over the lure."

When his lesson ended, Geoff smelled like dead eels. He stepped away to rinse off and returned to watch Coot slide the eels over the lures. Coot busied himself with his work, ignoring Geoff's feeble attempts to make conversation. A long silence told Geoff he had worn out his welcome and his long-winded chat with Coot should come to an end. He took a few steps backward. "Well, Coot, thank you for showing me how you make lures. I think I'll go up to the Pink House and see if I can find Johnny Curran."

Coot pointed his knife toward the fishermen's sheds. "He ties his boat around the back side of the sheds. If you don't get ahold of him, he usually leaves here around seven on Sundays. When I see him, I'll tell him you need a ride."

"Thanks, Coot! My name is—"

"I know your name."

Coot continued his work. Learning eel-skinning techniques from a real fisherman was a serendipitous honor, and Geoff had survived dialog with someone he considered to be the fiercest man on the fishing dock. Bob Tilton could have been, but Bob also laughed, and that put him in second place. Until Coot cracked a smile and wiped some of that sternness off his face, he would remain the undisputed meanest man on the dock. That dog, on the other hand, could have been meaner than Coot. Diana had told Geoff that it was rumored that Cutty had eaten Wilfred Tilton's pet peacock. Mean doesn't get much meaner than that. Perhaps Coot was not the dock troll after all. Maybe it was Cutty who should be feared the most.

27

FINDING JOHNNY

The Pink House was small and boxy, punctuated with undersized windows and a gentle sloping roofline that almost looked as if it were one size too small. It was a nondescript structure, yet among the most well-known on the island. Except for a lone propane tank teetering on a wooden pallet, there was nothing else near the structure—no chairs, no yard tools, no garden hose, not even a doormat.

The Pink House was a party house, and there was plenty of evidence of merriment. A few cars were haphazardly wedged between the road and the house, and continuous laughter blasted out the open door. Geoff stepped up and knocked authoritatively, rattling the screen door on its hinges. Talking inside stopped. A woman opened the screen door with a welcoming smile. "Hi, come on in. Join the party," she said in a raspy voice. Her unruly reddish-brown hair was pulled back except for hundreds of errant strands blowing wherever the wind might go. In one hand she held a glass half full of something that sloshed about as she talked and waved her arm. In the other she held a lit cigarette and a pack of Marlboros.

The smoke-filled room was small and crammed with armchairs and old couches that looked like they had come from a house occupied by overzealous cats with sharp claws. The room went silent as three men studied their unexpected guest.

"You here to join the party?" one asked. "Name your poison."

"He looks a little wet behind the ears for that," said another. "Maybe lemonade would be better."

"Lemonade? Hell! We ain't got no goddamn lemonade! All we got here is… iced tea!" said the third man, holding up his glass. "Get that boy some iced tea!"

They all burst into laughter. The woman's laugh sounded like a car rolling down a gravel driveway, but it took the edge off Geoff's tension.

"Hey, aren't you that kid from the beach?" one of the men asked.

"Yeah, I'm Geoff. My friend and I are camping down there."

"Hell, everyone knows that. Come, sit down. Tell us about yourself."

Geoff sat and answered their questions about who he was, where he was from, how he and Peter knew about Cuttyhunk, and how he liked the island.

"Say, kid, you didn't come here to tell us all that," said the second man. "What brings you to the Pink House?"

"I'm looking for... Johnny Curran."

The four partyers looked around and without a cue began pointing to one another, asking, "Are you Johnny Curran? Are *you* Johnny Curran?" The party vibrated with more laughter.

"Why are you looking for him?" the woman asked.

"Muggsy, from the general store, sent me to the dock to find him, and Coot said he might be here."

"Spit it out, kid. Why are you looking for Johnny?" the first man asked.

"I heard he goes to the mainland for church."

The woman reached for a Jack Daniel's bottle. "Anyone ready for more... iced tea?" She passed the bottle and lit another cigarette.

Geoff surveyed the group. Why would any sane human being put iced tea in a Jack Daniel's bottle? This was his first encounter with people drunk and wobbly as an old wheelbarrow and happy about it. That could not be iced tea in that bottle.

One of the men leaned forward, resting his elbows on the chair. "I'm Johnny Curran."

Geoff stood and walked toward him with an outstretched hand. "Nice to meet you, Mr. Curran."

"Look here, guys, he called me mister. That deserves some respect. Better behave yourselves; we have a young man here who's been brought up right. Well, young man, it's nice to meet you, too. Just call me Johnny."

Even though he was sitting, Johnny looked tall. He wore a faded red broad-bill hat, and his smile exposed a gap between his front teeth. His face was round, clean shaven, and ruddy—most likely from all that tea. Or it could have been the elements. He was, after all, a fisherman.

"So, you want a ride to church, huh? I could use the company. Be on the dock by seven. Don't know if I'm coming back right away, but I'll get you to the boat."

Geoff nodded.

"Don't forget to bring your slicker. It could get a little wet. You do have a slicker, don't you?"

"I found one while beachcombing that should work. If it doesn't, I can bring my poncho."

"Poncho! Ponchos are for kids at day camp. You're not coming on *my* boat wearin' one of them. I *might* have an extra set."

The room went into a roar of laughter. Geoff looked around for the joke.

"Hey, I'm a fishing guide," Johnny said. "Of course I have extra slickers. I have enough for an army. I'm just pulling your leg, kid. Look, guys! His right leg is longer than the left." Johnny pointed to Geoff's leg, and laughter ensued.

"Geoff," said the woman, "they're having fun. Don't take it personal."

"I don't," said Geoff, waving his hand dismissively. "But I do have to go."

"Don't leave on our account," Johnny said.

"No, no. My friend is waiting for me. Thanks, Johnny—see you in the morning."

At the door, he turned to give a respectful look of farewell and received a smiling salute as they raised their glasses in a toast.

Geoff quickened his pace back to camp and broke into an old catchy tune from his favorite morning radio DJ, the Big Bopper. *"Smoke, smoke, smoke that cigarette. Puff, puff, puff, and if you smoke yourself to death tell St Peter at the Golden Gate that you hate to make him wait, but you just gotta have another cigarette."*

Camp was as quiet as the end of the day. The open tent flap told Geoff that Peter was nearby. He climbed atop the barge and found Peter on the beach stacking wood for a fire. "Hey, Pete!"

"Hey! Did you get a ride?"

"Yeah, all set. Man, you won't believe what happened!"

They sat on the side of the barge and passed the supper can of Chef Boyardee between them. Geoff told Pete about his encounter with Coot and about the happy partyers in the Pink House.

"Pete, I think they were all drunk. A woman met me at the door. Everyone was drinking what they said was iced tea and having a blast. They laughed at stuff that wasn't even funny, but who cares, they were happy. But man, did that cottage stink of cigarette smoke. Do I smell like cigarettes to you?"

Peter leaned over and took a whiff. "Nope."

"They even offered me some of their iced tea, but it wasn't iced tea."

"What was it?"

"It was from a Jack Daniel's bottle, and I think it had real Jack Daniel's in it."

"Did you try it?"

"Hell, no."

The day gave way to dusk, and it was time to light the bonfire. Peter and Geoff traded stories about early childhood—about experimenting with adult things like sipping what was left in their parents' cocktail glasses and stealing cigarettes to smoke in dark, musty cellars.

"I gotta be at the fish dock at seven," Geoff said. "I'd better turn in. Would you believe I'm looking forward to going to church?"

"I think you're looking forward to the boat ride, not church."

Geoff nodded in agreement as they retired to the tent. He retrieved his journal and flashlight and returned to the fire to scribble notes about Coot, the bad-ass black pooch, and his experiences inside the Pink House with the smiling woman and her wicked laugh.

2 8

POOR MAN'S DINER

Why today? It could've been any other day, but why today? Hell! I'm going to the dock anyway.

Daybreak greeted Geoff with the thickest fog of their trip. Mother Nature's timing was laughable. Visibility was worse than poor. He could barely see the back end of the tent.

By the time he reached the dock, Geoff was sure Johnny Curran would not be there, and if he were, it would be to tell him it was too foggy to cross. He walked behind the fishermen's sheds to the boats. No Johnny. He didn't know which boat might be his. Maybe Johnny had already left. Maybe he'd had too much ice tea and didn't even remember Geoff asking for a ride. Maybe he'd forgotten it was Sunday. Geoff returned to the dock entrance and sat on a short stack of lobster traps.

A faint gray silhouette appeared behind crunching footsteps. The shadow formed arms, legs, and a head.

"Morning," Johnny said.

Geoff stood and followed. "We crossing in this fog?"

Johnny pointed. "Can you see the end of the dock?"

"Barely, yeah."

"Well, if we can see the end of the dock, then this ain't thick fog. Let's go."

Johnny opened one of the sheds and stepped inside. As he came out, he threw a yellow bundle to Geoff. "Here, put these on. It's gonna be wet. Leave the one you're wearing behind. It's as worthless as tits on a bull."

Johnny's was one of several bass boats huddled around a floating dock. They were all about twenty-three feet long, open, with a gunwale slightly higher than one's knees. It wouldn't take much for a person without good sea legs to find themselves pitched overboard in rough water. Johnny's boat had two stick tillers – one at the stern and another amidships behind a weather windshield.

The engine rumbled, sending a deep growl into the quiet air. While it warmed up, Johnny stowed canvas bags into a covered area at the bow and untied the boat.

"When we get out of the harbor, I want you up there looking out for buoys when I tell you." Johnny pointed to the front tiller. "And keep your hands off the stick!"

Johnny stood tall in the stern as he steered with the tiller between his legs. He reached into his pocket and pulled out a box of cigarettes. He lit one and secured the box under an L-shaped lever he pulled up on the stern transom. He pinched the filter end in his teeth as he took a drag. "Damn things'll kill you, but do they ever taste good."

"Why do you put cigarettes under that lever?"

Johnny looked down at the box. "So I won't forget to close the drain plug."

"Where's that?"

"This lever plugs up a thru hull in the stern—below the waterline. When the lever is up and the boat's moving, bilge water flows out the hole. When the boat stops, water will flow back in if the lever's left open. I forgot to close it once and she damn near sank on me. I put the smokes there to remind me to close it. OK, time to start looking for buoys."

Fog quickly blurred Geoff's vision, and he could barely see. He occasionally looked back over the dead, flat sea to watch the wakes rolling off at an angle and disappearing into the obscurity of the fog.

"How long does the crossing take?"

"In this soup... about thirty to forty minutes."

Geoff sat on the engine cover while the rhythmic rumbling of the motor dulled his attentiveness when a figure came through the fog. He pointed. "There! I see a buoy!"

"Is it pointed and red?"

"It's pointed. Can't see color."

Johnny made a slight adjustment to the boat's heading. "You can relax until I tell you to look for another."

During the next twenty minutes, other buoys popped through the fog as Johnny slowed the boat and made small adjustments to their direction.

"Smell that?"

"What should I be smelling?"

"Seaweed. Barnacles. Low tide. We're close to Ricketsons Point. Lots of shoals around here. When you smell seaweed, you know we're gettin' near land."

They passed a shadow of protruding rocks. Geoff heard the squawking of sea gulls.

"Keep your eyes open and listen for the sound of other boats."

Moments later a row of docks and tied-up boats appeared through the fog. Johnny brought his boat dockside and cut the engine. He stepped out, tied it up, and lit another cigarette.

"Are we in New Bedford?"

"No, South Dartmouth. New Bedford is the next town over. We have plenty of time. You up for coffee and a sinker?"

"Sure, but what's a sinker?"

"You'll see. C'mon."

They climbed into Johnny's car and drove a few miles to New Bedford. "Ever been in the bus station before?"

"Yeah, we were here just a few weeks ago."

The bus station looked familiar—dirty and noisy. Through the loudspeaker an unintelligible, tinny-sounding voice announced arriving and departing buses. The smell of cigarette smoke saturated the air. Trash and newspapers blew around in the wake of rumbling buses spewing out diesel fumes and soot.

Geoff rubbed the grit from his eyes. They walked past the ticket windows and waiting room and into the coffee shop, where they found seats at the counter. A skinny man with hollowed cheeks approached from the other side of the counter, a cigarette hanging out of his mouth and a pencil cradled behind his ear. He cleared off dishes and wiped the counter with a rag that looked like it had been used to wipe the oil dipstick on bus engines. A long ash fell from the man's cigarette and landed on the counter. He swept it toward himself. "What'll it be?"

"Two coffees and four sinkers," Johnny said.

Two mugs of coffee and a plate of plain doughnuts crashed on the counter between Geoff and Johnny. Coffee splashed out of the cups, and one of the doughnuts slid off the plate. Geoff doctored his coffee with cream, took a bite of the doughnut, and washed it down with the coffee.

"Let me show you how to eat sinkers," Johnny said. He dipped a doughnut into the coffee, leaned over, and took a bite. "Try that. It's a might tasty."

Geoff mimicked Johnny, but a piece of doughnut fell off into the coffee and sank. "That's why they're called sinkers," said Johnny, pointing to Geoff's mug. "It'll be there when you get to the bottom. Best check before you eat it just in case it's got wings and legs."

"Like flies?"

"Yep. Flies and sinker crumbs have the same consistency. Flies like doughnuts. Every now and again one gets past you."

Geoff raised his eyebrows in disbelief. "OK, then. Can any doughnut be a sinker?"

"Nope. Only plain doughnuts. Powdered sugar on doughnuts makes them lousy sinkers. Same with doughnuts covered with that shiny glaze crap."

Geoff looked around the coffee shop, watching others come and go. Most of the clientele looked disheveled, tired, and without the means to travel other than on a bus. He looked back into the waiting room where a small group of uniformed sailors hovered around a colorfully lit-up row of pinball machines. There was loud cheering when one machine clamored *ding-ding-ding-ding*, giving a free play for a high score.

"You say you've been here before?"

"Yeah, when we were on our way to Cuttyhunk."

"And you got through without trouble?"

"Yeah, why?"

"You make a mark of yourself."

"I do? What am I doing?"

"You look new. You're gonna get rolled or conned if you keep looking around like that. Didn't anyone come up and ask if you wanted a ride somewhere?"

"Actually, someone did. When we were waiting in Providence, some guy asked if we wanted a ride to New Bedford instead of waiting for the bus. But he ran off when two policemen appeared."

"Kid, you *definitely* have a guardian angel. Look, when you come into a shithole like this, you'd better act like you lost your last nickel in a rigged dice game and have no place to sleep. Act like this godforsaken bus station is home and that cup of coffee is your only friend."

"How am I supposed to act like that? I guess I'm not sure what you mean."

"OK, look around. What do you see?"

"Other people?"

"C'mon, kid. You can do better than that. How are they walking around? What are they looking at? Do they act alive?"

"Well, none of them are moving too fast. They look depressed."

"Do they look like they have any money?"

"No."

"But they could have a stash of hundred-dollar bills in their pockets and you'd never guess that, would you?"

"No."

"If you're gonna travel by bus, you gotta be inconspicuous, and looking around is not being inconspicuous. For starters, you gotta learn how to drink coffee."

"There's a way to drink coffee in a bus station?"

"Jesus Christ, kid, you're greener than a grasshopper. Watch closely. Whenever you're in a bus station… First rule: Mind your own business. That means keep your head down and don't look anywhere, not even at the guy next to you. If he talks to you, don't look at him; don't talk to him. At this counter you act like you've lost everything—your friends, your dog, your money. Roll your shoulders forward and lean over your coffee mug. Cradle it in your hands like this. Look into it and nowhere else. If you stretch your neck all over the place, you'll attract rollers like flies to shit. OK, now you do it."

Geoff wiggled on his stool, placed his arms on the counter, and leaned forward, cradling his coffee mug in his hands. He looked deep into the mug. Then he lifted it with both hands to his chin while leaning on his elbows and took a sip, gazing ahead with a vacant stare.

"OK, act like that and you might just make it to your next birthday. And another thing, don't say please and thank you in bus station diners. The only word you need in here is *gimme*. Just state your business, pay up, and get out. Nothin' here costs more than a dollar, so make sure you carry plenty of ones. You go pulling out a five and you'll have bums following you all over."

"Yes, sir."

"I'm not getting on you. Just trying to teach you how to stay healthy in places like this. OK, kid?"

"OK. Hey, I know we gotta go soon, but I have some questions about how we got across the bay in the fog."

"Shoot."

"After we found that first buoy, there were only a few more as we got closer to land. You only changed directions slightly. How did you know they were there?"

"How did you find your way from your camp to the fish dock in the fog?"

"I followed the road."

Johnny waved his hand as if to say "may I present you." "The sea is my road."

"But you couldn't see."

"Neither could you, yet you still found the dock."

"Hmm. But crossing the bay is like driving through a huge parking lot."

"I know these waters. The buoys mark the way, and we always know the compass heading. I know where the shoals and islands are. When you pass land, the sound changes, just like the smell."

"Doesn't the flat sea make it easier to know your direction?"

"Flat seas just make the ride smoother. I have a compass, but I also know the tides and currents."

"What do they have to do with it?"

"If you don't take tides and currents into account, getting to where you want to go will be an accident. It's like your parking lot. You'll get across, but you may not get to where you want to go. If we had more time, I'd teach you how it works, but we gotta get to church. If you make the crossing with me again, I'll show you." Johnny glanced at his watch. "Got a quarter? That'll cover the coffee, the sinkers, and a tip."

"Pretty good deal, right?" said Geoff.

"Cheap enough. That's why this is called the poor man's diner."

The church was small, but most old things in New Bedford were small. An adjacent building, only the width of a narrow alley, separated God from commerce. Except for bright lights shining on the altar, the church was dark. Open windows ushered in street noise and damp air to help keep parishioners awake during the soft-spoken Latin mass. Although most of the people in attendance appeared alert, many nodded off, their bowed heads making them look reverent until a snort told a different truth. Geoff sat, surrounded by majestic blue stained glass and white marble columns. The priest's voice bounced off the interior, making it sound as if two or three uninspiring, monotone sermons were being delivered at the same time. Johnny fidgeted and continuously checked his watch. When folks went up for Communion, Johnny leaned over and whispered, "Time to go."

They walked briskly to the car. "I'm going to hang around, but I'll take you to the boat."

Johnny pulled up to *Alert*'s loading area. "Be at the fish dock by seven on Sundays if you want to ride over with me. I could use the company and, maybe, teach you a few things about boat handling and navigatin'."

"I'd like that. See you next week." Geoff hopped out and slapped the roof of the car, and Johnny roared off, leaving a trail of swirling trash. Geoff walked toward the *Alert* like a veteran who had made the crossing hundreds of times. Clarence stood steadfastly in the wheelhouse, leaning out the half door while keeping a watchful focus on loading cargo and boarding passengers. Geoff felt his scrutiny through the gray morning and waved. Clarence peered at him without twitching a muscle. Geoff murmured to himself as he climbed onto the boat, "Good morning, Clarence. How are you today? I am fine, thank you. Nice to see you. Nice to see you, too, Geoff."

Alert sent out its usual departing *WHO-O-O-OP*. Geoff found a place on the stern as he attempted to see the New Bedford fishing fleet through the fog. Moments later Bert, the mate, joined him and took his usual stance—right foot up on a cleat, body bent over with forearms crossed and leaning on his leg, hands drooping down.

"You come over yesterday while I was off?" Bert asked.

"No. I came with Johnny Curran this morning. Church."

Bert nodded. "Pretty foggy crossing, eh?"

"Pretty foggy crossing, yes."

Bert pulled out a pack of Camels and shook a few partially out of the pack. He offered one to Geoff. "No thanks, Bert. I haven't tried those yet."

"Gotta start sometime. Now's as good a time as any." Bert pulled out a smoke for himself and once again offered the pack. Geoff hesitated, then carefully pulled one out. "Before you light up, you gotta pack it down or you'll get a mouth full of tobacco." He tapped the end on a hard surface. Geoff followed suit. Bert pulled out a matchstick and struck it on the cleat. Geoff cupped it and sucked on the cigarette. He bent over and coughed, small puffs of smoke bursting from his mouth.

Bert slapped him on the back. "You OK, boy?"

Tears squirted out of Geoff's eyes. "Man, how... can... how can you smoke... these things?"

"Maybe you should start with training wheels and smoke some of those filtered jobs. Save these straights for later."

"Are you sure I'm not too young to start smoking? I thought you couldn't smoke until you shaved. I'm not even fifteen yet!"

"Well, it looks like you broke your cherry, you did. Try another drag."

Geoff put the cigarette to his puckered lips and cautiously took a small puff as though it were a demon that would consume him if he got too close. He sucked in smoke and held it in his mouth as he shifted his eyes to Bert.

"Suck it in."

Again, Geoff's body launched into convulsive coughing and choking. Bert took the cigarette and flicked it overboard. "That's enough for one day. What a waste of a good smoke. Next time I'll give you what's left of mine. You can practice on those."

"Man, how can you smoke those things?"

"Oh, it takes a little getting used to."

"I'm not sure I *want* to get used to it. They're *awful!*"

"Nah, consider this part of your manhood training. It's like drinking black coffee. You got to work yourself into it. Hey, gotta go to work. See you, kid." Bert went amidships and vanished down a metal ladder into the engine room.

Geoff wandered around, looking for someone he might recognize. No luck. He retreated to the stern and sat watching churned-up prop-wash fade away in the fog. He hunched his shoulders and leaned over with his arms on his legs. He cupped his hands, practicing what Johnny had taught him at the poor man's diner. He murmured, "Now would be a good time for a cup of coffee and a sinker."

29

YOU ONLY GET ONE GOODBYE

The three weeks were up. It was time to go. Peter chose to spend his last afternoon leading his young followers on one final island excursion. Geoff obeyed the call of his nostalgic side and walked around the island, visiting and reflecting.

He sat on his hands on the tower road wall, just below the Coast Guard tower and less than a hundred feet from their initial campsite. He quizzically studied the abrupt ending of the wall and lamented that he hadn't taken the time to investigate why it had never been completed or why the wall's footing was never backfilled.

In front of him was another vista that could have come out of a Chamber of Commerce brochure. He scanned the island and lingered on memories like fingers caressing the tops of daisies. A breeze rumbled past his ears, drowning out the swooshing sound of distant waves stumbling on the rocky shoreline. Far away, cars and people moved about silently, creating a surrealistic atmosphere that allowed his wandering thoughts to make up romantic stories. *What a way to end this camping adventure*, he thought.

People gathered on the main dock to send off visitors. Geoff pictured himself among the island kids standing at the edge of the dock waiting for *Alert* to pull away so they could make their traditional plunge into her wake.

He jumped off the wall and dashed down the tower road past the Allen House. He glanced over to the Bosworth House and realized he had not said goodbye to Robbie.

Without touching the steps, Geoff sprang onto the sacred landing outside Robbie's kitchen and pounded on the screen door. It rattled and banged against the doorjamb. He put his eyes close to the screen and peered through.

"Robbie! Are you in there?"

He thumped on the door again, then turned his ear toward the kitchen to hear past that ever-droning fan.

"Jesus H. Christ!" Robbie exclaimed. "What the hell are you doing here? I thought I'd seen the last of you. What do you want and what are you doing in my kitchen?"

"Robbie! You scared me! We're leaving tomorrow, and I just wanted to say goodbye."

"Jesus, Mary, and Joseph. You took me away from my work just to tell me *that*? You want to say goodbye? Is that why you're trying to rattle the screen door off its hinges?"

Perhaps Peter was right. Robbie seemed to have returned to his same old ill-spirited self.

"That's why, but I was hoping I would catch you not being so grum—" Geoff caught himself midsentence.

"Go ahead—say it, you little shit. You were hoping I wouldn't be so what?"

"Robbie, it seems like you're always in a bad mood."

"What? You take me for an idiot? What kind of crap are you trying to feed me? What you almost said was that I'm always grumpy, right?"

"Well, you seem grumpy most of the time, but you sure make a great lobster thermidor."

"O-o-o-h. Bad move, boy. You're diggin' yourself into a fine hole. Now you're patronizing me. Please don't do that. Good God, you're a dumb shit if you think you can pull that off."

Geoff looked down and said submissively, "Yeah. I guess I must be stupid. I get a lot of that back home."

"I never called you stupid. I called you a dumb shit. There's a difference." Robbie pointed at Geoff. "You can grow out of being a dumb shit, but stupid you wear forever."

Geoff chuckled. "So, all this time when you were calling me dumb you weren't calling me stupid?"

"You've heard me calling you a lot of things, but stupid was not one of them. Who's the bastard back home calling you that?"

"My teachers think I'm stupid."

"They tell you that to your face?"

"Well, not exactly. They ask me why I'm not smart like my older brother. Isn't that the same thing?"

Robbie raised his eyebrows and nodded as he pondered Geoff's question. He pushed the door open, looked directly at Geoff, and softened his voice. "Get in here, boy."

Geoff stepped in and sat on a stool next to Robbie. "Look, kid, I know you have troubles at home. I know about the dock scene when your old man came to the island. All that did was confirm what I'd suspected about you since I first saw you. I knew something was troubling you. You stood up to me, yet you strike out when it comes to self-confidence. Sounds to me like you brought your problems from home to the island. Is that what's troubling you or is it something else?"

"Look, I came here to say goodbye, not to talk about why I feel stupid."

"You're the one who brought it up, so just spit it out. What happens in school that the teachers say that?"

"Well, I get crappy grades. Can't read well. Don't remember what I *do* read. I get distracted easily. I daydream. When I get caught by the teachers, they make fun of me in front of the class. Even my friend Pete gets on me for drifting off."

"Einstein was a dreamer. Why can't *you* be one? The whole goddamn school system's gone to shit." Robbie shook his head. "Sounds like you had the same teachers as your brother. Is he brainy?"

"Yeah, he's pretty smart. Comes home with good grades."

"Does he rub your nose in it?"

"No."

"Is *he* calling you stupid?"

"No, he doesn't know what the teachers say."

"Your old man, then?"

"No one comes out and actually says it."

"Oh, so *you're* the one who's calling yourself stupid."

"I guess, but I think you can make a person *feel* that way without coming right out and saying it, can't you?"

"Happens all the time, but don't put the stories you tell yourself on others. *You're* responsible for your feelings, not them. What's your gripe?"

"My gripe?"

"Yeah. What's eating at you?"

"I guess I haven't thought about it that way."

"Well, kid, you first gotta understand what your gripe is. Let's figure it out. What's going on at home?"

"My father gets on me for everything. I can't seem to do anything right. He's always criticizing and telling me my decisions are wrong. I don't like his interrogations, so I don't make decisions and then I get nailed for that."

"Welcome to the world, kid, but that doesn't qualify as a gripe. So how does this relate to you feeling stupid?"

"My father is an attorney. He plays courtroom prosecutor and interrogates me. His questions sound like accusations. It's as if I'm lying and he's determined to get me to confess something I didn't do."

"Do you tell him the truth?"

"Always. I remember the taste of soap."

"Look, most guys your age have problems with their old man. It goes with the package. When you're older, you'll get along better as long as the two of you don't screw it up. He's being hard on you to toughen you up—to get you ready for the world and bastards like me. Every father raises their kids in the way they see best. If it makes you feel stupid, you can't pay attention to what he's trying to teach you. Feeling stupid is distracting. And that, my boy, is your gripe."

"You're telling me I should tell him that he makes me feel stupid?"

"That would be a good start."

"He'd just wave his hand and say he doesn't."

"Don't let him off the hook. Stick to your gripe. Do that and I promise he'll hear you. When you stood up to me, I changed my mind about you. I think he would, too. But judging by his behavior on the dock, I'd say your problems are far more serious than feeling stupid. Does he ever hit you or throw you around?"

"No, never. That would go against his own rules."

"You know he had been drinking when he hit the island, don't you?"

"Yeah, Mr. Baldwin had a talk with me about that."

"Have you ever seen him like that before?"

"Never."

"So, you would recognize strange behavior if he does it again, right?"

Geoff nodded.

"Sounds to me like you need to start by standing up to him and talking about your gripe, but just watch your timing to make sure he hasn't had too much to drink when you do. The rest of that crap you're talking about is part of growing up. Look, you're a stand-up kid and show good character. That comes from one place: your old man. He can't be as bad as you say. Before you blame him for all your troubles, take a look in the mirror. I'm not going to apologize for coming down hard on you. You're leaving tomorrow, and there's no time to pussyfoot around. Take responsibility for what's yours."

"You make it sound so simple."

"It *is* simple. You just complicate it by putting all those knots in your rope."

There was a brief silence. Then Robbie said, "So, you're here to say goodbye?"

"Yeah."

"Well, you said it, so get outta here." Robbie waved his hands to shoo Geoff away.

"OK, but I also wanted to say goodbye to Gladys Snow."

"She went to see the boat off. She's not back yet."

"I can come back tomorrow."

"You do that, kid. Just make sure you don't try that goodbye crap on me again. You only get one goodbye, and this is it. If you ever get back this way, look me up. Now get outta here so I can get back to work."

As Geoff went around the corner of the Bosworth House, Robbie's bellowing voice caught up with him. "And keep the hell out of my kitchen!"

Robbie's last words were as heartfelt and genuine as Geoff imagined the man could conjure up. Robbie came across as meaner than sin, but maybe his outward demeanor was merely a ruse to disguise a soft heart.

Geoff walked down the path smiling. *Too bad we're leaving*, he thought. *I've gotten to like it when he tells me to keep the hell out of his kitchen.*

30

LAST CHANCE FOR A FIRST KISS

The boys stood outside the kitchen door of the Baldwin House. "Hello! We're here!" Geoff called in a loud theatrical voice.

"Come on in," a voice came echoing back. Pammy, Hilly, and Billy immediately surrounded Peter. The happy group oozed into the open room as they all talked at once, vying for his attention. Something brushed against Geoff's back. He turned to excuse himself as if he were blocking a doorway and found Diana leaning against him.

"Hi, you," said Geoff gleefully.

"Hi back."

Geoff fidgeted, searching for a way to make conversation with Diana without his usual overwhelming clumsiness. He had spent many days with her—walking, sailing, swimming, or just sitting—and it seemed pointless to give the daily news to someone with whom he wrote it.

Whenever she was near, Geoff trembled from an inexplicably throbbing heart while the back of his neck prickled with awkwardness. It incapacitated him, reducing his vocabulary to unintelligible utterances and senseless words.

The onslaught of these new, terrifying, foreign feelings permeated his emotions, his mind, and his body. A mere few years ago, he'd dodged girls. Girls had cooties, an infectious malady communicable by proximity. Having conversations with girls was difficult. They read and talked endlessly about Nancy Drew mystery books, feelings, and "dreamboat" rock-and-roll stars. As recently as last year they had morphed into intriguing creatures who caused boys to give up all after-school activities just to carry their books. Those girls, once fiercely competitive in a game of marbles, had discovered the power of feigned innocence and eyes that talk. They had developed cunning skills that left boys off balance and confused.

In boyhood, chore earnings went to replace marbles or expand a collection of car and ship models. In adolescence, spending priorities shifted to buying a cute girl an ice cream soda at the local drugstore. Earning money was the easy part. The tricky part was finding the courage to ask. Before Diana, the closest Geoff had ever been to a girl was while doing the fox trot at arm's length at an eighth-grade Sadie Hawkins dance.

Diana had ushered in a new era and sent him spiraling on the most awkward trip of his life. Standing side by side was the safest and most satisfying way to overcome his malady of stupefaction. It required no talking and allowed him to avoid eye contact, which, he had discovered with her, sent thousands of volts of electricity through his body. Arm contact, however, caused light-headedness, hearing loss, and speechlessness.

Mr. Baldwin came down the stairs. "Hey, Geoff! Good to see you!"

Geoff stood up straight, shook off his fog, and gave a firm handshake. "I told you this on the boat over, and I'll say it again. A strong handshake says something about a person. Your father taught you well."

Geoff heard a message in Mr. Baldwin's words. When he was near, everything felt OK. He brought a sense of safety. There was no tension in his presence. His unexpected compliment caught Geoff off guard. How could Mr. Baldwin express admiration toward his father, a person who seemingly delighted in pulverizing his self-esteem? His earlier talk with Robbie had filled Geoff with hope, but he did not give into it blindly. He had just spent three weeks exorcising the voice of his father in his head and dealing with their embarrassing encounter on the dock in front of the whole island. And now he was standing with a man whom he wished his father would emulate or become.

Mr. Baldwin asked about their sailing adventures, and Diana playfully told stories about Geoff's initial lack of sea legs and near mishaps with swinging booms. As she talked, Geoff reflected on his forbidden thoughts of wishing his father was more like Mr. Baldwin. How could he wish that? Anxiety filled him as a black veil of guilt fell over him. He felt as though he were covered with dirt—in his hair, on his face, down his legs, and between his toes. In admiring Mr. Baldwin, Geoff was doing the worst thing he could to strike back at his father: betraying him.

Mrs. Baldwin rang the supper bell, which ignited the usual frenzy of table setting, distracting Geoff enough to rejuvenate his festive mood. Peter formed a "bucket brigade" from the kitchen while Mrs. Baldwin maneuvered the seating to ensure Geoff sat next to Diana. Conversation at the Baldwins' dinner table never made sense, because each person would add a sentence to whatever someone else had said. Contagious laughing punctuated the always jovial mood. Someone would start it; another person joined in, and before long the entire table was engulfed in laughter and no one knew what had triggered it. In the front of Geoff's mind were thoughts of home. *I wish we had this kind of supper table.* Peter was in his own domain of social comfort with his animation, engaging smile, and flair for entertaining while using big words.

Finally the serving plates lay bare. The Kool-Aid pitcher was empty. Supper was over. Geoff hesitated over the irreverent thought of leaving the table without some kind of acknowledgment that they had just finished their last meal with their hosts.

Mr. Baldwin looked to the boys. "It seems like only a few days ago I met you on the boat. I had no idea you would become part of our family. I know I speak for all of us when I say you boys have been a delight. We've really enjoyed having you. Thank you."

"Thank you for having us," Peter said. Geoff nodded in agreement as his eyes locked on to Diana's.

"Well, I second that!" said Mrs. Baldwin. "Let's clear off the table and you guys go over to the game table while I wash the dishes."

Peter suggested pulling out a board game, an idea met with lavish enthusiasm. Whether it was Monopoly or Candyland did not matter; it was more about being with Peter than the game itself. As nightfall pushed the last remnants of daylight to the horizon, overhead lighting aimed at the game table made it look like a well-lit stage. Geoff stood away from the action with his hands in his pockets—not because he wasn't welcome, but because he preferred not to join. Lingering in his head was the conflict between Robbie's pep talk and thoughts of his father.

Diana came out from the kitchen and stood beside him, jabbing him slightly with her elbow. "C'mon, you. We're on KP."

Geoff followed her into the kitchen. "She volunteered," said Mrs. Baldwin with a smiling whisper in his ear as she left the room.

Diana and Geoff stood in front of the kitchen sink, their arms touching from shoulder to elbow. It looked innocent enough on the outside but ignited a conflagration within. It was like making out while your kid sister was in the room without a clue about what was going on. Geoff and Diana were equally as conscious of their actions, but pretended they were merely washing dishes. It sent Geoff's heart pounding and Diana's breathing faster and deeper. The two teens stood side by side, more afraid of themselves than the other. They dared not look at each other or talk. Something had stolen their souls, and neither knew what it was or what to do about it. They stood, frozen in the good feeling taking over them.

For Geoff, dishwashing had never gone so fast, even though they dawdled over every dish and glass. When they had used up the hot water, they waited for a new batch to heat up. Clean dishes were rejected for the most insignificant or invented reasons—anything to buy more time in their blissful shoulder-to-shoulder love play.

Mrs. Baldwin popped her head into the kitchen, jolting Geoff and Diana out of their state of ecstasy with the abruptness of a pre-dawn bugle blast. "You kids about finished?" she asked.

Finished? Finished with what?

"Almost," said Diana.

"Well, Peter left and asked me to tell you, Geoff, that he'd meet you back at camp. We're *all* turning in. See you two tomorrow."

We're *all* turning in. Could it be code for "Douse the lights, the place is yours"? Diana turned off the water. Geoff took a deep breath—not sure if he had just been torn away from an about-to-happen historic event.

"Well, maybe I should get back, too." It was hard to know if he'd intended his asinine comment to thaw his cold feet or entice Diana into making the next decisive move. Whatever it was, intoxicating shoulder-sex was over.

The young lovers sighed and looked at each other in disappointment. Geoff took Diana's hand and led her toward the back door. She flicked off the light in what felt like a last-ditch effort to rekindle the fire between them. Darkness covered them except for the stage lights surrounding the game board in the next room. Geoff turned to Diana.

Was it time to move on to something more substantial—lip kissing? Did he have the nerve?

She pulled his arm around her and pressed his hand to her back. They moved closer together at the speed of an hour hand on a clock. Their lips crept within inches of each other. Their hot breath commingled, and the sensation electrified their bodies. Geoff pulled her closer until her chest pressed against his. Her breathing was deep and fast. Diana moistened her lips with a sweep of her tongue. She closed her eyes and tilted her head. She was ready. Geoff knew it was time. He had seen Ingrid Bergman doing the same thing with Humphrey Bogart in *Casablanca*. But where was gutless Geoff?

Geoff's lips moved within millimeters from hers. A voice screamed in his head, *Kiss her! Kiss her! Kiss the girl, you damned fool!*

"I should go."

Geoff's words snuffed out the fiery magic.

The violin music screeched to a stop.

The blue bird of opportunity flew out the door and vanished.

Diana's arms fell limply to her side, and her head dropped to her chest as though she were a marionette whose strings had broken. Geoff felt like a failure. He felt dirty for taking her feelings to an exciting place and leaving her alone without warning. His head spun. *Why did you quit? What were you afraid of?* No answers came. He gave her a puny hug—a poor consolation prize that failed to explain his suddenly fleeing from their pepper-hot passion. A million words could not compensate for "I should go." There was nothing more to say, and their nocturnal goodbye was shortened by silence.

Stepping into the cool night air felt like a slap across the face. It was as though an unseen hand were separating him from Diana against his will. Emotions bombarded him from every angle: helplessness, shame, worthlessness, embarrassment, disgrace, confusion. With each step toward camp, the reality of his actions chided him for his cowardice and indicted him for what looked like playing emotional badminton with Diana's heart. *Bad. Bad. Bad.*

31

WATCHING HIS ISLAND VANISH

"Rats! It's raining!" Peter grumbled as he climbed out of the tent. "Sand's gonna stick to everything."

Geoff joined him and looked to the sky. Latent electrical waves from Diana continued to whip through his body like lightning splashing across the sky after a summer thunderstorm. He had blown his chance to kiss Diana. So who gave a shit about a little rain? Who gave a shit about sand? He pulled on his slicker. "Well, we still have to break camp," he said. "Let's clean out the tent first and put our stuff on top of the table and cover it with my poncho."

After all their gear sat neatly on the table, they spent the rest of the morning standing on the barge, watching the mounting breakers.

"Did you know we're supposed to be at the Baldwins' for lunch?" said Peter.

"No, but that's OK."

"Hey, *Alert*'s coming in. Let's go meet it."

"You go ahead. I want to look around to make sure we didn't forget something."

"OK, but don't be too long. I'm sure Diana will be waiting for you."

Geoff stood looking at what remained of their camp while small raindrops made indents in the sand and tapped on the poncho. To Geoff, camp had become home, and he had imbued it with its own personality. Pulling up tent stakes was like ripping out the soul of the camp. What remained was the fireplace that had self-destructed the one and only time they'd used it while preparing dinner for Miss Wheeler. The icebox had proved to be a futile attempt to keep things cool, but black spiders with yellow stripes had found it to be a fine home. Now the table was the only remnant of Geoff's legacy. People would visit the camp in the years to come and wonder how such a strong table came to be.

The *Alert* entered the channel and pulled Geoff from his nostalgic tribute. He ambled toward the dock, his lively gait left behind. Peter's words, "Diana will be waiting for you," echoed in his ears. After last night, who would he be to her? His cowardice had made him run from her arms. He expected the worst. He wanted to see her and was fearful that he would. The *Alert* triggered its daily frenzy of unloading passengers and provisions, and the dock quickly emptied as islanders headed back to town. Geoff was relieved he had not seen Diana, yet he knew he would have to face her at the Baldwin House.

"Hey, Geoff! C'mon! We got a ride." Peter waved madly from the Baldwins' car.

As Geoff approached, Diana looked the other way. He *was* in trouble. Cowardice had its penance.

Peter and the gang of young people piled into the car. Geoff was about to find a seat when he felt tugging on his shirt. "Let's walk."

Geoff and Diana walked slowly up the road. Their fingers brushed against one another, and soon they intertwined. Neither could explain what had happened the night before.

"Does it feel strange walking up this road for the last time?" Diana asked, breaking the silence and wrapping her arm around his. As they walked, they made lists of what they had done in the last three weeks, whom they had seen, what they had liked, the bonfires, walks to the West End, endless days of sailing and just sitting together doing and saying nothing. Diana made the mood festive and resurrected a sense of going away that improved the memory they were making together. Had Diana forgiven him, or did she simply understand what had happened better than he did?"

After the hot dogs were downed and the Kool-Aid was gone, they all sat at the Baldwins' table as the boys complained about the strange feeling of wearing long pants, sneakers, and socks. Then Peter announced it was time to head back to collect and carry their gear to the dock. Pammy was the first to spring forward to offer help. In keeping with Peter's flair for fun, there was instant excitement over making a Sherpa game of it. They set off to their camp together while discussing who would carry what. Diana and Geoff followed, holding hands with reckless abandon, knowing they were taking their last walk together.

Islanders arrived on the dock to give the boys a Cuttyhunk kind of send-off. Geoff felt like Dorothy in *The Wizard of Oz,* surrounded by the Good Witch of the North and the entire cast. He shook hands and hugged islanders—Muggsy, Potter, Gladys Snow, Miss Wheeler, and the entire Baldwin family. Geoff glanced over to Clarence Allen, who was in his usual stance: arms folded while leaning against "The Poplars" panel wagon. Clarence looked at Geoff without expression, then gave him a nod. It was another first for Geoff.

The *Alert* gave out its daily *WHO-O-O-OP.* Peter climbed aboard, and Geoff tossed him their gear. He stood and turned one more time to the islanders and found himself face-to-face with Diana. She threw her arms around his neck and kissed him on the cheek. Witnesses whooped and whistled. "You come back to me, Geoff Sharpe." Diana looked into his eyes and sent her last message. Geoff gave her another hug and jumped aboard just before *Alert* pulled away.

Geoff stood on the stern with his eyes on the dock. Diana stood alone, looking back at him. He watched until she became a dot and faded in the distance.

"You like her, don't you?" Peter interrupted Geoff's dreamy trance.

"Yeah, I do."

"So, are you ever gonna tell me what happened in the kitchen last night?"

"OK, I'll tell you."

Peter squirmed against the rail to settle in for a long juicy story.

"We washed dishes."

"That's it? You washed dishes? I don't believe you."

"Did you see anything else going on?"

"No."

"Then yes, that's it."

"You disappoint me, Geoff. I was sure you'd at least get a kiss."

Geoff continued watching the dock as *Alert* rounded the jetty and turned northward to New Bedford.

"You know you can tell me if you did."

The jetty ended any possibility of a last glimpse of Diana.

"Hey, I didn't see your pal Robbie there. I told you he didn't care, but you wouldn't listen."

Geoff kept his eyes on the island saying nothing.

"It's getting chilly back here, and you're not being very talkative. I'm going into the cabin. You coming?"

Geoff gave no response.

Alert moved through the water with its *chica-chic-chic-chica-chic-chic* rhythmic song. Geoff leaned on the rail, watching his island vanish.

32

HAPPENINGS ON THE FISH DOCK

Three weeks later…

The *Alert* arrived at Cuttyhunk. Geoff climbed off and waved at familiar faces. He'd thought he would never see Cuttyhunk again, but because of their friendship with his parents, the Fairchilds had invited him to return to the island and spend two weeks with them.

"Well, Geoffy boy, how does it feel to be back on the island?" Mr. Fairchild asked.

"It feels like I'm back home. Almost like I never left."

He gathered his belongings and left the dock for an awaiting car with his new island family. Mr. Fairchild was tall and weathered, and laughed with gravel in his throat. Mrs. Fairchild, Aunty Flo, seemed to always wear a smile. Three-year-old Christine had been back-seat pals with Geoff on the ride from Connecticut. Peggy was Mr. Fairchild's daughter, a zesty, first-year college student with fair skin and a red-headed ponytail, and more energy than a teen on a sugar high. Aunty Flo's mother, Mamie House, made up the reception committee. They stood around the family station wagon, attempting to figure out how to stuff it with both luggage and bodies.

"C'mon, Geoff, let's walk," said Peggy.

Peggy skipped, bounced, stretched out her arms, and leaned her face into the wind, taking it all in. The two had met only the day before. The newness of their relationship and their three-year age difference made it difficult for Geoff to initiate any conversation, but Peggy's enthusiasm more than compensated for his loss of words.

Peggy pointed toward the barges. "Is that where you camped, over there?"

Geoff looked and felt the breath of a recent memory. "Yeah, right over there on the other side of the first barge."

"You'll have to take me there and show me. I want to know all about it."

At Four Corners they headed toward the fish dock. Peggy steered them up a path to the faded bluish-green rental cottage on a grassy knoll behind the Coffee Shop. Small and boxy, sitting on concrete blocks, it was barely large enough for all four Fairchilds, but a large picture window on the back wall gave a panoramic view of the harbor. Lounge chairs and small tables huddled on a large wooden deck behind the cottage.

By the time Peggy and Geoff reached the cottage, most of the "put away" work was done, and the family talked about going their own ways to meet up with old friends and visit familiar places.

"You'd better set up your tent before you go off, Geoff," said Mr. Fairchild. "Over there in that grassy area would be a good place."

Geoff dragged his gear to the side of the cottage and worked quickly. He constantly looked over to the family, sure they would all be gone by the time he finished. "Don't worry," Peggy called. "I'll wait."

She walked over to inspect his work. "So, this is what you slept in for three weeks."

"This is it."

"Looks kinda small for two guys. Didn't you get a little claustrophobic?"

"Only when we had to wait out weather. Mostly we were somewhere else."

"Yeah? Like where?"

"Well, we spent a lot of time with the Baldwins."

"Really? Dad and Mr. Baldwin are good friends. How'd you get in with them?"

"They have a telescope in their house, and the girls watched us down at the beach. One day Mrs. Baldwin brought the family down to meet us. And that's how it began."

"Did you spend any time with Diana?"

"Almost all of it. You know her?"

"Of course. I've known her since she was about seven or eight. How'd you two get along?"

Geoff blushed and inspected his sneakers.

"Ha! I see a romance there. She'd be a good catch. You have good taste. C'mon, let me help you finish putting this thing up and then we'll go check out the happenings on the fish dock. I've been watching boats pour into the harbor ever since we arrived."

August was a busy month on Cuttyhunk. The main dock was the go-to place when the *Alert* arrived and departed, yet the fish dock was the uncontested heartbeat of the island—its social barometer. Late afternoon attracted both islanders and boaters. Islanders came for the action, and boaters came to buy ice, provisions, and freshly caught fish. By midafternoon, boaters from ports near and far were flowing into the harbor, competing for anchorage and three-dollar-a-night mooring balls.

As Peggy and Geoff arrived on the dock, they overheard two boaters. "Did you see that mahogany hull sloop?"

Geoff's eyes widened. "Did you hear that? Let's check it out." He dashed ahead to inspect the glistening single-masted sloop with unblemished teak and a flawless rock-hard varnish finish. Dock lines gripped cleats with textbook precision, and the bitter end lay artistically rolled in a Flemish coil.

"Is this your ship, sailor man?" said Peggy as she nudged an awe-struck Geoff.

"No, ma'am. She's a classic, but I would never want her."

"If you're going to be my dashing captain, you *must* have a sailing ship. Why won't this one be yours?" Peggy clasped her hands while swaying from side to side like a smitten damsel.

"Opulence, ma'am, pure opulence."

"Big word there, sailor man. Do you know what it means?"

"Heck no. But look at her. She looks new, right out of the shipyard."

"If this isn't to be your ship, which one out there is?"

Geoff scanned the vast array of boats in the harbor. "See that ketch way over yonder, that two-masted job with the green hull? That's her. She ain't nearly as pretty, but she's plenty sea friendly."

"How do you know it's sea friendly?"

"Those old boats have a heavy keel running from bow to stern, and that makes them better in a storm. Newer boats are getting away from that kind of keel."

"Wow! Mr. Boat Man!" Peggy leaned back and studied Geoff. "Where'd you learn all *that*?"

"I have a dinky rowboat that I take to a pond behind our house. I tried making it into a sailboat with a broomstick and bedsheet, but all it did was drift downwind. When I went sailing one day with Diana, she told me I needed a centerboard. When I went back home, I bought some sailing magazines and studied up on boat hulls. I fell in love with sailboats and decided that one day I'll have my own."

"I'm impressed. Is that your dream, to have a sailboat someday?"

"Yep, that's my dream."

Geoff spotted a small dinghy coming dockside. "Jeez, Peggy, look at that! A quarter says they don't make it to the dock. That isn't much bigger than my rowboat. How did they get that many people in it?"

Six boaters sat precariously in a dinghy made to safely carry two. Its motor had as much power as an eggbeater. The boat sat low in the water with its freeboard down to inches. Any small wake could have swamped it. Even wakes from paddling ducks.

"That boat's gonna dump everyone if anyone sneezes," said Geoff.

The dinghy reached the dock. "Guess I was wrong. I wonder why he's not going around to the dinghy dock. Woulda been easier."

A boater on the bow stood and handed the painter to someone up on the dock. His jerking movements caused the dinghy to dip one way and then the other, resulting in instant pandemonium. The men passengers took to bellowing orders, and the women responded by laughing. The craft's captain, sitting at the stern holding the tiller of the eggbeater motor, attempted to make order by commanding everyone to remain calm. If he wasn't the real captain, he was dressed like one. He sported white trousers, white boat shoes, a white shirt, a blue blazer with two columns of shiny gold buttons, and a white admiral's hat with gold-colored leaves on the brim.

The man who had started the chaos grabbed the ladder and climbed up to the dock, causing the bow to rise and the stern to dip below sea level. The passengers resorted to expletives as the boat went down in slow motion. The captain kept his balance as the water rose to his knees, then to his waist, and finally to his chest. The rest of the dinghy slipped quietly under the water, leaving five floundering souls on the surface. The man who had begun the chain reaction stood on the dock, looking back at his companions, and said, "Good God, how'd that happen?"

A small crowd leaned over the dock and watched the drenched passengers climb the ladder one by one. One woman still gripped her glass of spirits and ice cubes. "Well, at least the important things came through!" she said, laughing. The captain was the last up the ladder and found no humor in the rescued drink. Onlookers retrieved the submerged dinghy and other floating possessions. The little eggbeater motor, however, was a goner.

Small fishing groups huddled together, preparing their gear, rods, and bait for an evening fishing party led by Coot, Joe Bettencourt, A.P. Tilton, or Lennie Hathaway.

Joey, the young ice-cutting expert, attracted a circle of spectators as he chiseled the exact amount of ice from a larger block by boaters' requests. His skill elicited applause and cheering. Joey was not only skilled, but an amicable entertainer who added to the dock's festive mood.

Boaters and islanders cleaned out the fishermen's iceboxes of their striped bass and swordfish. Bob Tilton's lobster supply sold out.

Children darted among people and lobster traps in spirited games of tag.

Other dinghies shuttled groups from anchored boats. Some brought small dogs with wagging tails and flopping tongues standing as a ship's figurehead. Soon the dinghy dock became a hodgepodge of huddled boats and crisscrossed painters.

Geoff and Peggy drifted apart as their interests pulled them. She found him when it was time to go. They traded "did you see" tales and laughed about the dinghy mishap as they moseyed off the dock.

"You know, I can't tell you how many people asked me if there was a general store on the island," Geoff said. "A guy could make a killing here during the season rowing around the harbor just selling milk, eggs, and bread."

"There you go. A summer job waiting just for you," Peggy said.

"I could make a deal with Muggsy, but then I'd have to find someone to lend me a boat."

"Or you could come a little early in the season and buy one. Someone's always selling. You could clean it up, caulk it, give it a colorful paint job, get some coolers, and you'd be in business. It could be fun!"

"That's a great idea!"

"Hey, you said you hung around with Diana a lot when you were here. You're going to look her up, aren't you?"

"We've been writing. She's off the island."

"Do you miss her?"

Geoff looked nostalgically up the hill to the Baldwin House. "Yeah. Every time I look at something, it seems like she's always in the picture. That family treated us well—Peter and me. They adopted us. I sure got to know a lot about the island because of them."

They stopped in front of the Coffee Shop. "Geoff, one night while we're here—you and me—apple pie à la mode. Do you think you'd be up to it?"

"Up to it? Apple pie's my favorite. Of course!"

"You know, the pie here is the best. It's yummy. Stick with me, Geoff, I'll show you. C'mon, I think Dad's waiting for us."

33

APPLE PIE À LA MODE

Peggy and Geoff rounded the corner and encountered a hungry mob standing in front of the Coffee Shop. "Holy schmoley! Look at that!" said Geoff. "Maybe we should wait for it to settle down."

They returned to the cottage, where a well-underway party looked as bustling and festive as the Coffee Shop. The Fairchilds had invited a few island relatives and friends, and all were deep into conviviality. The drinks were flowing, as were Mr. Fairchild's card tricks, jokes, laughing, and getting lost in "remember when" stories. Supper that night was simple—carrot sticks, crackers, cheese, and an open spigot of Scotch.

Darkness draped the island. Peggy and Geoff nodded at each other—time for a second attempt at pie.

"My treat tonight," said Geoff.

"OK, but next time it's mine."

A yellow glow shone through the Coffee Shop windows. People moved about as obscure shadows and indiscernible figures. The din of constant talk vibrated through the walls. An old railroad station lamp lit the entrance. Moths and other small bugs fluttered around it, flirting with instant death by scorching.

Geoff opened the door; out swooshed the roar from the crowd within. The Coffee Shop was a jumping, jiving, hot spot with people jammed inside like a Boston subway station at rush hour. Peggy grabbed Geoff's arm and wedged her way through the people. Shouting at close range was the only way to communicate.

Through either luck or adeptness, Peggy found herself standing near a just-vacated stool at the end of the counter. She quickly sat down, pulled Geoff close, cupped her hands around his ear, and said, "I'll scooch over. Sit with me or we may not get served."

"I can't believe this place holds this many people."

"Haven't you been here before?"

"We came here one day in June hankering for a cheeseburger, but they weren't open yet."

A waitress emerged from the kitchen balancing three or four plates of French fries on one arm and as many hamburger plates on the other. She glided through the crowd with the grace of an Olympic figure skater. When she came back, her arms were full of empty plates and table trash. "OK, guys, my name's Bea. What can I get you?" She had straight blond hair pulled behind her head and plump red cheeks, and wore a dirty apron from a rough night at the office.

Bea returned with a large slice of apple pie with a generous serving of vanilla ice cream. The pie was warm with an oven-browned, crispy, rippling crust sprinkled with cinnamon sugar and that down-home smell of vanilla. White Cottage ice cream was touted as the best around the Cape with its specks of vanilla bean seeds. It melted under the warmth of the pie, ran down the sides, and pooled in the plate. With forks in hand, Geoff and Peggy attacked it from opposite ends, each taking small bites to make it last.

They ate slowly, sucking on their forks after each bite. The remaining morsel sat swimming in pie sauce and melted ice cream. They both looked at it, both coveting it and neither wanting to be the one to take it.

Geoff nudged the plate toward Peggy. "That's yours."

She pushed it back. "No, it's yours."

They stared at the remaining crumb and then looked at one another. "OK, it's mine, but the next time we do this, the last piece is yours."

Geoff was glad to be with Peggy. His admiration of her deepened with the way she treated him, and while sitting with her, he didn't feel like a bothersome kid brother.

Suddenly he sat upright.

"What's wrong?" Peggy asked.

"I left my money in the tent. I could run back for it, but what if they think I'm trying to skip out on paying?"

"Don't worry. I can stay here while you go back to get it."

Just as Geoff was about to leave, Bea appeared a few feet away in the kitchen doorway. She put her hands to her mouth and bellowed above the crowd, "Anybody want a job washing dishes?"

The Coffee Shop fell silent as people stopped to see who was making the ruckus. To Geoff, dishwashing sounded like an escape from the shame of forgetting his money. He jumped off the stool and waved his arms in the air. "I do! Pick me! Pick me!"

Bea looked Geoff up and down and motioned with her head for him to follow her into the kitchen.

"Have a good time," Peggy said. "Don't worry about me. I know people here."

The bright lights in the kitchen contrasted with the dim lighting in the dining area. The fluorescent bulbs looked greasy and were speckled with stuck bugs. Whatever fell off plates had been kicked out of the way. Grease on the floor cemented anything that dropped—old French fries, crumbs, parts of hot dogs, and other unrecognizable bits to support a thriving cockroach population. The pull strings on the lights were tied around curled-up flypaper with innumerable dead or dying flies and gnats. *How could apple pie from the Coffee Shop taste so good?* Geoff thought.

Bea stepped aside, revealing a counter running along the entire back wall of the kitchen. It was piled high with a dishwasher's nightmare. Plates were glued together with leftover food, and glasses were stuffed with napkins soaked with Coca-Cola, chocolate frappes, and other clotting things. The sink was not industrial size like the one in Robbie's kitchen. Instead, it was like the one at home—two sections, a swiveling faucet, and only enough space to wash dishes for a family of four. Geoff had never seen so many dishes precariously balanced. *How can a restaurant survive with a sink like that?*

A phantom voice came from behind a shelf partially stacked with clean dishes and lots of open spaces. "You the dishwasher?"

"Uh, yes. Yes I am."

"Good. See these shelves? They're getting empty, and I've got a shit-load of orders. If you're gonna wash dishes, you'd better get to it."

Geoff peered around the shelving. "Gus!"

Gus stopped what he was doing, wiped sweat off his forehead with a towel, and looked at him. "Do I know you?"

"It's me… Geoff! Remember? My friend and I were camping here in June. We came to the back door asking for something to eat and you told me you weren't open because the season hadn't started."

"Thought you looked familiar, kid. I thought you left the island."

"I did, but I came back."

"Well, I can see that. And I can see that I need dishes. Grab an apron from over there and get to it."

Geoff donned an apron and assessed his task. He began by separating food, napkins, and cigarettes from the crusty, sticky plates. He filled the sink with water, squirted in enormous amounts of dish soap, and assaulted the mess. Water flew in all directions and Geoff looked like he had taken a dip in the pond, but soon he could see the countertop.

Whenever Gus completed an order, he pulled a string that went from his workstation to the ceiling, around shelving, through cup hooks, around a cabinet, and down to a ship's bell in the kitchen doorway. His system was simple: One ding brought one waitress and two brought a different one. Geoff beamed from the privilege of witnessing, firsthand, one of the restaurant's secrets from the trenches.

For the rest of the evening, Geoff kept up with the demand for clean dishes. He even grabbed a tray and braved the crowd in the dining area to bus tables. He came alive with the responsibility and felt proud to be a part of the island.

Finally the doors closed, the Coffee Shop fell silent, and the dining room lights went out. Gus and Bea sat together as he counted the money from the cash register and she counted her tips. They had had a good night.

"Excuse me, Gus?" said Geoff. "Where's a mop?"

"What do you want that for?"

"I made a real mess over there. I just want to clean it up."

Gus motioned to the back door. "Outside, in the shed."

Moments later, Geoff stood in the dark shed, feeling around for the light's pull string. Once it went on, he found himself in a mishmash of miscellaneous kitchen tools. He grinned. "I'm in the shed! Yes!" He bounced back to the kitchen and mopped up water around the sink. Then he crawled from the sink area all the way around the cabinets, brushing weeks or maybe even months of accumulated crud from the corners. He stopped by Gus's foot.

"Now what are you doing?" said Gus.

"I'm cleaning."

"I can see that. Enough of that for tonight. You busy tomorrow morning? If not, you want to come back around nine to wash the breakfast dishes?"

"Sure! I'll even clean the bugs off the lights."

Gus looked up. "What's wrong with them?"

"It's getting pretty thick up there. Wouldn't want bug bodies dropping into your cheeseburgers, would you?"

"We cleaned those at the beginning of the season. At least I think we did. Those that are stuck there ain't coming off. They're *stuck*!" said Gus with a chuckle. When he laughed, his round face reddened, his eyes became upside-down smiles, and his entire body shook. "But if it bothers you and there's time, you can clean them tomorrow. Right now, it's time to turn off the lights and go home."

Geoff walked back to the cottage while his eyes slowly adjusted to the dark night. Lights out in the cottage. No one up to share his happy news. He crawled into the tent, wiggled into his sleeping bag, and lay on his back. He reached up and touched the tent while thinking back to when he and Peter had camped in the meadow below the tower. Geoff heard reminiscent raindrops splatting on the tent as if it were only moments ago. "We're having a splat attack," he recalled saying to Peter.

Sleeping with this much adrenaline flowing in his body would be impossible. He unzipped the tent and stared out at the stars. He clenched his fists and shook them over his chest. *I have a job. Yes! Yes! Yes! Gus liked my work. Nobody told me how to do it, nobody told me there was a better way, and tomorrow I get to do it again. Yes! Yes! Yes!*

He wandered through his thoughts. His breathing slowed and he climbed back into his sleeping bag. Soon he was asleep—asleep in his tent next to a tiny summer cottage behind the Coffee Shop.

34

YOU WANT WORK *AND* PAY?

A sliver of the moon popped up over Gay Head on Martha's Vineyard moments before first light drew a defining line where sea and sky joined. The world took on a bluish-gray color as dew magically appeared on everything. Another lazy summer day was in the making.

Geoff was the only sign of life. He was raring to tell Peggy about his dazzling new dishwashing job. To pass time, he walked down to the fish dock. On his way back, he stopped in front of the Coffee Shop to time how long it took to get from there to the cottage. It was only about a one-minute walk, but Geoff wanted to make sure he allotted enough commute time. He sat on the wooden deck behind the cottage, waiting for a sign of life from within.

Tap, tap, tap. Geoff turned to the sound of fingernails drumming on the window. Peggy held up a mug of coffee and motioned for him to come in.

Geoff slurped down a bowl of cereal as he delivered blow-by-blow details of how he had washed every cup, saucer, plate, and spoon at the Coffee Shop. He knew Gus was saving the big stuff—the pots and pans—for advanced dishwashing. Peggy sat at the table sipping coffee as Geoff rambled.

Geoff took a breath. "And… Gus invited me back to wash morning dishes!"

"Wow!" That was all Peggy could muster, but it was satisfying enough for Geoff. "So, how much did Gus pay you for all this work?"

"Pay?"

"Yes, pay. You didn't work there for three hours just to pay off a slice of pie, did you?"

"Oh, no. In fact, I don't think they even remembered that we had pie."

"Well, how much did you get?"

"Um. He didn't give me anything."

"Nothing?"

"Nothing."

"And you're going back there today?"

"This morning. Yeah."

"Geoff, you shouldn't have to ask for money. They owe it to you."

Geoff set off to work armed with Peggy's strategy about how and when to ask Gus for money. He wasn't convinced of the wisdom of her advice. Working as a dishwasher brought more bragging rights and a sense of island belonging than pay. He struggled with the risk of losing his very first outside-the-home paying job over a question of being paid. Was it worth it?

Just as he approached the kitchen door, it was flung open and Bea from the night before burst out. "Hey, we left you plenty of breakfast dishes. They're all yours."

"Close the screen door before you let all the flies in!" Gus called from somewhere in the bowels of the kitchen.

But all the flies were *already* in, and new ones were already sticking to things.

Geoff surveyed the counter. Leftover egg yolks had hardened to concrete. Remnants of toast soaked in syrup and cigarette butts epoxied plates together. Lipstick on coffee mugs would require paint remover. There was a line of uneaten food and syrup between the dining room and the sink.

Later, with the dishes washed, dried, put away, and not another dirty plate coming for hours, Geoff found himself idle. Gus was away, leaving Geoff alone to either "lean on the broom" or find something to do. Those bug-ridden fluorescent lamps… They were the most bothersome. With cleaning tools in hand, his first pass at the light fixtures removed bug parts but left behind a streaky, sticky yellow residue. Still, the entire kitchen looked brighter.

The flypaper resembled curled-up 35mm film strips with bug parts from top to bottom. It posed a most unappetizing view from the counter in the dining room. They had to go. Cleaning fluorescent lights without permission was one thing. Removing the decorative flypaper, however, would require executive approval.

Gus reappeared just as Geoff finished cleaning the last of the lights. "Couldn't resist, could you?"

"I wanted to keep busy in case you had other work for me."

"Well, as a matter of fact, I do. You up to making French fries?"

"Sure!"

"First, let's get some food inside you. I'm making you a hamburger."

Geoff scarfed down the burger and eagerly jumped to his new assignment.

Gus loaded Geoff up with a sack of potatoes, a peeler, and a pail, and sent him to work outside on the kitchen steps. Geoff didn't need lessons. He was experienced. Years before, his parents had planted a small section on the farm with potatoes that had produced a bumper crop. He adroitly used the peeler to remove the eyes and skin. Pieces of potato skin stuck to him like leeches on Humphrey Bogart in *The African Queen*. Potato peelings covered a three-foot radius—on the steps, on the side of the building, and on him. Gus appeared at the screen door. He stuffed his hands in his back pockets and laughed hard enough to make his belly bounce. "You have potato peelings on your neck, your legs, and up your arms. They're everywhere! How did you miss the bucket?"

"They were sticking to me, so I shook them off."

Gus chuckled as he tried to talk. "Well, you didn't shake them *off*. You shook them *on* to another body part. I think I need to show you how to peel potatoes without peelings flying about. When you're finished, there's a rake in the shed you can use to clean up this mess."

Peeling potatoes was straightforward and uncomplicated, so how it produced three or four walnut-sized blisters on Geoff's hand was a mystery. With great pain from the blisters, now broken, Geoff emptied the potato sack and was ready for the next step. No open wounds could dampen his spirits.

Gus pointed to a device nailed to the side of the building. "This turns those potatoes into French fries." He took a potato and demonstrated. Geoff quickly transformed the pail of potatoes into a batch of ready-to-deep-fry French fries. He returned to the kitchen, trying to keep the bucket from touching his broken blisters.

"What's wrong with your hand? You have blisters! You didn't get those from peeling potatoes, did you?"

Geoff looked at his hand and nodded. Gus chuckled as he shook his head. "Never in my life have I seen anyone get blisters from peeling potatoes. Best to keep those clean. They can get infected. I think you've had enough for now. Do you want to come back and clean the supper dishes?"

Geoff hesitated. "Something on your mind?" Gus asked.

Geoff shifted his eyes and pursed his lips.

"Well, speak up. What is it?"

"Am I going to get paid for any of this work?"

Gus slapped his cheeks and sat back. "Are you kidding? You want work *and* pay?"

Geoff nodded humbly. He felt sick. Gus's reaction had just confirmed his suspicions that asking for pay would end his short-lived summer career. Up to this point he had been doing well. He had done more than wash dishes. He had showed initiative and willingness to work and take on undesirable, sticky tasks with unabated enthusiasm. And he had just flushed it all away by asking for pay.

Without further word, Gus left the kitchen. Geoff had been fired by silence—without being given a reason except for committing the sin that he expected pay for his work. Geoff walked slowly to the door.

Gus returned to the kitchen. "Where you going?"

"I was leaving."

"Well, before you go, you might want this." Gus held up a five-dollar bill. "Is this a fair amount?"

Five dollars! Five whole dollars for about ten hours of work?

Notwithstanding the fact that the minimum wage was a dollar per hour, Gus was probably violating all the state's child labor laws. Gus had, however, fed him and he hadn't had to pay for the apple pie from the night before. That had to account for something. And he had a job! It was his ticket to belonging to the island. Geoff was ecstatic. That money could pay for a lot of things—*Alert* fares, dinners, train tickets, more apple pie. His eyes lit up.

He looked at the money, then at Gus, and then back at the money.

"Well, take it!"

Geoff took the money and gave a humble bow. "Thank you! This is very generous of you. Thank you, Gus."

"Generous, my ass. You earned it. You're a good worker, me lad."

"Oh, and thanks for not coming over to check out my work last night."

"Check out your work?"

"Yeah, you never walked over to the sink to inspect the dishes. Thanks for trusting me."

Gus laughed. "Trust? The hell. Each time I take a plate off the shelf, I make sure it's clean. I never had to send a single one back. Good work. Anything else?"

"No, I guess I'll be going. See you later."

Peggy and her father sat playing gin rummy when Geoff burst through the cottage door waving the money like a captured flag. "Look what I have! Gus gave me five dollars for my work. And he asked me to come back later!"

Peggy and her father put their cards down to revel in his good news.

Geoff spent his days with his adopted family and worked for Gus in the mornings and evenings. In between, he filled his day with meeting and sending off the *Alert*, fishing with Aunty Flo off the barges, surf casting and beachcombing with Mr. Fairchild, and hanging around with Peggy and her friends.

Gus paid Geoff every day with a two-dollar bill—a common denomination used to pay sailors in the Coast Guard. Over the span of four days, Geoff accumulated more in pay than he had brought with him as spending money, and Gus gave him free hamburgers and vanilla frappes.

"When do you go back to school?" Gus asked him one day.

"I think the Wednesday after Labor Day."

"When are you leaving the island?"

"We're set to go this Sunday. Why are you asking?"

"Well, if you wanted to stay a little longer, I was going to offer you full-time work for the rest of the summer."

"Really?"

"Yeah, really."

"Yes! I'd like that, but I need to ask my parents."

"Where are they? Have I seen them on the island?"

"I'm here with the Fairchilds."

"They're your folks?"

"Well, they are while I'm here. They know my parents and invited me to come back with them. They're staying in the cottage right behind the Coffee Shop. There wasn't enough room for me inside, so I pitched a tent right beside the cottage. You can almost see it from the kitchen window by the sink."

"Well, do you need time to think about it?"

"Yeah, I need to talk to the Fairchilds and maybe get ahold of my parents."

"OK, you talk with them and let me know tomorrow."

Geoff raced back to the cottage to share his news. He wanted permission but was unable to answer many of Mr. Fairchild's questions. Mr. Fairchild deemed that a meeting with Gus was the next step before rendering a decision.

At a meeting the following morning, Gus sat around the kitchen table in the cottage with Geoff and Mr. and Mrs. Fairchild. There was the matter of where Geoff would stay, who would be his guardian, who would answer for him, what his hours would be, the exact kind of work he would do, and where he would launder his clothing.

When satisfied, Mr. Fairchild leaned forward with his elbows on the table and looked Geoff directly in the eye. "Geoff, is this something you'd like to do?"

The room fell silent. Geoff sat at the edge of the chair looking down as he pondered his final response. Then he slowly looked up. "Yes."

"Can you get home on your own?"

"Yes. Pete and I got here on our own. I've been in New Bedford a few times with Johnny Curran, so I know my way around. Shouldn't I call my parents first?"

"I already spoke with them last night. Your father said it was your decision."

35

A WALK TO THE WEST END

"Geoffy boy! Ready?"

Ready? Ready for what? It didn't mean, "Are you prepared?" It meant "Let's go." Geoff savored his time with Mr. Fairchild. They roamed the island beachcombing, surf casting, and sitting around on rocks watching the world go by. Geoff had become his shadow.

"Up for a walk to the West End?"

Geoff sprang out the door on the heels of his host. The "road" to the West End was a narrow, winding path that followed the hills and valleys while cutting through waist-high grass. Once past the dump, it wasn't much more than a set of tire tracks.

The Gosnold Monument popped into view, marking their arrival. They rounded the end of the island and began the coastal rock hop back toward civilization. Mr. Fairchild pointed to a large, flattened boulder and invited Geoff to sit.

"Something's been on my mind ever since our conversation about you staying behind after we leave," he said. "I'd like to talk about it."

Geoff looked at Mr. Fairchild inquisitively and sat down without saying a word.

"I want to leave here tomorrow knowing you'll be all right."

"Oh, I'll be all right."

"I'm not convinced you really mean that."

"I'll be OK. I promise."

"You're telling me you have no concerns about being here by yourself?"

Geoff looked around, mentally searching for a concern. "No, I can't think of any. Pete and I were here by ourselves for those three weeks in June and July. I know more people on the island now than I did then."

"When we leave, things will be different. When you camped here, you boys had each other, and during these past two weeks you've had Aunty

Flo and me. Yes, Gus will be looking after you, but you'll be on your own. You will have to rely on yourself and solve your own problems. That can be very daunting to a young man your age."

"Like I said, I'm much more familiar with the island and know a lot more people. I know how to use that old crank phone and can call home if I have to, and I plan to write letters."

"You're a different Geoff from the one who rode with us from Connecticut. On the ride over you were quiet—so quiet it was worrisome. You spoke only when we asked you something. Getting anything out of you was like pulling teeth. You responded as if you were being interrogated. You were guarded and distrustful, as if what you said might come back to bite you. Now look at you. You don't seem to be afraid to talk. You're much more self-assured. Being here has served you well. It doesn't surprise me that Gus asked you to stay on."

"Why's that?"

"Simple… If Gus thought you'd be trouble, he never would have invited you."

"I still don't get what you're worried about."

"We've gotten to know each other pretty well, wouldn't you say?"

"Yeah, I'd say so."

"Would you say you trust me more than when we first got here?"

"Oh, yeah. Much more. I feel I can tell you things, knowing you'll keep them to yourself. And I know if I mess up, you'll get me back in line without making me feel stupid."

"So, we're OK in the trust department?"

"Definitely."

"You're a ponderer. You like to mull things over. I can tell you look beyond what's right in front of your nose. Generally, you're not a big talker, but you sure talked a lot on our walk out here today. I think you wanted to tell me something while a voice inside you told you not to. Am I wrong, or is there something we need to talk about?"

Geoff turned his head almost completely away, looking out to sea.

"My gut says you want to go home but you're clinging to the island. It's almost as if you're afraid to leave. You should stay here because of what lies ahead, not to avoid something back home. And that is what I'm concerned about. You want to tell me what's going on?"

Geoff avoided looking into Mr. Fairchild's eyes, knowing he had been found out in a lie and that his eyes would only confirm the truth.

Mr. Fairchild continued. "After your camping trip with Peter, you took the initiative to come to our house with your journal and shared the details of your trip with Aunty Flo. You bounced with excitement. We thought you'd like to experience Cuttyhunk again. But when we met with your parents to talk about you returning with us, you stood in the background, appearing disinterested. When we saw your reaction, we wondered if we were doing the right thing."

"Oh, I was very excited about coming back. I just didn't want to show it until I knew my father was going to give me permission."

"Well, Geoff, you didn't show much more *after* your father gave it. It looked as if your parents were more excited about it than you were. When I spoke with your father the other day, I assured him you'd be OK here. That put some of the responsibility on me. Help me understand what you're thinking, and maybe I'll be less concerned about leaving you here alone."

Geoff sighed deeply as he looked away. Mr. Fairchild sat quietly while Geoff fidgeted. He looked over to Mr. Fairchild and offered a painted-on smile, then shrugged and turned back to the sea.

"OK, let me help. You know, Geoff, when I was about your age, the only thing I wanted was my freedom. My dad wouldn't give it to me. He said I was too young and would abuse it. He kept a tight rein on me. The nerve! I was fifteen. I was a man! At least I thought I was, yet he treated me like a boy. We were on opposite sides of the playing field, with nothing in common. I shared my problems with other boys when we gathered after school, and we ruthlessly bashed our fathers. Our anger fed off one another. And somewhere across town, there was my dad. All he wanted was to raise his children to be good citizens. He was strict about how I showed respect for others—regardless of their color, religion, or where they came from. He went out of his way to make sure I didn't latch on to the wrong values.

"One day my friend's dad overheard me badmouthing my dad. He challenged me with questions, but I clammed up. I thought it was OK to talk about my dad with my friends, but talking about him to an adult felt like a betrayal. One of the top values we learned as kids was respect. That was the day I learned I had crossed the line. I was wrong for talking about my father that way."

Geoff turned to Mr. Fairchild. "What did you do then?"

"As much as I resented my dad, deep down inside I loved him. Can you imagine the personal conflict *that* caused? When challenged by my friend's dad, I couldn't look him in the eye. I remember that day well. I felt so bad. It was a turning point. We owe our parents respect, and the worst way to betray them is by being disloyal. That day I had come within inches of doing just that. I was so ashamed for what I had done."

"How did you get over it?"

"I'm not sure if 'getting over it' is the right choice of words. It was more like learning from it. Time usually takes care of most issues. That is, if you let it."

"What do you mean when you say, 'let it'?"

"With my dad, I actually had to work at being angry and resentful. When I stopped talking and thinking about it, the big chip on my shoulder fell off. When I quit focusing on my anger, it went away. Over time, I forgot most of the reasons why I didn't like my dad, and the ones I remembered just didn't matter any longer."

"So, you're telling me this because you think I have problems with my father?"

"Think? Ha! I *know*. Your behavior around your dad is almost the same as mine around my dad at your age. My dad had more rules than I could remember. He was a perfectionist. He'd blow up if something was out of place or not done to his liking. He questioned and overturned all my decisions and went out of his way to tell me why they were bad. Nothing was ever good enough. My thinking was always shortsighted. Can you imagine what that did to me over time?"

"Yes! Yes, I can! But what changed for you?"

"The change was slow. It's not like I woke up one day and everything was fine. I think it began when someone complimented me on a behavior, telling me I must have had good upbringing, and it came at a time when I thought my upbringing was neglectful. When I was in my twenties, I concluded that I'd been hating my dad because all he wanted to do was give me the tools to make me a good man. Is that dumb or what!"

Geoff slowly looked up at Mr. Fairchild and whispered, "You know, don't you?"

"Geoff, I know where you are, and I know it makes you hurt. It makes you angry. You wonder if there will ever be an end to it. No sooner do you want him to vanish than you want him back. You don't want him watching the game, but you look for him in the bleachers. You want to trust him, but you fear rejection or that he'll use it against you. You desperately want him to be a dad and fear you don't have one. Am I right?"

Mr. Fairchild put his hand on Geoff's shoulder, and Geoff let out a deep sigh. Then he said softly, "You know he came to the island, right?"

"Yes, I know about it."

"On the day he came here, people got me off the dock, fed my father lunch, and put him back on the boat. I waved to him from the channel. I know he saw me, but he didn't wave back. I just wanted to cry, but my friend Diana was with me. I was afraid to go home at the end of our camping trip. I didn't know what to expect. It was strange, though. Everything at home was normal. It was like he'd never come to the island. I started believing I had imagined the whole thing. Nobody mentioned it. Not a single word. I tiptoed around, worrying that he would jump all over me again, but it never came up.

"I don't get it. Except for my kid sister, not one person at home seemed interested in my time here. Pop seemed like the same person I had left. I had hoped things would change, but nothing did. I just gave up. What does he want of me?"

"Geoff, you know that your father was drinking on the day he arrived, don't you?"

"Yes, I was told that, and I still don't know why he came all the way out here."

"He was angry."

"What did I do to make him so mad?"

"He wasn't angry with you. He was angry with himself."

Geoff chuckled dismissively.

"You don't believe me, but let me give you another perspective. The other day you told me that Peter called and told his mother you had a new home here. Is that right?"

Geoff nodded.

"Whatever your father told you the day he came was *not* what was on his mind. He thought the island was taking you away from him. He was afraid he was losing you."

"How do you know that?"

"We agreed we were OK in the trust department, right? I know that because I know things. What he did that day was not done out of anger. It was done out of love and desperation over the thought of losing you. You asked what he wanted of you. That is a question you'll have to ask him, but I can tell you this… Whatever answer he gives will come only from good intentions. You may think the way he goes about it is all wrong, but trust me on this, all he wants for you is the best."

"If he wants the best for me, why does he make me feel so stupid all the time? When will it change? When will he start respecting my decisions and trusting me to do the right things?"

"He already has."

"When?"

"He trusted you enough to come here, didn't he? And just the other day he said the decision to stay on, working for Gus, was entirely yours."

"Yeah, he did, didn't he? He gave me permission to come here in June, but why did I go home to the same old criticism and interrogation about decisions? Why didn't he say anything about the day he came? Now he's given me permission to stay another few weeks. I see what you're saying, but I don't get it. What am I supposed to believe?"

"That, my boy, is one of those problems that only time can solve. Patience is part of maturity, so take a good bite of it. I think you're focusing on his methods and that's blinding your ability to see his good intentions. The sooner you start looking for the good he wants for you, the sooner you'll move that relationship to where you'd like to see it. Right now, you have a decision to make—stay here or come home with us. Stay only if it's to go to something, not to get away from something. Think about it and let me know tomorrow."

Mr. Fairchild looked out to sea. The wind began to settle, and the sea responded with calmness. "It's beginning to feel like the day is getting away from us. We've got packing to do. We'd better get moving."

Geoff didn't understand everything Mr. Fairchild had said, but he did regard him as a trustworthy confidant. Back home, Mr. Fairchild was only a short bike ride away, and he could be a good ally. Perhaps time would peel back the layers of wisdom he had shared. Maybe, Geoff thought, his father wasn't so bad after all.

36

THE EVER-SHRINKING *ALERT*

Geoff crawled out of his tent and stretched to welcome the new day. When he stepped into the cottage, a well-organized row of suitcases and tied-up boxes blasted him with a shot of reality—the Fairchilds *were* leaving. He stared somberly at the baggage and glanced up to Mr. Fairchild, who studied him as though he were something under a microscope.

"Geoff, you can change your mind. You can jump on the *Alert* with us and no one will think less of you. What's it going to be?"

"I'm staying."

"Why?"

"Because there's still plenty of adventure in what's left of the summer."

Mamie House came for the luggage. With all the helping hands, car loading went fast. The Fairchilds walked to the main dock. Conversations among family members were mere words on Geoff's deaf ears. He remained unusually quiet and preoccupied.

The goodbye crowd quickly bulged to the edges of the pier. Navigating around luggage and boxes was a daunting challenge as the normally courteous masses focused on last-minute hugs and well-wishing. Geoff stood close to the Fairchilds, staring at the *Alert*. Greeting and sending off the *Alert* was always exciting, but knowing it was about to take loved ones away made him somber.

"OK," said Mr. Fairchild. "Time to say our goodbyes." He turned to Geoff and gave him a firm handshake. "You'll do well, young man. We'll tell your folks you said hello. Look us up when you get home."

Christine climbed halfway up Geoff's leg, and he lifted her into his arms and high over his head. "I'm gonna miss you, little one."

Peggy gave Geoff a hug. "Think of me when you're eating apple pie à la mode." She touched the tip of his nose and turned toward the *Alert*.

Flo smiled at Geoff and pulled him close. "I *really* liked having you here with us. You'll be fine."

Alert sent out its daily *WHO-O-O-OP* that ended all long good-byes. She had a schedule to keep. Islanders untied the dock lines, and *Alert* slowly turned and chugged toward the channel. Geoff focused on the ever-shrinking *Alert*. The Fairchilds stood astern, waving until she turned into the bay beyond the jetty. Then she was gone.

A few islanders walked by and stopped for a chat. They meant well with "I hear you're working at the Coffee Shop," or "Well, it looks like you're on your own now," but it did little to ease his growing anxiety over being left by himself. He rubbed his fingers through his hair thinking, *maybe I shoulda gone home with them.* When he turned to leave, he spotted Muggsy leaning against a shed, his arms folded. He looked like the hero in a mystery movie keeping a watchful eye from a dark corner.

"Muggsy!"

Muggsy said nothing but kept his eyes on Geoff.

"Hey, do you think I made the right decision?"

Muggsy stepped toward Geoff, then looked briefly out to the bay and back at him. "Folks worry too much about decisions *after* they make 'em. There's no doubt in my mind that your choice will prove to be a good one. C'mon, I'll give you a ride."

They climbed into Muggsy's truck and headed up the road. Geoff vanished in thought, absorbed with the beach by the barges and the oat grass swaying along the roadside. His world fell silent, as if someone had stuffed cotton in his ears. For once, Geoff, a person who frequently talked out loud to himself, had nothing to say.

Muggsy dropped Geoff off at Four Corners. He walked toward the dock and turned up the driveway alongside the Coffee Shop. He stood at the top of the knoll and looked pensively at the cottage, now empty of loved ones.

"Hey, Geoff!" yelled Gus.

Geoff went into the Coffee Shop.

"I have some bad news for you. I happened to be standing outside when the new renters from the cottage came over asking about your tent. I told them you were working for me and the only time you'd be there was when you slept. It made no difference to them. They don't like it and want you to move. I hate to tell you this, but you're gonna have to move your tent and do it today while there's still daylight. There's no place to put it on this property. I could ask some of the islanders if you could put it on their grass, or you might want to go back to the beach. Any thoughts?"

"Wow!" Geoff sighed deeply and gazed out the back window.

"I know this is a blow for you. I had no idea the new renters would object. For tonight you'll have to move your tent, and tomorrow when Bob Tilton returns to the island, I'll ask him if you can stay in one of the rooms in his house."

"No. I'll move back to the beach. I'm OK with it."

Geoff stood over his tent. It sagged in the middle, looking forgotten. The comfort of his happy little place in the world had been instantly turned upside down. At least he was familiar with the beach.

Geoff crawled into his tent and quickly stuffed everything into his duffel and rolled up his sleeping bag. With a few kicks and pulls on the stakes, the tent went flat. Minutes later he donned his knapsack, put the sleeping bag and duffel under his arm, and balanced the tent on his shoulder. "Now, this is how we shoulda moved to the beach from the top of the hill, instead of using that damned stretcher," he said out loud.

Gus intercepted Geoff as he passed the Coffee Shop. "I made you a sandwich, just in case you don't get back here before we close. I'll be around if you need anything, otherwise I'll see you in the morning."

Partway to the beach, Geoff heard the familiar sound of loose chassis springs, a rumbling muffler belching carbon monoxide, and squeaking brakes.

"Want a ride?" said a smiling Potter in his usual gravelly voice.

Geoff tossed his gear into the bed of Potter's truck, wiggled onto the tailgate, and slapped the side fender to let Potter know he was safely on board. Once at the dock, he walked up the sandy road to his old home by the barges.

The once-hallowed ground had already returned to Mother Nature, and the table that he'd thought would "last for years to come" must have gone to feeding a bonfire during a Coast Guard beach party. All that remained of the old campsite was the narrow valley between the barge and a sand dune, a few round "hearth" stones half buried in the sand, and memories from what seemed like long, long ago.

Within minutes the tent was taut, the sleeping bag was unrolled, and his personal effects were laid out. Geoff pulled out his journal and set it on top of the barge. He looked out to Vineyard Sound and over to Gay Head, searching for literary inspiration. He began scribbling.

Fairchilds left today. Sorry to see them go. Thought I was going to camp next to Coffee Shop, but new renters kicked me out. Back here at old camp. Everything different...

Geoff wiggled his pen between his thumb and index finger, trying to pry a noteworthy something out of his wandering thoughts.

Feeling alone out here. Am not afraid like before, but I don't feel at home. Maybe tomorrow. Maybe I should have left, but here I am. I don't understand my feelings. Would rather be camping by the cottage.

Geoff normally ran short on writing space for the day's activities, but there remained a half-empty page, and he was out of reportable news even though there was a lot to say. He chuckled as a thought came into his head and continued.

Peter's not here. I can write whatever I want! He can't see. Ha!

Geoff laid the pen on the pages and closed the journal.

The island was quiet. He walked to the fish dock, passing the closed-up Coffee Shop. He sat on a lobster trap and pulled a smooshed sandwich from his pocket. He looked at it and chuckled. *This isn't mom's fried chicken, but I'm famished!* Nightlife on the dock consisted of watching the bright hot lights tease moths and gnats, daring them to die. Waves lapped at the waterline on boats tied to the dock. The soft breeze made that distinctive lullaby sound from halyards slapping against the masts of rocking sailboats. Geoff listened for boaters, night walkers, dogs—anything that moved—but he was the only one stirring. Mr. Fairchild's words, "you'll be on your own," echoed in his head and took on new meaning.

As he walked back to camp, that old feeling of homesickness seeped back into his soul. He turned in feeling alone and forgotten. That new chapter of adventure that drove his decision to stay... Well, it would have to wait till morning.

37

THE ABLE KITCHEN BOY

Gus took advantage of his enthusiastic, can-do-anything, able kitchen boy. When Gus wasn't assigning him tasks, Geoff assigned them to himself. In between washing dishes, pots, pans, stove tops, fryers, and grease buckets, he kept the kitchen spotless. He removed the sticky yellow film from the walls and ceiling, chipped away all the food cemented under the cabinet kickboards, and even scraped a summer's worth of errant food from the sides of the stove. When he cleaned all there was to clean in the kitchen, he took his crusade into the dining room.

Two weeks as a kitchen boy did not restrict his activities. The "other duties as assigned" on Geoff's imaginary job description filled his time with rewarding experiences.

* * *

How much better could New England quahog chowder be than when it was made from freshly gathered quahogs? Gus escorted Geoff to the fish dock, handed him a long handled rake-like tool, and a set of oars, and pointed him to an algae-encrusted flat-bottom rowboat tied to the dinghy dock behind the sheds. He gave Geoff instructions and a collection pail, and pushed his boat away.

"Hey! You on the boat… Whatcha doin'?" yelled a young teenage girl. She stood in the shallows with water at midcalf and blue jeans rolled up to her knees. A kerchief kept her hair out of her face, and she balanced a basket on her hip.

"Quahogging. What are *you* doing?"

"Same thing you're doing, but one of us is workin' up a sweat, and it ain't me. You look like you're makin' a lot of work for yourself. C'mon ovah."

Geoff pulled the rake into the boat and rowed as close to the girl as shallow water permitted.

"You're quahogging? How do you get them up?"

"I feel 'em with my toes and reach down."

"You put your feet into the muck?"

"Ha! Try it for yourself."

Geoff slipped into the water and waded toward her. He watched as she wiggled her foot in the muck and brought up a black, muddy quahog. She swished it around in the water and put it in her basket. Geoff tentatively dug his foot into the soft muck. "It's cold."

"Aw, don't be a sissy. Dig in!"

Geoff winced and poked his foot back into the muck, where he felt something hard. He reached for it, pulled up his very first quahog, and held it over his head as though he'd found a gold doubloon.

The girl gave a full belly laugh. "Nice rock!"

In a second attempt, Geoff pulled up the real deal. The girl cheered and laughed heartily. She slapped his arm. "See there, you can do it. How come you're collectin' so many?"

"I'm working at the Coffee Shop, and Gus sent me out to gather them for chowder."

"Coffee Shop, eh? Well, guess I'll see you again then."

Geoff climbed back into his boat. "Hey, I don't know your name."

"Donna. I come down heah all the time." She waved and waded toward shore.

Geoff arrived at the Coffee Shop with a bucket filled with quahogs, put them on the kitchen steps, and set out to find his boss for more instructions. Gus explained the art of holding and shucking quahogs, but Geoff accidentally knocked the bucket that triggered squeezing sounds as the entire batch tightened down their shells.

"Well, you just warned them we were coming," Gus said. "Now you have to sit and wait for them to relax. You'll slice off your thumb if you try it now."

Geoff waited and waited and waited. He slowly picked one out of the bucket and shucked it. He could not believe what he was seeing. What Gus identified as "meat" looked like slimy guts. Some of the guts were brown, some white, some green. If folks only knew. He was not making quahog chowder. He was making slimy gut soup.

A neophyte sticking his hand into the shucked quahog-gut bowl to feed the grinder required a strong constitution. Over time, Geoff could reach into it without gagging or making facial contortions. Customers described the Coffee Shop's chowder as "watered-down potato soup." It was, understandably, unpopular with the locals, and several times Gus gave the order to "deep-six" moldy green chowder into the pond after it had been forgotten in the back of the refrigerator. When Wilfred Tilton caught Geoff doing so, he bellowed from his porch, "If what you're pitching kills any of my ducks, I'll have your ass."

* * *

Geoff's skills at French fry preparation improved significantly, judging by the absence of blisters on his hands and the lack of peelings clinging to the side of the building. A week into Geoff's time working, Gus presented him with a "present," a time-saving potato-peeling machine. The process was simple: Dump in whole potatoes, turn on the water supply, and wait while a gritty abrasive disc at the bottom tumbled away the outer skin of the tuber. Potato peeling couldn't be easier. He loaded the device, stepped away momentarily to attend to another task, and returned to "peeled" potatoes the size of small marbles. That was the first and last time Gus permitted Geoff to use that new-fangled potato peeling machine.

* * *

Bob Tilton kept the Coffee Shop supplied with fresh lobster and routinely brought them after dark several times weekly. He appeared at the kitchen door with two gunnysacks draped over his shoulder. In the sacks were fresh and very much alive lobsters that required steaming, shelling, chopping, and carcass discarding – all in the same evening.

"Geoff," said Gus, "tonight you learn about steaming lobster."

Geoff opened the sack and peered in. "Dang! These lobsters are small."

Bob and Gus lunged at Geoff while looking around to see if anyone had heard his forbidden observation. "Boy, you keep your mouth shut and do as you're told," Bob said through gritted teeth.

After Bob left, Geoff looked to Gus. "What did I do?"

Gus shifted his eyes around and said softly, "You have to throw back any lobster shorter than three inches from the rostrum to the tail. They're called 'shorts.' If the Fish and Game Department caught Bob with them, there'd be huge fines and he might have to do jail time. That's why Bob brings them around closing time. Those guys snoop around here often, so don't ever say anything about shorts again."

* * *

Geoff bounced into work one morning to find Gus working as both breakfast cook and waiter. Sweat rolled down his red face and soaked the neck of his white T-shirt—not a very appetizing sight. Geoff quickly donned an apron, took to cleaning tables, and assigned himself the task of breakfast waiter. Time to shine.

Gus let Geoff loose on the hungry breakfast crowd. He zipped around the dining room like Bea, the regular waitress. He kept coffee mugs filled to the brim and gathered dirty dishes on his way back to the kitchen. All was going well. He was a natural.

Gus rang the "ready" bell for a breakfast order for the party of four in a corner booth. He delivered two plates of hotcakes to the women. "Where's ours?" asked one of the men.

"It's ready in the kitchen. I'm going back for it now."

"What's your problem? Any waiter worth his salt could bring an entire order in one trip."

Jerk, Geoff thought.

By the time he returned, the women were sampling their hotcakes swimming in butter and Gus's homemade syrup. "Yummy," one said.

"Glad you like it, ma'am."

"C'mon, boy. Food's getting cold."

Geoff quickly placed the fried eggs in front of one customer and, while setting the poached eggs in front of the other, discovered that toast does not cling to angled plates as well as eggs. The toast slid toward the man. The poached egg lost its grip on the toast, and both toast and egg told a story that would not end well. The man attempted to grab the egg, but the hot broken yoke oozed through his fingers, down his hands, and onto his shirt, ending in a pool of yellow goo in his lap. He stood quickly, jolting the table, which overturned water glasses and coffee mugs. Fast-moving hands attempting to stabilize the disaster only led to more damage. Within seconds, the entire table was a wasteland of spills and watered-down food.

"You idiot! You complete imbecile! You did that on purpose."

Geoff raced to the kitchen and returned with damp towels.

"Are there any competent waiters in this joint?"

"No," Geoff said, meaning he was the only one waiting on tables, but it was taken as a declaration that no competent waiters would be found in that eating establishment.

The angry customer stormed out, dragging his fellow eaters behind him. One of the women whispered to Geoff as she passed, "I'm so sorry. The hotcakes were delicious."

Geoff was not ready for prime time.

* * *

"Geoff!" came Gus's summons from the kitchen. "Johnny Curran said you were good at spotting buoys. That right?"

"I was his buoy spotter in the fog when we went to the mainland for church."

"Well, I have a job for you. After the *Alert* leaves, we're going out to the south point off Penikese. Be ready to leave when I say."

Good at spotting buoys? That means riding in a boat! Yes!

Geoff stood amidships next to the forward tiller. Sea chop obscured any small buoys. They zigzagged and motored slowly around the designated area. Geoff spotted a small bluish-green ball and pointed. "There! I see something."

Gus positioned the boat next to the buoy while Geoff was poised, ready to snag it. He pulled on the rope; up came a large, moving, lumpy gunnysack—the same kind as those Bob Tilton brought to the Coffee Shop at closing time. Hmm. More shorts?

Gus turned the boat toward Cuttyhunk and opened the throttle. Instead of picking up speed gradually, the boat lunged forward, sending Geoff backward. He crashed into Gus, who lost his balance, fell back onto the transom, and tumbled into the deep blue, leaving Geoff as the only one on the speeding boat. Geoff grabbed the tiller, thankful that he had ridden with Johnny Curran enough to know how to work it and the throttle.

A pissed-off Gus treaded water while Geoff searched for a ladder but found only life vests and slickers. This might have been comical, but Gus's two-hundred-pound frame was more than Geoff could hoist up the two-foot freeboard. The situation shifted to dire as dusk started to close in. Gus had been in the water for about ten minutes and was growing tired, cold, and stressed. Geoff looked around for anything he could use for the rescue, imagining solutions that would have resulted in splintering the boat on the Penikese rocky shore one-hundred yards away or death by dragging Gus back to Cuttyhunk, several miles away. However, ideas beget ideas, and moments later he had a rope looped and hooked over the stern cleat to act as a ladder.

Once Gus was back in the boat, the two sat on the transom to catch their breath as a breeze turned Gus's wet clothing into an evaporative cooler. Geoff blamed himself for what had happened and couldn't stop thinking about possibly disastrous what-ifs. He also knew his able kitchen boy career would end the moment they docked.

Gus found a folding chair in the storage locker near the bow and wedged it between the engine cover and gunwale. "Sit down in that chair and don't get up until I tell you."

Geoff sat quietly as Gus turned and headed the boat toward Cuttyhunk.

Gus secured the boat to the dock. "You can get up now, but if I hear so much as one word about this, you'll be on the boat home faster than you can pack. Got it?"

Geoff nodded as Gus handed him the gunnysack. "You know what to do with these."

* * *

Ellen Veeder, postmistress, adopted Geoff by assigning herself as one of his island mothers. She was tough yet caring, and she had eyes that could see beyond. Those same eyes reflected her gentle nature, conveying empathy and comfort. Whenever a letter for Geoff came from home, she sent it along with someone going toward the Coffee Shop or sent word instructing Geoff to report to her at the post office. Ellen scanned Geoff for signs of mischief, and when satisfied that he remained on the straight and narrow, she scooted him on his way with, "Here you go, young man. A letter from home. Got one for me to send back?"

* * *

The Bosworth House was a stone's throw from the post office, and that made a visit with Robbie easy and convenient. Geoff spent many afternoons sitting on the back steps helping him peel potatoes. It was like father and son watching a baseball game without conversation. Robbie's goodbye was always the same: "Keep the hell out of my kitchen."

* * *

Geoff's afternoon routine consisted of seeing off the *Alert* and making a sweep through his camp on the way back. One day he spotted a tall, lanky boy checking out his camp and poking his head inside the tent. His furtive movements made Geoff think he might be casing or even burgling. Nothing in Geoff's tent was worth stealing or fretting over if it was lost, but a violation is a violation.

Geoff picked up his pace to intercept the intruder. When he was within a hundred feet of his camp, the boy realized he'd been seen, scaled the barge, and scurried down the shore toward town. Geoff inspected his camp. Nothing missing. Nothing disturbed. Perhaps the invader had been merely curious. The sagging tent and a towel draped over its peak did make the camp look neglected. Geoff reported the incident to Gus, who dismissed it with "probablies" – it was probably this or probably that. Theft just didn't happen on Cuttyhunk.

* * *

After his first week of work, Gus presented Geoff with his first "paycheck"—thirty dollars. Geoff looked at the bundle of two-dollar bills, which constituted more money than he had ever earned in a week anywhere else at any time in his life. He was rich! Given the stranger snooping around his camp, Gus suggested that he keep his pay in a jar in the Coffee Shop's cupboard.

Geoff scrubbed dishes harder, cleaned the floor faster, bounded with greater enthusiasm, and kept up his "can do" attitude. His workday tirelessly spanned fourteen hours with afternoon time off. He worked seven days straight. He did the mental math and determined he was earning about half the minimum wage, which caused him to pause briefly and wonder if he should really be celebrating. But his glum thoughts were short-lived. It was, after all, the going wage in the island-kid slave trade, and the real payoff was freedom. Gus gave him three squares a day and looked after him, he constantly learned new tasks, and he was allowed to eat all the apple pie he wanted. No complaints from Geoff.

* * *

"Well, Geoff, are you glad you stayed on?" Gus asked him one day.

"I sure am. I'm learning a lot *and* being paid. What more could I ask for?"

"You're pulling your weight, that's for sure. You've turned out to be quite the kitchen boy."

Geoff stood to attention. "No, Gus. I'm not just 'quite the kitchen boy,' I am an *able* kitchen boy. I can do *anything* in this kitchen without being told."

"Able? That you are, my boy. Ok, mister able kitchen boy, check out the icebox. I think you'll see the French fries are running low."

38

THAT RED PAINT

The Coffee Shop suddenly awakened from its afternoon doldrums when the front door crashed open and four raucous teenagers walked in and plopped themselves down in a booth. "Anybody work here?" one of them yelled toward the kitchen. Gus summoned Geoff. It was time for him to go back to the dining room. Geoff perked up, washed his hands, and attended to his first customers since the poached egg fiasco.

The group consisted of three girls and a thin guy who didn't really sit in the booth. Instead, he was draped over it with his arms slung over the back and body sliding off the bench to the floor. He talked loudly and found himself very amusing, punctuating everything he said with laughter.

Geoff approached the table. The loud boy gave him a scornful head-to-toe inspection. "You work here, kid?"

"Me?" Geoff put his hands on his chest and gazed at the boy innocently.

"Who else, stupid?" The boy laughed hideously.

"How may I help you?"

"I'll have a glass of water and a toothpick."

"That's it?"

"Yeah, that's it."

"Just water?"

"Don't forget the toothpick."

"For all of you?"

"Are you dense? Of course! A round of water for all of us," he said, waving his arm in the air.

"I think you have to buy something."

The boy reached into his pocket and pulled out loose coins. He sorted them out and pushed two pennies over to Geoff. "There. A glass of water can't cost more than two cents. We'll have water."

"I don't know if I can do that. Let me ask the boss."

"Hey!" the boy said, looking down at Geoff's bare feet. "Can't you afford shoes? Is that why you have to work in a dump like this?"

Geoff bristled on his way back to the kitchen. "Welcome to the restaurant business," said Gus.

"Who *is* that guy?"

"I don't know. He's been here for maybe a week or less. Comes in and takes up space."

"How come I haven't seen him before?"

"You've just never been here when he's come in."

"He wants to buy four glasses of water for two cents."

"Well, you know my answer to that. Just bring him a menu."

Geoff returned to the table. "So, what did your boss tell you?" the boy asked. "Are you gonna bring me a glass of water or are you too tight to do that?"

"The boss said you'll have to buy something off the menu if you're going to hang around."

"And water's not on the menu?"

"No, I checked. Sorry."

"Well, screw you! C'mon, girls, let's get the hell out of this shithole."

The kid stood tall and close to Geoff, trying to use his height to intimidate him, but Geoff stood his ground and glared back.

"You're the one camping down on the beach, aren't you? What's the matter? Haven't got money to stay in a real place, or is it that nobody wants you?"

"How do you know I'm staying on the beach? I've never seen you before."

"I just know." The kid stepped past Geoff and headed for the door with his following.

"Didn't get your name," Geoff said.

"Didn't give it. What's it to ya?"

"I'd like to know who knows where I stay at night."

The kid sneered as he stepped through the door. The last girl in his entourage leaned toward Geoff. "Biff. Biff's his name."

Geoff returned to the kitchen.

"That guy's trouble," said Gus. "He'd be one to avoid. But just the same, you should be wearing shoes if you're gonna work in the dining room. Actually, you should be wearing shoes even in the kitchen. You know… gravity—that stuff that sends knives and plates and hot food to the floor. Shoes, my boy, shoes."

"First I gotta find them. They haven't been on my feet since I started working here."

Geoff returned to his camp at day's end. It was too dark to go on a sneaker hunt. He'd do it first thing in the morning.

At dawn, Geoff rummaged through his duffel and under his sleeping bag, searching to no avail. He sat back on his knees, trying to retrace his steps and remember when and where he had last worn them. Maybe they were sitting on the barge or half buried in the sand. Maybe he had left them on the fish dock. A more thorough search would have to wait. His work shift would start soon.

A preoccupied Geoff was scurrying to the Coffee Shop when he stopped abruptly at the Coast Guard station and gasped in disbelief. "Oh, jeez! Someone's gonna be in big trouble for *that*!" Red paint had been slopped over the large, sturdy, majestic Coast Guard sign, all over the ground, and on the concrete slab that secured it. This was serious vandalism. It involved US federal government property, and even Geoff knew that would bring more than local trouble to whoever was responsible.

Dave Jenkins, the chief of police, stood in the kitchen talking with Gus when Geoff walked in. He had already launched an investigation. Geoff listened as Dave unraveled the facts. The vandal or vandals had not only painted the sign, but broken into the Coast Guard boathouse at night to steal the paint. They'd been sloppy, tracking it around. "This shouldn't be too difficult," Dave said. "Find a shoe with red paint on it and we find our culprit."

Why is he talking to Gus about this? Geoff wondered. Then he remembered: Muggsy had told Geoff early in the summer that whenever something was amiss, unsupervised teens always topped the list as prime suspects. Kid workers without parental supervision surely topped the list. It was no accident that Dave was there. *Settle down,* Geoff told himself. *Only guilty people have something to be nervous about.*

Dave looked to Geoff's feet. "Where are your shoes, boy?"

Geoff looked down at his feet and back at Gus. "I couldn't find them."

"What do you mean, you can't find them?" Dave asked.

"I've been looking all over for them. I haven't worn them for about a week. Gus told me I should wear shoes so I could work in the dining room."

"When was that?"

"Yesterday."

Gus stood with his arms folded as he studied Geoff. He looked to Dave. "I asked him yesterday to start wearing them to work, and he said he couldn't remember where they were. Said he hadn't worn them since he started working here."

"How many pairs of shoes did you bring?" Dave asked.

"Just that one pair."

Dave looked to Gus, who nodded to verify Geoff's story.

"Is there anyone who can attest to where you were all night last night?"

Attest? This can't be good.

"No. I was alone in my tent."

"Well, son, you're camping close to the boathouse, your one and only pair of shoes suddenly went missing, and there's no one who can vouch for where you were last night. Whoever painted that sign got paint on their shoes and tracked it all over. If I were you, I'd find them pretty quick. Do you have any idea how serious this is?"

"Yes, sir, I do. But I didn't do it."

"Find your shoes, boy," Dave said as he walked out the back door.

"Gus, I swear I didn't do it."

"No one's saying that, but if your shoes show up with red paint on them, it's not gonna look good for you. Maybe you should take some time off and find them."

Geoff left the Coffee Shop feeling gut punched. Finding his sneakers was his only hope. If he had left them somewhere, chances were good they might still be there. He walked to the fish dock, filled with dread. He thought about the deep embarrassment of being expelled from the island. A conviction would flush away all his efforts to become part of it. He wouldn't even be able to walk to his camp without terrible shame. What would Gus think? Or Muggsy or Gladys Snow or even Robbie? He would bring shame to the Fairchilds. He feared returning home and having to face his father's interrogation to ferret out his assumed guilt for a crime he hadn't committed. And then there was the government that would want him to pay for the damages.

Geoff stood on the fish dock, trying to remember where he had been. On the island, things left behind tended to stay put until retrieved by the owner. He searched over, under, and in and out of lobster traps, buoys, boxes, tools, benches, and fishermen's sheds. Asking people if they had seen a pair of blue sneakers brought the same response.

He mentally retraced his steps through the past week. He had them on when the Fairchilds left and later when Gus told him he would have to move his tent. It was coming back. Yes! He recalled taking them off and placing them on the barge while he set up his tent on the beach. He hadn't worn them since moving there. They were somewhere in his camp. They just had to be. His spirits lifted with the hope that a more thorough search back at camp would produce his exonerating evidence.

Geoff raced back to camp. He reminded himself that sometimes a person could look for something so hard, it could be right in front of them and remain invisible. He took a few deep breaths and told himself to search slowly without assuming anything, empty out the tent, and go through each item piece by piece.

First out was the sleeping bag. He shook it vigorously, but all that fell out was sand. He laid it on top of the barge and crawled back into the tent to retrieve the next item. There were his sneakers. They must have worked themselves under the sleeping bag.

He exhaled deeply; the weight of the world was gone. Those sneakers had just saved his life. He could return to work with his dignity. His sneakers proved his innocence.

Geoff set his sneakers on the edge of the barge. He tossed his sleeping bag back inside the tent, but part of it stuck to his hands. Blood. Where had that come from? He looked for a cut, a puncture, and even a vengeful splinter. He turned the sneakers over, searching for a sharp something embedded in the soles. A horrifying reality smacked him in the face when he saw red paint covering the soles of the sneakers.

Geoff collapsed against the barge. His sneakers would have brought exoneration, but now they had become the evidence that would condemn him. He wanted to run, but to where and why? This was a bad dream. Nothing made sense. How could sneakers suddenly turn up with sticky, fresh red paint that happened to be the same color as the paint splattered on the Coast Guard sign? Only one reasonable explanation existed: someone was framing him. Who knew his comings and goings?

Biff did. Geoff was almost certain it was Biff he had seen snooping around his tent a few days before. The guy he'd seen was tall and lanky, just like Biff. In the Coffee Shop, Biff had asked if Geoff was the one camping on the beach. Geoff thought, *How could he know? It wasn't just a good guess. I wish I had moved faster when I saw that person in my camp. Then I would know for sure.*

Geoff felt cornered. Maybe he should bury the sneakers deep in the sand. But that would make him guilty of destroying evidence, which, because the crime involved federal property, could bring even more trouble. Geoff was a lousy liar. He knew he would be unable to look Dave Jenkins in the eye and lie to him. The most honorable approach would be to bring the sneakers to Dave and hope his honesty would demonstrate his integrity and innocence.

He needed to talk with someone. Robbie. He would be hard on Geoff, but he would listen, and he could be trusted.

Geoff dumped the contents of his knapsack and put the sneakers inside. He sprinted off to see Robbie and found him on the kitchen landing peeling potatoes. Robbie took one look at Geoff and stopped his work. "You look troubled, boy. What is it?"

Geoff looked at Robbie. He knew.

"Well, speak up. What is it? Was it you who painted the Coast Guard sign?"

"No, sir. I didn't."

"I didn't think so. It's not your form." Robbie pointed his potato peeler at Geoff's knapsack. "Those your shoes in there?"

Geoff held the knapsack close to his stomach. He slowly unrolled it and revealed the damning evidence.

"Holy shit almighty! There's paint on them, all right. Someone's got a hard-on for you. Any ideas?"

"Yeah, but I can't prove it."

"Who?"

"There's a guy who's been coming into the Coffee Shop..."

"Goddamn it, kid, just gimme a name."

"His name is Biff."

"OK, sit down there. *Now* you can tell me the whole story."

Geoff described his encounter with Biff in the Coffee Shop and how he had seen someone checking out his camp a few days earlier. What he recalled about the person's height and frame matched Biff.

"Start from the beginning. Tell me what happened again."

"From the beginning? Why?"

"I just want to hear it again."

"OK, but it's gonna be the same." Geoff retold the story while Robbie looked at him intently.

"Why would this guy Biff want to pin the blame on you?"

Geoff shook his head. "I don't know. It seems like he's had it out for me ever since I first saw him."

Robbie pointed to the painted sneakers. "Looks like he got the goods on you. Has anyone else seen them?"

"No."

"What are you going to do?"

"I don't know. That's why I came here."

"If you had to make a plan, what would it be?"

"I think the best thing would be to tell them I didn't do it and hope they believe me."

"Good plan, boy, but before you do that, go pack up your camp."

"You don't think that's a good idea? But it's the truth."

"Ha! The truth, he says." Robbie burst out laughing. "If you tell them you didn't do it, they'll think you did. That's the first thing guilty people say: *'I didn't do it. I swear, I didn't do it.'* If you hide your shoes, it's the same as admitting guilt. And you don't look like you can pull off a lie. You have to focus on what you believe are the facts. So, kid, just what *are* the facts?"

Geoff listed what he considered to be facts, and Robbie helped sort them out. As much as it looked to Geoff as though Biff had framed him, he had no proof. Without proof, accusing Biff would look like he was trying to shift blame.

"If someone took your shoes, when did they get back in your tent?"

"I really don't know. It had to be sometime this morning after I went to the Coffee Shop."

"How do you know that?"

"I tried to find my sneakers last night, but it was too dark to see. I looked around this morning and still couldn't find them. Dave Jenkins said someone painted the sign last night, and I found sticky paint on my sneakers when Gus sent me back to find them this morning. I left the Coffee Shop about ten, went and looked around the dock, and got back to camp a little after noon."

"Well, kid, half the island goes to meet the *Alert,* and with some luck, maybe someone saw your buddy snooping around your campsite. Did Gus believe you when you told him you couldn't find your shoes?"

"I think so."

"Does Gus know about your confrontation with Biff in the Coffee Shop?"

"Yes, he heard it from the kitchen. He said Biff was a smart-ass and I should steer clear of him."

"OK, kid, I gotta get back to work. Here's what I'd do. Since you're working for Gus, he is responsible for you. I'd take that knapsack and go down and talk to him. Can you tell him the same story you told me? Exactly the same story?"

Geoff nodded.

"And you haven't had any other conversations with Dave Jenkins?"

"Just that short one in the Coffee Shop. He thinks I did it."

"Well, of course he does. You'll have to talk to him as well. Keep your story straight. Make sure what you tell Gus and Dave is exactly what you told me. *Exactly.* Stick to the facts. They're easy to remember. And when you tell them, look them square in the eye. That's important. Liars can't look others in the eye, and they can't tell the same story twice. No speculating. Go on, now. Come back and let me know how it went. Don't let me hear about you getting on the boat today."

"So, you believe me?"

"Of course I do."

"How come?"

"You were straight with me and you faced the problem. A guilty son of a bitch would never show up on my landing with evidence that proves he's guilty. Setting you up like that is chickenshit. I got no respect for the bastard who did that. Hell, that's worse than painting the sign. Besides, doing that kind of crap isn't in your character, and I'm a pretty good judge of character. Now get outta here so I can finish the lunch prep. Remember… facts only and look 'em square in the eye."

"Thanks, Robbie. You've been a great help."

"And one more thing."

"Sir?"

"Keep the hell out of my kitchen."

Geoff found Gus in the kitchen of the Coffee Shop. Gus pointed to the knapsack. "Looks like you found your shoes. That them?"

"Yes, but we need to talk."

Geoff unfolded his story. He laid out his facts—the conversation they had about wearing shoes while working, the unidentified intruder in his camp, and that the islanders had gotten to know him over the summer. He resisted the temptation to suggest the deed was Biff's doing. Gus questioned Geoff, who remained consistent in his responses. Geoff was glad he had talked to Robbie. Repeating facts was easy as was looking Gus in the eye. Now, would Gus believe him?

Gus sat and pondered. Then he slapped his knees. "What you're saying makes sense. It took a lot of guts to bring me those shoes. They could still get you thrown off the island, but I believe that if you'd painted the sign, you would have buried them and told me you couldn't find them. My guess is someone set you up. You stay here and mind the store until I get back."

Geoff sat on a stool and waited. The only activity in the Coffee Shop consisted of flies trying to escape through the front window screen.

Geoff heard someone coming into the kitchen through the back. His heart pounded at the thought that Dave Jenkins would be with Gus, but he didn't dare leave the stool to find out.

"Couldn't find Dave Jenkins, but I want you to go up to their house and talk to Bette, his wife."

"Right now?"

"Right now. Take your sneakers."

At the Jenkinses' front steps, Geoff sighed and knocked forcefully on the door. A woman appeared on the other side of the screen.

"Hello, Mrs. Jenkins."

"Just call me Bette. Come on in."

He followed Bette into the kitchen and sat at the table. She folded her hands and looked at Geoff. "I hear you have something to talk to Dave about, but he's not here, so you can talk to me."

Geoff related the same story he had told Robbie and Gus. He kept to the facts, as few as there were. Bette said, "Gus told me you had a run-in with a boy named Biff. What was that all about?"

"I saw a guy looking around my camp, and he ran the other way when he saw me heading toward him. I couldn't be sure, but from a distance it could have been Biff. And in the Coffee Shop he said, 'You're the one camping on the beach, aren't you?'"

Bette studied him. "And you think this fella, Biff, might be the one who actually did it. Why?" Geoff kept his eyes locked on Bette's and gave his reasons, enveloped in facts, without sounding like he was attempting to shift blame.

Bette asked to see the painted shoes. "Hmm. Yes, they do have fresh red paint on them, don't they? You know, this could prove that you did it, but you brought them to us instead. Why?"

"Ma'am, believe me, I thought about getting rid of them. I really did, but all it would have done was make me look more guilty."

"You did the right thing. Is there anything else about this you'd like to tell me?"

"No, ma'am. I think I told you everything. Is there anything more you'd like to ask *me*?"

"Yes. I heard Miss Wheeler came and had supper at your camp last June. How did that all come about?"

Geoff relaxed and let out a big sigh. He told her about the invitation to supper, the work he and Peter had put into preparation, how he had almost lost the entire meal when the fireplace began to crumble, and the stories Miss Wheeler had related about the pictures in her cottage.

Geoff left Bette Jenkins's house feeling good about being truthful, even though his future on the island remained uncertain. He was convinced Biff was responsible for the vandalism, but the truth of it might never be known. Maybe guilt would eat at the perpetrator and he would feel compelled to come forward. Geoff knew that people who did these kinds of things liked to brag about it. But would Geoff get the boot before the culprit's bragging reached the long ears of the island? Time was not on his side.

His thoughts were interrupted when he saw Biff and his entourage heading his way. Geoff gripped his knapsack and kept his head down as they passed.

"Hey, stupid kid! Find your sneakers?"

Geoff stopped abruptly, turned around, and walked toward Biff with purposeful resolve. He cast his knapsack aside and lunged at Biff, grabbing him by the shirt and repeatedly slamming him into a parked car as the bully Biff cried and pleaded for mercy.

Biff had played his hand.

"So *you're* the one! You bastard! Why did you do it, you son of a bitch? I'm gonna get kicked off the island because of you."

"You're not too bright, are you, kid? I wore your sneakers so that if someone tried to pin the blame on me, I could point the finger at you." Biff looked down his nose with a smirk.

"Well, it looks like you succeeded. They think I did it."

"Ha! Better you than me. Those your sneakers in that sack? If I were you, I'd hide 'em." Biff turned and steered his friends up the road.

Geoff raced to the Coffee Shop.

"How'd it go with Bette?" Gus asked.

"Gus!" said Geoff, out of breath. "He admitted it!"

"Who?"

"Biff. He just admitted taking my sneakers."

"When?"

"Just now. Outside. Right up the road by Alan Wilder's."

"Just you two?"

"No, he had two girls with him."

"Do you know them?"

"No."

Gus dashed out the front door with Geoff close behind. Gus squinted from the bright sun as he looked up the road. He could barely see Biff and two girls heading up Broadway.

"Do *you* know them?" Geoff asked.

"No, but I'm gonna find out. You, stay here." Gus headed up the road. Geoff retreated to the Coffee Shop, where he waited an interminably long time. When Gus finally returned, he said only, "*Alert's* in. Hungry people will be here soon. Let's get ready."

Two hours later the hamburger and hot dog gang had left, the kitchen was clean, and the Coffee Shop was silent once more. Geoff sat quietly on a stool in the dining room, awaiting word about his fate. He hesitated about asking, fearing the worst. The best way to make time go faster was to stop looking at the clock, so he assigned himself chore duty.

Gus found Geoff on a step stool outside, washing windows. "Take a break and go see the *Alert* off."

Geoff jumped off the stool and set his cleaning tools aside. "Why do you want me to do that?"

"Well, you've been working a lot, and you should get to know some of the other workers from the Allen House and Bosworth House. They get time off and usually hang out on the main dock when the boat leaves. It'll be slow here until the dinner crowd comes, so don't come back until about six."

"But what about the paint? What's going on with that?" Geoff had to know.

"Just go to the dock."

Geoff walked briskly, consumed with suspicion. Dave Jenkins would probably intercept him, escort him to the dock, and shamefully place him on the *Alert*. A truck slowed as it came up behind Geoff. His heart pounded. *This is it. They've come to kick me off the island. Aren't they gonna at least let me get my stuff?*

The truck pulled up beside him. It was Potter. Had they sent him to escort Geoff off, or was Potter just doing what Potter does? Geoff sat on the tailgate. If the boat left without him, he'd be in the clear. But a lot could happen between that short ride to the dock and *Alert*'s departure.

Moments after they got to the dock, the *Alert* sent out its deep *WHO-O-O-OP*. It was time for those departing to board. Geoff hung back, trying to hide in the crowd.

Dave Jenkins pulled up in his truck. Geoff couldn't remember ever seeing Dave on the dock for either the *Alert*'s arrival or its departure. He *had* to be there to put Geoff on the boat. No other explanation could possibly exist. Geoff buried himself even deeper in the crowd.

Dave walked around his truck and opened the door, and out stepped Biff. Geoff did a double take and bristled. As he watched, Dave grasped Biff's upper arm firmly, as if taking a suspect into custody. Biff held a soiled duffel bag in his free hand, wore an angry look, and jerked defiantly as Dave steered him toward the dock.

What was *he* doing in Dave Jenkins's truck? An elating thought flashed into Geoff's head: *It's Biff who's getting kicked off the island.* Or maybe Dave Jenkins planned to have the two confront each other in a final effort to ferret out the truth. Biff was a master at denigration. He would devour Geoff.

The two approached Geoff, and his world went into slow motion. Biff's angry eyes locked on Geoff. Then he spit in his face and yelled, "You dirty son of a bitch. You're a goddamn snitch!"

Some people nearby gasped, and Biff tugged against Dave's grasp while being ushered to the boat. A woman looked at Biff as he passed and said, "You're disgusting. That was uncalled for." Many eyes watched an embarrassed Geoff wipe spit off his face.

Another woman Geoff had seen numerous times but had never spoken to stepped over and handed him her handkerchief. "You handled yourself well, laddie," she said.

And then Biff was gone. Dave stood watching until *Alert* was beyond the jetty. The ordeal had ended. Geoff left the dock.

A truck pulled up alongside him. "You walking, or do you want a ride?"

A kid never passes up a ride, not on Cuttyhunk. Geoff began to hop in the truck bed. "No, I want you to ride up here with me."

At Four Corners, Dave stopped the truck, leaned back, draped his arm over the seat, and looked at Geoff. "Well, boy, did you learn anything?"

"I'll be thinking about all this, and I'm sure a few lessons will jump out at me."

"I'm sure they will."

Geoff had a few hours left in his afternoon off. His nightmarish ordeal had sucked the life out of his emotions. He wanted to be with someone, and Robbie would most likely tell him to get the hell out of his kitchen because it was nearing dinnertime. But Robbie's advice had saved him. He found Gus and Bea sitting and talking in the kitchen. Gus looked at the clock and then at Geoff.

"Yeah, yeah. I know you gave me time off, but I had nothing else to do. You didn't send me down to the boat to get to know other island workers. You knew Biff was getting kicked off the island, didn't you?"

"Yes, I knew. I wanted you to see what happens to those who break the rules. It's sort of a warning to keep you kids on the straight and narrow."

"How'd you know it was Biff?"

"Well, it turns out someone saw him by your tent and one of his girl-friends had a conscience. When Dave confronted him, the first thing he did was point to you and say something about red paint on your sneakers. Dave asked how he knew they had paint on them, how he knew what kind of shoes they were, and how he knew they belonged to you. Your pal had a hard time lying his way out of the big hole he dug himself into."

"Well, it's been hairy."

"Yeah, and you handled yourself well. I'm sure your dad would be proud."

Geoff stood looking off into space. "I'm sure he would be. But why did Dave suspect me from the start?"

"He doesn't know you. Everyone else stood up for you. Luckily, you've made some good friends here. I don't know what's going on between you and Robbie, but he stood up for you while waving his knife around. It's not like him to stand up for someone unless he believes in them. No one really thought you did it. It was just so out of character for you."

"Well, *I'm* certainly glad it's all over. Would you mind if I hang around here until it's time to go to work?"

"Why don't you finish cleaning the windows. But first, there's some turpentine in the shed. Clean your shoes. Then try keeping them on your feet while you're working here. That red paint could have gotten you thrown off the island."

39

BERT'S INNER SANCTUM

The church service in New Bedford was excruciatingly long as the sermon went way beyond human tolerance for the irrelevant. Johnny tugged at Geoff when the ushers came forward with a stack of collection baskets. "We gotta go."

Johnny whisked Geoff to the pier to catch the *Alert*. They arrived moments before dockhands released the bow line. "Geoff, my boy. When you first stepped onto my boat, you were as clumsy as a lobster on a rock. You've become a good mate." Geoff got out of the car, and Johnny zoomed off. Geoff stood stunned; Johnny wasn't one to hand out compliments.

"Hey, laddie! You comin'?" Bert shouted as he waved an arm. Geoff dashed toward the bow and casually stepped off the pier onto the *Alert* as it slowly backed away. He walked by the wheelhouse, only to get a glare from Clarence, who regarded stepping onto an untethered boat as reckless and dangerous.

Geoff stood at the stern as they began the crossing to Cuttyhunk. They passed the three-hundred-foot US Coast Guard cutter *Yakutat*, a landmark in New Bedford since 1949. Bert, having completed his getting-underway duties, found Geoff in a dreamlike state of awe watching the *Yakutat* shrink behind them. "She's sure a beaut," said Bert.

Geoff looked upon her with reverence—there was something majestic about her long, sleek white body with the diagonal red stripe close to her bow. "One day I'm gonna be on that ship."

"Thinkin' about the Coast Guard?"

"Yeah, been thinking about it."

"Why the Coast Guard?"

"I like being on the water, and folks respect the Coast Guard."

"They don't pay beans, but you're right about respect."

They watched the *Yakutat* vanish behind them. Bert put his foot up on the boat cleat, pulled a cigarette from a pack, and offered one to Geoff. Geoff put his hand up and shook his head. "You remember the last time I took a smoke from you. I almost choked to death."

Bert lit the smoke and leaned on his knee while looking out over the water. "I hear you're working at the Coffee Shop."

"I am. Only been on the job a week since the Fairchilds left."

"Where they puttin' you up?"

"I have my tent pitched by the barges where I camped last June."

Bert nodded as he studied his cigarette and took another puff. He stood and stretched his back. "Well, laddie, I gotta go below and check the gauges. Wanna come?"

Go to the engine room? Of course! A person got to see the engine room only by special invitation after passing numerous undefined moral tests. Geoff envisioned miles of pipes and dozens of gauges and control valves. He had an occasional glimpse of it whenever Bert pulled up the hatch and vanished below. Whatever machinery was beyond his view was an intriguing mystery, made more alluring by the distinctive sound that belched up from the hatch—more like a heartbeat than turning parts in an engine. A closed hatch muted its sound, but it pushed its rhythmic vibration throughout the boat. Geoff's insides jumped with excitement. All he wanted to do was lunge at the hatch door before something caused Bert to rescind his invitation.

"Sure," he said in a calm, cool voice. Bert motioned with his head and led the way. Geoff walked directly behind him, almost tripping on his heels. He stood tall and erect, but it was all he could do not to be Mr. Bobblehead and break into song that beat with each step, "I'm goin' to the engine room. I'm goin' to the engine room."

Bert unhooked a chain across a safety railing. "Face the ladder as you go down. Don't go down like me. I do this every day."

Bert slid down the ladder and Geoff followed. His feet touched the sole of the boat. If that was all he got, it counted as a visit. The engine room was tight—very tight. Not much headroom, and no place for wide people. Except for daylight seeping in from the open hatch, the only light came from dim overhead bulbs protected in wire metal cages. A steel grid catwalk wrapped its way around the engine. It was a monstrous gray rectangular box with rows of hinged covers, levers, high pressure tubes, and circular lids shaped like cones. Strapped overhead were air ducts, electrical lines, and water and fuel lines—all out of harm's way. Along the hull was an assortment of hoses, electrical cords, fire extinguishers, and odd-looking tools. Geoff was deep in the bowels of Bert's kitchen. There was not a misplaced drop of oil anywhere.

Automobile engines hum; why and where did *Alert's* rhythmic *chi-ca-chic-chic-chica-chic-chic* come from? Geoff worked his way aft, right on Bert's heels. The air was heavy with an odor of hot oil. The farther they penetrated, the hotter and darker it became. Bert opened a small hinged door on the top of the engine, exposing a row of clicking, clacking levers and rods. One would rise as another would fall. Bert turned his ear to the clicking noise and reached for a gauge, a wrench, and a screwdriver. He pulled a light from an overhead spool, handed it to Geoff, and positioned his hand to where he wanted the light to shine. He loosened a locknut and turned an adjustment screw, all while parts were going up and down. The intensity of the clicking increased. When he inserted a gauge and tightened down the adjustment screw, the clicking decreased. Bert listened, nodded, tightened the nut, closed the cover, and motioned for Geoff to work his way back to the ladder. Geoff took one last long look to indelibly etch this rare sight in his head.

Other passengers glanced over to see Geoff emerging from below. He felt their eyes. Who was this person to get this prestigious invitation into the bowels of the *Alert*? Geoff felt like he had just hit a grand slam. Containing his excitement became the challenge of his morning. He wanted to prance in privilege but settled back when he heard the voice of his father: *Gloating only comes from poor winners.* He turned his head away from the onlookers and murmured, "Stay cool. Stay cool."

Bert attached the chain across the railing around the hatch. "Wanna know what I just did?"

"Yeah, sure do. I like knowing how things work."

Bert explained that rods rose when lifted by cams deep inside of the engine. The tops of the rods pushed up on seesaw levers called tappets, which pushed on the valves. That was how fuel got sucked into the cylinders and exhaust got forced out. If the space between the rod and the valve was too small, the rod could bend, which would be very bad. Too much space resulted in a lot of noise and poor performance. Tappets needed constant adjustment. Information overload. Geoff's eyes glazed over.

"OK. Where'd I lose you?"

"I was just trying to visualize all those parts."

"Guess you haven't taken high school automotive class yet, huh?"

"Not yet."

Bert slapped Geoff on the shoulder and smiled broadly. "You'll get all this on the first day of auto shop." Bert looked at his watch and checked landmarks on the water. "Gotta go steer the boat. See you around, kid."

Geoff found a seat in the closed cabin behind the wheelhouse. His head had begun to nod and sink to his chest with the *chica-chic-chic* of the *Alert* when suddenly the cabin door slammed open and yanked him out of his daze. There stood Clarence with a fist full of money, bellowing, "Fayahs. Fayahs." Geoff pulled out a dollar.

40

WOULD HIS FATHER RECOGNIZE HIM?

The lazy days of summer were numbered. A crispness in the air told of an approaching autumn. The sky was azure blue. The water was indigo blue. Whitecaps frothed with turquoise blue. Blue, blue—everywhere! The morning breeze was noticeably cooler, and the warmth of dusk did not linger as it had in June.

Labor Day marked the closing of the Coffee Shop. Geoff washed dinner dishes, wiped down the front counter, swept the floors for the last time, and sat with Gus as he counted the day's receipts. Nostalgia filled him. He was looking forward to going home yet sad about the closing of this summer chapter.

Gus pulled a roll of bills from his pocket. "Your pay, Geoff. Well deserved. I'm glad you stayed. Don't forget your money in the jar."

They sat talking about how Geoff would spend his last day—mostly breaking camp and walking around to say his goodbyes.

"Well, Gus, I guess it's time for me to go."

Gus reached back into his pocket. "Take this and have dinner on me when you get to the mainland."

Geoff looked at the money. "Really? That's a twenty-dollar bill! That's close to a week's pay!"

"Take it," Gus said, waving the bill at him.

"Thank you, Gus!"

"If you want a job next summer, you know you have one here."

Geoff beamed. Returning to the island with the Fairchilds had been the lucky surprise of the summer. Working in the Coffee Shop had been a dream come true. Being invited back for the next summer was off the charts.

Geoff jumped off the stool and leapt to hug Gus.

Gus turned his head aside and cringed. "OK! OK! Don't get gushy on me. It's only a job."

"Not for me!"

"Well, go cut yourself a slice of pie and get outta here. While you're doing that, I'll write down my address."

The night was black when Geoff arrived at his camp. He set ablaze his entire supply of driftwood and watched the flames send yellow-orange sparks crackling high into the sky. He sat watching the fire, the surf, and the lights in town. When all the driftwood had been transformed into smoldering coals, Geoff jumped off the barge, brushed off sand, and headed to his tent.

* * *

Geoff poked his head over the barge to a welcoming brisk morning and a dead-flat sea. It was difficult to tell where the sea and sky met. He had just spent his last night at his "beach cottage" and awakened to "going-back" day. He hoisted himself up onto the barge and looked down the side where it met the sand. Memories of pleasant days on the island gave way to vivid images of the day his father's angry words had pummeled him into a cowering heap. His father's voice and face had long since vanished, but now Geoff stared deep into the ground as he contemplated the place to which he had to return. He sighed deeply and sat up straight. *My home is here now. How can I go back to that?*

There were neither jars of applesauce nor eggs and bacon from the Coffee Shop kitchen to satisfy the hunger pangs that began yanking at his gut, but the general store could easily remedy that. He leapt off the barge, packed his belongings, collapsed and folded the tent, and headed toward town.

His path crossed Bev Snow's, and they stopped for small talk. She suggested that Geoff swing over to the Bosworth House for a late morning breakfast instead of settling for applesauce. It would be a long shot, she said, but Robbie seemed to be in a good mood and might even open the kitchen for him.

Geoff walked down the dark hall and stopped by the Dutch door. For once, Robbie was in the kitchen.

"What the hell are you doing here? I thought you left. I told you that you only get one goodbye and you already got it, so you'd better be here for a different reason."

"Bev said you were in a good mood. I thought I'd come and see for myself."

"Ha! Don't believe it. I'm only in a good mood when nobody bothers me, and you're changing it. What the hell do you want?"

"Well, you haven't called me a little shit or a dumb bastard yet, so I take it your mood is still good."

"I hope you don't think you have me figured out. Well, are you gonna stand in the doorway or come on in? I was just gonna fix me some grub. Want some?"

Geoff nodded and grabbed a few plates and utensils while Robbie cooked a late morning breakfast. They sat on stools at the stainless-steel table and savored Robbie's culinary workmanship. When they were finished, Geoff cleared the table, and they sat drinking coffee.

"Are you all set to leave?"

"Yeah, everything's packed up and sitting on the barge, waiting to go."

"You know, you've come a long way, kid. The island has been good for you. You fit in well around here, and I see you landed a job at the Coffee Shop come next summer."

Geoff smiled and shook his head slightly. "Wow. News does travel fast. I talked to Gus about that just yesterday."

Robbie laughed. "Nothing gets past these ears. So, do you know what you're going back to?"

"You mean the situation between my father and me?"

"Yep, that's what I mean."

"I was thinking about that earlier. I don't think anything's changed. I'm not looking forward to it."

"Why not? You got more balls than you did in June, and going back will give you a chance to try your luck at standing up to your old man. And what the hell do you mean, nothing's changed? Remember what I told you about putting the stories you tell yourself on others? You haven't been home, so how would you know? Don't be your own worst enemy."

"Except for my friends in school, I know more people here than I do in my hometown. This island is my home now."

"Look, kid. This isn't your home. Your home's back there in Connecticut. You just have to figure out how to bring what you like here to there. Sure, there are plenty of good folks here, but there's nothing for you here except a summer job, and in a few years you'll move on. If you stay, you're only running away from a good fight, and I didn't teach you to do that. Neither did your old man. He's not a bad guy. We've been over the long list of what he's done for you. Just what do you want? What would change that could make it work for you?"

Geoff nodded as he looked away, thinking about Robbie's question. "Well, I'd like to be able to sit with my pop and talk to him like I'm talking to you right now. He wouldn't judge, point out my faults, criticize or interrogate me, or make me feel stupid. That's what I want."

"Knowing what you want is a good first start, and that's something to be excited about. We talked about your gripe and how your old man can't argue with that. If you push back like you did with me, I think he'll respect you more and see you differently."

"You make it sound easy."

"It is until you muck it up with all that other crap. OK, kid. Enough talk. I have to close down this place, and you have a boat to catch. Come back to see me next year. Now get the hell out of my kitchen."

They shook hands, and Geoff headed back to the beach to collect his belongings.

He threw his gear onto the *Alert* and climbed aboard. There were the usual faces in the end-of-season send-off crowd. They were all part of his island family. Muggsy stood among them, looking on with folded arms. Gus, a sworn "never to see *Alert* come or go," stood by a cargo boom and gave him the two-fingered salute.

The engine revved, and *Alert* pulled away from the dock. Geoff waved until all the faces became indiscernible as the boat headed out the channel. He kept a sharp eye on cottages as images and happy memories leapt into his head. As they blended into the landscape, the last landmarks to go were the Coast Guard boathouse and the tower on top of the island. As quickly as the island had appeared on his June arrival, it vanished behind a layer of afternoon haze.

That *chica-chic-chic-chica-chic-chic* of the *Alert* and a rolling sea lured Geoff into reflection. Two and a half months had passed since he'd first set foot on Cuttyhunk. Trepidation, hunger, and homesickness had debilitated his spirit. Salty islanders had been quick to speak their mind and warn of trespass. The island culture was uncomplicated and straightforward. It demanded accountability. Islanders were kind yet intolerant of the disrespectful. They were tough-minded yet fair. Adults were surrogate parents and guardians of all children.

Chica-chic-chic-chica-chic-chic.

Geoff's thoughts continued to meander. He thought of his last night with Diana, when her eyes had electrified a passion that kidnapped his body. He had never imagined that telling Robbie he wasn't in his goddamn kitchen would ignite a relationship that would save his summer. A forgetful moment had left him with an inability to pay for his pie and opened the door to the kitchen of the Coffee Shop. His rides to church had equipped him with the skills to handle a boat and rescue the man he'd knocked overboard.

The influence of the island that had begun in June held the promise of guiding him through the months and years ahead. For now, it was time for him to turn his eyes homeward. He feared the uncertainty of how his father would receive him, even knowing he was returning with a quiver filled with different perspectives and wisdom from those who had cared about him the most this summer. How could his father, a man with such good intentions, deliver life lessons with such a harsh whip? How could a man filled with love be so blind to the damage he inflicted? How could a man who second-guessed and criticized all his son's decisions give him permission to spend a summer far from his grip? The more Geoff pondered, the less anything made sense.

Would Geoff surrender to his father's will, or had the island given him the strength, stamina, and courage to alter and revive the fading ember of their relationship? Geoff had the heart. He believed he could pull it off, but would his father recognize him when he got back home?

41

THE REST OF THE STORY

Workers waited nearby under a tree, holding their shovels. Gray skies and wind sent a chilling rain. Water slid off the umbrella as I stood motionlessly over the hole in the ground. Negotiations with God were over. Pop was gone.

During the week before Christmas 1971, just five days earlier, I welcomed Pop into my apartment for supper. He came. We ate. He left. He appreciated the hospitality but was anxious to spend his evenings with Ma, who was recovering in the hospital from surgery.

Pop and I had come a long way since the summer of 1959, when he'd held a tight dictatorial grip on my thinking, my emotions, and my actions. Although his harsh ways had left me with tenacious baggage, he had also given me life tools to navigate my ship. We had worked hard to build a respectful and caring relationship. And luckily, neither of us had quit. If it hadn't been for the island lessons, things between us would most likely never have been resolved.

* * *

On a rainy October night in 1961, I stood beside Pop, who was hosting a Saturday night neighborhood cocktail party. With martini in hand, he sat comfortably in his thick leather chair away from the group. He was leaning forward, wearing a strange grin, and turned to me. "What are you so giddy about?" he asked.

"Our band just booked our first gig."

"Well, that's OK as long as you have your union card. You *do* have a union card, don't you?"

I stood puzzled. *What's a union card and why did I even need one?* "What would happen if I played without it?"

"The union boys will come for you."

"And do what?"

Pop made a fist and slammed it into my chin. I tumbled back and landed upside down and twisted around the leg of a bench. No blood. No broken bones. No pain. Just astonishment. Pop may have been emotionally abusive with all his "good intentions and crappy methods," but to him, striking another person in any situation was taboo. What had just happened and why?

Pop wore an uncharacteristic smirk and returned his attention to his guests, who huddled in tight circles engaged in humdrum cocktail chatter. They seemed unmindful of Pop's strange behavior, and not one of them had witnessed what had happened less than ten feet away. I vanished before Pop could shift his attention back to me.

I stood beside Ma at the kitchen sink. "What's wrong with Pop? He just hit me."

She bristled, straightened up, and looked through the window into the dark night. She turned off the water, ripped off her rubber gloves, and turned to me with a glare. She snapped out questions as she jerked my chin from side to side, inspecting for bruises, broken teeth, or blood.

In the dawn of the next day, Ma stood over my bed. "Get up. We're going to church." Churchgoing was a family thing, although it felt more like a process than part of a spiritual upbringing. Even as a boy, I thought our family of five children was on display as a well-dressed, well-behaved, well-raised, and well-managed clan. We paraded up the main aisle of the semi-filled church in ritualistic order. On that day, though, it was just me hustling behind Ma to our "regular" front row pew. Why weren't Pop and my siblings with us? What was going on?

The service ended, and the congregation poured out. My cluelessness persisted, and Ma's stern demeanor kept me from asking questions.

Back home, my siblings looked at me, bewildered, to which I responded by simply shrugging. Time worshipping God had done little to soothe Ma's anger.

My old journals describe a day of upheaval. Sunday was usually Pop's day to give orders, hold family court, and regain any lost ground as undisputed dictator. But on this day, we siblings hid in the corners as

Ma's incoherent, raging voice waged a strange new kind of war behind closed doors.

Hours later, Pop emerged from their bedroom—clearly beaten, clearly confused. He had struck me hard the night before. Was he going to be just as volatile today? Was he out to settle a score because I'd snitched? He searched for me, but I attempted to remain evasive and invisible. Suddenly, Pop and I stood face-to-face. I turned away.

"Wait!" said Pop in a submissive voice. "Your mother said I hit you last night."

What? *Mother said?* If ever I'd heard Pop utter a dumb statement, this one took the cake. How could he not know?

"It was nothing. Forget about it."

Pop stretched his arms out and took a step toward me. "But it *was,* and we need to talk about it."

I stiffened and looked him squarely in the eyes. The blow to my chin was nothing compared with the knock-out punch to my hope that we could ever mend our relationship.

"Your mother said I hit you last night, and I don't remember it."

"What? You've never hit any of us, and you've always warned severe consequences if we did. How can you *not* remember?"

"I was drunk. I had a blackout. Did I hurt you?"

"I was more stunned than hurt. What's a blackout?"

"It's when a person who's had too much to drink can't remember what he did. I lost control of my drinking."

This was insanity! Pop was a New York executive, the vice president of a major music corporation, the principal corporate attorney negotiating the multimillion-dollar acquisition of a movie studio in California. He was self-reliant, self-confident, self-everything. How could a man of his stature and character lose control of his drinking and not remember that he had struck his son?

I never saw a martini glass in Pop's hand again.

A few years passed, and someone asked if I could ever forgive him. Forgiveness? What was that? Fathers were unchallenged, respected authorities to be obeyed. Was that strike on my chin the end of his reign of terror, or would it only fuel the bonfire of my resentment, distrust, confusion, fear, intolerance, vulnerability, guilt?

As bad as our relationship was, the family disconnect was worse. We remained civil. I reveled when he left on extended business trips and lamented when he returned. I was unable to put my angry sword down. This was my life as a high school senior.

During a Saturday supper, we all sat at the large round table, staring at our plates to avoid being called upon to share our secrets. I glanced over to Pop. His eyes locked on mine. "So, Jeffrey, what's going on with you?" I scanned the table to see my siblings maintaining their low profiles.

I swallowed my food and set down my fork. I sat tall, looked directly into Pop's eyes, and said decisively, "I've decided to apply to the Coast Guard Academy." My siblings lifted their heads, looked at me, then looked to Pop for his reaction. In past times, Pop would have attacked me for not consulting with him before arriving at any decision—especially one as important as this. Instead, he asked questions for understanding. The anticipated barrage of criticism never came.

"Do you know how to go about this?"

"No."

"Would you like help?"

I accepted his offer as coach on the long road between desire and acceptance. He guided me through the application, the essays articulating my goals, securing a congressional recommendation, passing the dreaded entrance exam, preparing me for the interview with the admiral, and meeting the medical requirements. The dream died in the last step when the medical examiners detected a heart murmur. A lousy little heart murmur! It was all over. Pop sat quietly with me and put his hand on my shoulder. My self-pity blinded my ability to see him morphing into the father I had always wanted him to be.

With crushed dream in hand, I crashed and burned. My educational apathy showed in deteriorating grades, but I swept it aside with indifference. Yes, I went through the ritual of applying to colleges, but their responses came back with the same rejection vernacular. As high school graduation neared, Pop gave me an application for a school somewhere out in the Southwest. Where the hell was New Mexico? Was it even a state? Why would he want me to go *there*? This was the epitome of desperation. To placate Pop, I sent it off.

Classmates boasted of where they were heading after graduation. When asked, I dodged the question. "I'm thinking about the Coast Guard." It was a respectable branch of the military, and it sounded sexy. Their supportive nods were better than scorn.

I headed to Cuttyhunk the day after graduation. I would deal with "life beyond" after Labor Day. Why couldn't I enlist in the Coast Guard on Cuttyhunk? The captain didn't need to know the academy had rejected me. If not them, I'd try the navy. One way or the other, goddamn it, I would wear a service uniform. It was my only hope for career redemption.

While mixing cement for the foundation for a new kitchen, an islander passed and handed me a letter sent down from postmistress Ellen Veeder. I stuffed it into my hip pocket and shoveled more sand into the mixer. Later, I pulled out the crumpled, sweat-ridden post. It was a letter from home with a note from Ma. "Thought you'd like to see this." Behind it was an acceptance letter from that college way the hell out in New Mexico. A sense of relief and pride flowed through me like hot dye in my veins. If a learning institution believed enough in me to offer a bed, I would be heading to the Southwest at summer's end.

* * *

With freshman year behind me, I walked through the front door at home with duffel bag over my shoulder to say hello to the family before heading to the island for the summer. Pop asked me to wait a few days to attend a "function" with him.

We walked into a church meeting hall filled with cigarette-smoking, coffee-drinking guys who looked like many of those I found in the New Bedford bus station. No one had last names, and many were scraggly and missing teeth. I sat in the back as they introduced the next speaker.

Pop approached the podium. He stuttered and looked around with a timid smile and took a long look at the floor, searching for the courage to begin. The room was silent. Pop, that ever self-confident and self-reliant man, took a deep breath and choked out, "Hi, I'm Ed, and I'm an alcoholic."

Pop's stories left me with mouth agape as he told how he devised ways to appear normal after liquid lunches, mastered walking straight after stepping off the commuter train's bar car at day's end, and "borrowed" cars to get back to his hotel while on business trips to California.

He detailed the effect of his drinking on his family and how it had almost destroyed everything he held dear. He told how he could not remember striking his son as his drinking took a nosedive into the cesspool of loss. He pointed to me in the back. "I never knew how to say this to my son, to apologize for what I did to him. That's why I invited him here with me tonight. He's sitting back there. That's my son. He saved my life. Say hello to Jeff."

Pop's words stunned me. *I* saved *his* life? He was giving me credit for *that*? His entire audience turned to me and said, "Hi, Jeff." I heard nothing more of Pop's speech.

Announcing that he was an alcoholic to a room filled with others struggling on the same road must have been liberating. Pop no longer had to hide from the world, his family, and, most importantly, himself.

We drove away from the meeting.

"Coffee?"

"Sure."

Pop looked into the cup the same way Johnny Curran had taught me in the bus station. There was more to his story. I could see it. I waited. Pop cleared his throat, unable to look me in the eye. Then the mystery began to unfold. Pop had come from modest beginnings shaped by World War I, a pandemic, the stock market crash, and the Great Depression. He vowed that neither he nor his family would struggle financially like he and his family had. He attended a prestigious law school and emerged as top in his class. Opportunity fell at his feet, and he quickly became part of the upper echelon, with its expectations: self-control, moral character, community image, and contributor to society. But Pop's drinking took a firm hold on him at a young age. If discovered, it would be fatal to his career ambitions. He was an alcoholic before alcoholism was defined as a disease.

Raising and showing off perfect children—his yardstick for stability, character, image, and contribution—allowed him to deflect any discovery of his little drinking problem by his executive superiors. His children became his protective façade, his smokescreen. We were not permitted to act like children even though that was exactly what we were. He pressured us to do what we were incapable of doing, and by the time we all came of age to be good reasoners and decision makers, the damage had already been done.

Pop's grand plan became complicated as drinking priorities pitted his ambitions for advancement against his vows to give his children a better start. My discreditable grades confounded his ploy and begged the question, "What kind of parents does this stupid boy have?" Hiding behind his children allowed him to buy more time in his descent into hell. It also brought him excruciating guilt. His world fell apart the night he struck his son.

Pop, holding his mug in both hands on the table, looked up at me. "And now you know the rest of the story."

I sat back, sighed deeply, and could only say, "Wow."

"Is there anything you'd like to ask me?"

"Yes. Yes there is. Why for the past four years haven't you mentioned your visit to the island?"

"Because I remember very little about that day. You know about blackouts. The more this disease takes you, the faster you go into blackout with less and less alcohol. All I remember of that day is sitting in the car before the boat left. Yes, I was drinking. The next memory is of being somewhere on the turnpike driving back. I have no recollection of what happened on the island, and because I was still denying I had a drinking problem, I couldn't very well ask you about it, could I?"

"Why did you come in the first place?"

"I knew my drinking was destroying our family, and I knew I was risking losing everything. Your friend Peter called his mother from the island, and she called us. Peter said you were having a great time getting to know everyone and didn't want to come home. I drove up because I thought that was the end of it for us. The rest of what happened that day is gone."

"Mr. Fairchild told me that was your reason, but I had to know for myself."

"He is very perceptive."

"Do you want to know what happened that day?"

"I'm not sure, but since we're on the subject, maybe you'd better tell me."

I told the story of a Saturday in June 1959 as if it had happened the day before.

"So the islanders protected you and then they tended to me."

"Yeah, something like that."

Pop looked down and shook his head. "That must have been a terrifying day for you. One of the most frightening aspects of a blackout is hearing it as if it were a story about someone else. You'd think that, alone, would be enough to scare one into sobriety. I don't even know how to begin to apologize for all that."

Pop had suffered enough. If I could not see that giving me public credit for saving his life was a humble apology, then he had raised a truly ignorant fool for a son. Pop deserved another chance. I owed it to him.

* * *

I completed college, married, became the father of two, and began a career in an aircraft factory. Pop and I spent Sunday afternoons in his kitchen drinking pot after pot of coffee and rediscovering each other. Pop showed a genuine interest in my thoughts and perspectives. One day he asked about my six-summer Cuttyhunk adventure. A first. My stories flowed for weeks.

"I must ask about something," Pop said carefully. "This isn't criticism, just a question of great curiosity. That house you bought. It's in such disrepair. Why did you buy it?"

"Because it was a wreck. It was cheap. I'm fixing it up, and I'm free labor."

"You like doing that?"

"I love it! I can't wait to get home from work and put on my toolbelt."

"I didn't know you had such a passion for it. Where did you learn your skills?"

"Each summer I went to the island about three or four weeks before the season began and worked with Gus to expand the Coffee Shop. I helped him transform that boxy little cottage into a sprawling restaurant which he renamed, The Scuttlebutt. I was really proud to be a part of it."

"I had no idea."

"You couldn't have. I kept it to myself. That was back in the day when you were unsupportive of my interest in the trades. You told me many times that relying on one's body was a poor career strategy."

Pop shook his head. "I didn't do a good job of explaining myself. I never wanted you to overlook the power of having a good head on your shoulders. If you like building, then run a business as a contractor, not an hourly tradesman swinging a hammer."

"If I could start all over, I'd make a life fixing up old houses."

"What would that take?"

"Gus gave me the skills. I'd need a contractor's license, business guidance, capital, and courage to take the plunge."

"Well, I'm an attorney with lots of business savvy, and I have capital. Having that kind of support minimizes the risk you're afraid of. If you worked on getting a contractor's license, we could combine our skills and form a business."

A new dream was born.

* * *

On December 16, 1971, Pop phoned to break our standing supper engagement. Ma was to be released from the hospital the next day, and he wanted to ensure everything at home was in good order.

We never dragged out long goodbyes, yet on that evening we both lingered.

"Pop, you still there?"

"I am."

"Before you go, there's something I've been meaning to tell you. Something I haven't told you in a long time."

"What's that?"

"I love you, Pop."

There was a long silence.

"I know, Jeff. And you know I love you." A few moments later, without another word, the connection ended.

* * *

It was nine when my phone rang the following night. "Come quickly!" sister Gale said. "Something's happened with Daddy, and they took him to the emergency room."

At the hospital, they ushered Ma and me into a room and handed her the phone. She dropped it and fainted. Nurses rushed to attend to her. I looked at the phone dangling down near the floor and hesitated to pick it up. I slowly put it to my ear, knowing what the doctor would say.

* * *

They say boys don't become men until they bury their fathers. It is a gut-wrenching and torturous time, yet most emerge with stronger character as the traits, spirit, and wisdom of those loved ones find their way into the fabric of our souls.

Pop was not without his flaws. Hell, find someone who is. He was my enemy when I was a teen, but I was my enemy, too. Pop wanted his boys to be good providers and contributors to society and taught us the principles he learned from his father—men rule, sissies cry, we wielded long swords and rode black steeds, and at home the men made the decisions and the household complied.

My babies didn't come with a user manual. As a parent, I learned that I had to write my own, as Pop had. Like him, I based mine on the values taught to me by my father and the condition of the world while I was a young parent. Pop's generational, chauvinistic customs were the only guidelines I had. Some were shameful compared with the values of the newer era. Between Pop's time and mine, many things changed. I didn't recognize the shift and wrote an instruction manual with obsolete values and ways that sometimes didn't serve my children well.

When Pop died, I lost my best friend. I had to wait until wisdom and maturity gave me perspective to see that giving him the benefit of the doubt was my only path to relationship salvation. Luckily, or miraculously, our last words were of love.

IN MEMORY

Clarence Joseph Flores (Captain of *Alert*) (1908 – unknown)
Bob Tilton (1897 – 1982)
Wilfred Tilton (1920 – 1996)
Malcolm "Muggsy" Thomson (1922 – 1983)
Florence "Flo" Thomson (1924 – 2004)
Ruth Alton "Mousey" Thomson (1891 – 1971)
Fredrick Fairchild (1907 – 1972)
Flo Fairchild (1923 – 2008)
Steve Baldwin (1921 – 1994)
Nancy Baldwin (1924 – 2000)
Diana Baldwin (1946 – 1972)
Irwin Winslow (Coot) Hall (1904 – 1983)
Gladys Snow (1921 – 1972)
Leonard Lionel (Robbie) Robinson (1914 – 1977)
Hetty Sheppard (Piney) Wheeler (1880 – 1964)
Arthur (Gus) Parks (1929 – 2007)
David Norris Jenkins (1921 – 2005)
Donna Veeder (1944 – 2015)
Ellen Veeder (1922 – 2002)
Allan Potter (1914 – 1995)
Clarence (and Lucille) Allen (1899 – 1974)
John Curran (circa 1915 – unknown)